> Third Edition

JAZZ

A Listener's Guide

James McCalla

Bowdoin College

Prentice Hall
Upper Saddle River, New Jersey 07458

Library of Congress Cataloging-in-Publication Data

McCalla, James
    Jazz, a listener's guide / James McCalla. —3rd ed.
        p.   cm.
    Includes discography, bibliographical references,
    and index.
        ISBN 0-13-014545-9
        1. Jazz—History and criticism.   2. Jazz musicians—United States.
    I. Smithsonian collection of classic jazz.   II. Title.
    ML3508.M35   2000
    781.65—dc21   99-29445
                                                                          CIP

Editorial director: Charlyce Jones Owen
Acquisitions editor: Christopher Johnson
Editorial/production supervision
    and interior design: Mary Araneo
Buyer: Benjamin Smith
Cover art director: Jayne Conte
Cover designer: Joe Sengotta
Cover art: Artville, LLC

© 2000, 1994, 1982 by Prentice-Hall, Inc.
Upper Saddle River, New Jersey 07458

Printed in the United States of America

ISBN 0-13-014545-9

PRENTICE-HALL INTERNATIONAL (UK) LIMITED, *London*
PRENTICE-HALL OF AUSTRALIA PTY. LIMITED, *Sydney*
PRENTICE-HALL CANADA INC., *Toronto*
PRENTICE-HALL HISPANOAMERICANA, S.A., *Mexico*
PRENTICE-HALL OF INDIA PRIVATE LIMITED, *New Delhi*
PRENTICE-HALL OF JAPAN, INC., *Tokyo*
PEARSON EDUCATION ASIA PTE. LTD., *Singapore*
EDITORA PRENTICE-HALL DO BRASIL, LTDA., *Rio de Janeiro*

Contents

Preface

Jazz: A Listener's Guide is the product of a course I have taught, both in the classroom and over the radio, at the State University of New York at Stony Brook and at Bowdoin College. It is intended for the student or general listener who comes to jazz without a prior knowledge of terms, techniques, or even much listening experience. Such knowledge and experience will come—I hope—through the use of this book in combination with repeated and attentive listening to the music discussed in its pages.

The principal point of this book is not the memorization of names, style periods, titles, dates, and other facts. My goal is to guide the beginning listener's ear. Each large chapter of the book is thus divided into smaller units dealing with a genre, a single major musician, or a more or less cohesive grouping of performers. Technical terms—in other words, *what* to listen for and *how* to listen for it—are introduced as needed, with references to music already discussed and occasional pointers toward what is yet to come. Each chapter begins with an essay setting forth general information about the music and its extra-musical content. Additional information about history or about jazz in American society also appears within some of the smaller units. But the meat of the book is its discussion of particular pieces, both for themselves and as specific examples of general styles, periods, or techniques. I cannot emphasize too much that this is not a book simply to be read: it must be read while listening.

To make this listening a little easier to manage, and a little less expensive, I have taken advantage of an admirable and widely used anthology, *The Revised Smithsonian Collection of Classic Jazz*, compiled by

Martin Williams. In the first edition of this book (Prentice-Hall, Inc., 1982), my choices and those of the Smithsonian anthology simply overlapped. In this revised third edition, I treat almost every selection in Williams' revised collection, and two selections from the original *Smithsonian Collection* (1973), but I also still include a large number of selections which he does not. *The Revised Smithsonian Collection of Classic Jazz* includes 92 selections; in this book I discuss almost 200. No two people's choices will be the same; in addition, I have defined my range more broadly than did Williams, both chronologically (pre-jazz musics, jazz since the 1960s) and in what I felt to be equally exemplary or interesting musicians or tunes in the years to which we both devote a fair amount of attention. I believe that my choices here are a comprehensive introduction to the history of jazz, and I hope that they are various and numerous enough to allow the student and teacher of jazz and jazz history a degree of individual flexibility in the use of the book. It is my overall hope that these pages will provide an informed foundation for *further, continued* listening and study.

ACKNOWLEDGMENTS

I have incurred debts to many people while writing and revising this book, and it is a pleasure to acknowledge them. First, the book is dedicated to my parents; they were not jazz aficionados, but they were music lovers, and their encouragement was very important.

I also thank Lawrence J. Fried, jazz scholar, Ellington *mavin,* and friend of long standing. It was he who long ago introduced me to the music of Duke Ellington beyond the most commonly heard standards, supplanting my entirely inadequate acquaintance with those marvels; such a gift cannot be forgotten or repaid. My friend Margaret Burke's enthusiasm for jazz was unquenchable and highly contagious; our many long listening sessions have a tangible record here. Charles O. Hartman and Molly McCalla read early drafts of the first edition of this book; their criticisms, mingled as they were with encouragements, were extremely helpful and extremely welcome. I have also been able to profit from the experience and knowledge of a number of professional colleagues whose expertise certainly matches my own, and who have been generous enough to pass on their reactions to the first edition of this book. I would like to thank Scott DeVeaux, Paul Machlin, Jim Pinfold, Krin Gabbard, and Paula Gabbard. More than once Gayle Pemberton has alerted me to performers or to tunes that I now cannot imagine living without. Jason Klaitman will find in the last chapter some of his enthusiastic and knowledgeable recommendations from recent jazz. I hope that all these colleagues and friends will continue to give their honest reactions to what I've done in the following pages.

I am also grateful to Dan Morgenstern, Ed Berger, and the staff of the Rutgers Institute of Jazz Studies in Newark, New Jersey; to Ann H. Sneed, Executive Director, International Art of Jazz, Stony Brook, N.Y.; to the staffs of the Music Collection of the New York Public Library and especially of the Music Library of the State University of New York at Stony Brook; to Barbara Whitepine, James Storer, and Margery Storer for their assistance; and to the many others who have helped me in my teaching, in my listening, and in my writing, but who are—I apologize— too numerous to cite by name. Finally, I thank my students at Bowdoin and at Stony Brook, who have read, heard, and reacted to much of the material in this book. They have also *taught me;* and had I not done this music for our classes, I might not have done it for myself.

Brunswick, Maine

➤ Chapter 1

The Beginnings
(Hotter Than That!)

According to common knowledge—which, as usual, didn't get the facts quite straight—jazz is a combination of African rhythms and European harmonies, was born in the red-light district of New Orleans (called Storyville), and traveled up the Mississippi to Chicago in 1917 and thence to New York in the early 1920s. Not quite so.

In the first place, there is no generally accepted definition of the word "jazz," nor do we know where the word came from or what it originally meant. Some people, including some jazz musicians, have said that Benny Goodman was not a jazz player, that Swing is commercial music, not jazz. One may also hear that the fusion music of the 1970s is not jazz, or that there is no such thing as a jazz singer, that these people are pop singers who do jazz material. Such statements are as much a reflection of personal predilections as anything else. What seems to be the case is that jazz coalesced in various parts of the United States at roughly the same time (if in different ways in different areas). The word "jazz" came into general use around 1917, the same year that the first jazz recordings were made in New York by the Original Dixieland Jazz (or Jass) Band. Jazz is a fusion of a variety of African and European elements, depending on the area of the country and the time one is discussing. By the mid-1920s, "jazz" was fairly widely understood to mean the kind of music played by Jelly Roll Morton, Louis Armstrong, Jack Teagarden, and others in New York, Walter Page's

Blue Devils in Oklahoma City, and elsewhere. There were many local dialects, but it had become a recognizable national—and native—musical language.

The African elements which fed into jazz came primarily from the oral folk traditions of blacks in the South. Perhaps the most important of these had to do with the kind of delivery a musician used—his or her ways of "coloring" a melody or a note, making it expressive—and the forms that these folk musicians used in their music. In some African languages and musics, *timbre* (or *tone color*, the distinctive sound of any voice or instrument) is very closely associated with the literal meaning of a word or gesture. This is a factor in all language, of course: think of the number of meanings one can give to a phrase such as "Oh, yeah?" or "Well!" in English. But this close relationship of inflection and meaning was much more pervasive in these West African languages than in European ones; and the sliding-around sound, the timbral coloring of a word or note (sometimes called "circumlocution") is everywhere in speech and song. This carried across into Afro-American music, where instrumental musicians often tried to imitate the sound of the human voice and human speech with their horns, and where melody, what we often think of as the succession of notes, was often equally a function of the special timbre of those notes. It was also important to the African-American musician, as it had been to the African drummer, to cultivate his or her own *individual* timbre, whether as a singer or as an instrumentalist. One didn't just develop a "good" trumpet tone: one also developed one's *own* tone. This individuality in delivery and in timbre leads straight into individuality in making music, into improvisation.

Improvisation can involve both how one decorates or embellishes a given tune and how one can make up new music or new words on the spot, as the occasion calls for. A specific way of improvising whole songs is "additive form," in which the musicians add phrases or new melodies as they go along, not according to any preset pattern. Additive form will be explained in more detail, and examples of it given, in the section on Afro-American roots (pp. 7–11). A final kind of form or way of building up pieces is the call-and-response between a leader and a group or between two groups. This may be heard in much African music, in religious music from Africa, Europe, and America, and in children's games from all over the world.

Finally, there is the matter of *meter*, the way the basic pulse or beat is organized. European music, as a rule, has only one sort of meter at a time, 1 2 1 2 or 1 2 3 1 2 3 or whatever. ("Meter" is discussed in more detail in the section on ragtime [pp. 11–15] and in the Glossary.) African musicians, on the other hand, developed a genius for what is called *polymeter*, more than one metrical pattern at a time: imagine tapping out 1 2 1 2 1 2 with one hand at the same time you do 1 2 3 1 2 3 with the other, keeping both patterns straight and correct. African musics are also notable for their use of *syncopation*, accenting the beats that normally aren't accented. African drummers were able to play seemingly without any strict meter at all, although they could silently "hear" an unstated meter in their minds and coordinate their drumming with that. All these elements—polymeter, polyrhythm, syncopation and accents, rhythmic freedom; in short, real rhythmic play and virtuosity—will show up in the examples discussed throughout this book, from the era of orchestrated ragtime to the present.

As African elements of jazz have to do with more than just rhythm, European elements involve much more than harmony. That harmonic element is, of course, important. The chords used in Afro-American music (folk songs, gospel music, ragtime, blues, and jazz) do come from a framework provided by European music, which determines the particular kind of chord used and the ways in which those chords are linked together. But three other elements are of equal importance. First, the instruments used in prejazz musics and in jazz are European, and many of the early jazz players actually learned how to play instruments by playing European music—in marching bands or in dance orchestras. It was only with the 1960s that some jazz musicians began to be interested again in the instruments of Africa, the drums and gongs that characterize much of that music.

Second, just as the basic harmonic framework or background of jazz is European (remember that we're separating harmony from melody here), so is much of the metrical background. Much jazz is built up in duple meter (see the ragtime section, pp. 11–15), and this regular duple pattern comes from the European side, not from the polymetric African side. The idea of regular phrases—units which are all the same length and which are usually built up in 2s—is probably also derived from European music. Finally, a way of putting music together, of coordinating the various instruments and/or voices, derives form Europe; that is the kind of texture called *homophony*. Texture refers to the number and relationship of various instruments or voices: above, I mentioned the *polymeter*, a kind of *polyphony*, of African drumming, more than one meter of equal importance at the same time. Homophony, on the other hand, means that there is just one principal voice or melody at any time, and anything else going on is accompaniment, a backup to that main melody. The greatest number of songs you'll know (popular songs, rap songs, hymns, patriotic songs, folk songs) are homophonic, having one principal voice or melody plus some kind of accompaniment.

All these different elements came together, very slowly and over a wide geographical area, and not directed by any single person or group of persons, during the last decade of the nineteenth century and the first ten or fifteen years of this century. It's simply not the case that jazz in its entirety was born in New Orleans: that city was certainly of paramount importance, but music that became jazz was being played throughout the South and the Southwest at the same time. (The Kansas City/Southwest tradition, for example, was begun in Kansas, Missouri, Oklahoma, and Texas, at the same time that the New Orleans style was formed in that city; and the Southwest tradition continued to feed and invigorate new jazz styles through the development of bebop in the early 1940s.) The belief that jazz was born in New Orleans probably exists for a number of reasons, not the least being that it makes a nice story—and people like nice stories. It's also important that we simply know more about what transpired in New Orleans in the years 1900–1920 than we do about, say, Memphis or Dallas, or even Los Angeles. And so we think that what we do know is all that there is to know. (Vigorous ongoing research has begun to shed light on early jazz and its development in other parts of the country besides New Orleans, so the story may yet change.) But New Orleans is, in fact, a good example of the way jazz came to be, and we can learn about the coalescence of the music and about its social context from that example.

During the nineteenth century, there were three distinct social and racial classes in New Orleans: the blacks, the whites, and the so-called "Creoles of color," people of mixed blood. These "Creoles of color" were among the aristocracy (or were one of the aristocracies) of the city, and by training and inclination their culture was almost entirely European. (Their term for themselves parallels 1990s usage: they were "Creoles," i.e., of French ancestry, but their racially mixed heritage made them "Creoles of color.") Their prejudice against the black populace of New Orleans was at least as great as that of the whites. But in the late nineteenth century, legislation was passed to enforce racial segregation of neighborhoods in New Orleans, and the Creoles of color were made to move away from downtown, where they had lived in some proximity with the whites, to the areas where blacks had been living, uptown. The man responsible for this legislation was named Story, and the part of town where blacks and Creoles now lived became known as "Storyville." Storyville soon became a center of all kinds of entertainment in New Orleans, as Harlem would later be known in New York for its bars, restaurants, theaters, gambling houses, and bordellos. Black and Creole residents and white visitors mingled there, and many of the establishments had live music. What this means is that we have, playing in the same neighborhoods, in the same establishments, in the same

Storyville, in New Orleans. Courtesy Al Rose Collections, Manuscript Section, Tulane University Jazz Archives.

groups, blacks who had learned their music by ear, who used a kind of delivery closer to the oral folk tradition, together with Creoles whose training was European, cultivated, and "classical." As things turned out, everybody learned to play all kinds of music, and the kinds of tune one heard in any given place depended not on the musicians, but on the audience. The players could do it all, so all the elements began to feed into each other, to cross-cultivate. The people who could read music and who played marches and dances learned how to embellish, how to improvise; people who had played by ear learned how to read music and how to develop better playing techniques; everybody learned new ways of playing and got a wider range of possible timbres and tones and ways of phrasing.

In 1917, the United States entered the First World War, and New Orleans became a major port for the Navy. The Navy looked at Storyville and did not like what it saw: "Not for our boys" was the verdict. And so the Navy forced New Orleans to close the district down. Many of the musicians went elsewhere—to Chicago, to Dallas, to Los Angeles, to New York, even to Europe. (This is the part of the legend about jazz moving up the Mississippi to Chicago.) Many stayed in New Orleans and took the jobs that remained. Many got out of music altogether. But it was not simply because of Storyville's closing that jazz "went to Chicago": New Orleans musicians had been working already on the big steamboats plying the Mississippi River, and New Orleans jazz had already begun to spread beyond those city limits. And finally, New Orleans jazz began to take on new characteristics, those of other areas of the country. New Orleans jazz, as such, can still be heard in that city, in clubs all over the country that specialize in "traditional" jazz, on riverboats, and at picnics and political rallies. But after 1917, or at least in the mid-1920s, what had been "New Orleans" jazz became a major starting point for "American" jazz.

There are two principal characteristics of New Orleans jazz. The first is the kind of instrumental ensemble, which comes from that of orchestrated ragtime. There is a *rhythm section* consisting of piano, banjo (the guitar will come in later), tuba or bass (tuba is the earlier instrument, later replaced by string bass, though this will sometimes depend on playing venue), and drums. On top of this is the *front line*, the three melody instruments of clarinet, trumpet or cornet, and trombone. This ensemble is also standard for 1920s, post-New Orleans jazz. The second main feature is polyphonic texture and group improvisation. Over the basic chords and rhythms laid down by the rhythm section, the three horns all play together, but they play very different melodies. The trumpet or cornet usually stays closest to a song's original tune. Above and around the trumpet, the clarinet improvises lines with lots of notes, lots of "noodles," and below both of them, the trombone adds its contributions. New Orleans jazz tends to be sectional, although the groups also played blues and various kinds of strophic songs. All in all, it tended to be entertainment music, music to support good times.

In the 1920s, soloists began to emerge—players like Jelly Roll Morton, King Oliver, Johnny Dodds, Bix Beiderbecke, Jack Teagarden, and especially Louis Armstrong. These players began to change the characteristic polyphonic texture of New Orleans into a soloist-led music. This emphasis on the soloist is the primary distinction between New Orleans jazz and what is often called "Chicago," "post-New Orleans," or "early" jazz. The ensemble stays pretty much the same, though there tends to be more variety and more pure solo music in the later kind (see, for example, *Weather Bird*, p. 28, recorded by Louis Armstrong and Earl "Fatha" Hines). Banjo is replaced by guitar, tuba by bass. New Orleans polyphony still comes along, but usually now at the beginnings and ends of tunes, not as their focus. And with the solos comes a tremendous virtuosity, real musical mastery. This is still music that entertains, but it's much more besides—you don't want to use it only as background for dancing, talking, drinking, keeping the kids amused, you want to *listen* to it.

In this first chapter, we trace out this history. There are six sections: Afro-American roots, ragtime, blues, and three sections on early jazz, from the New Orleans sound of Jelly Roll Morton through Louis Armstrong's work into the early 1930s, with some side trips to the Midwest and New York as well. Your listening should be cumulative— don't forget, for example, Mahalia Jackson or Bessie Smith when you listen to Louis Armstrong or Sidney Bechet (or anyone else). Some of the things to listen for, and how to listen for them, are detailed in the discussion of individual selections. But these are really just a starting point for you. It's *your* listening and hearing that matter.

AFRO-AMERICAN ROOTS

➤ *Ol' Hannah*. Work song, performed by Doc Reese.

This prison "holler," an example of unaccompanied folk singing, derives from the older field or plantation hollers. The form is additive, which means that the singer adds phrases as he or she wishes, not according to any preset pattern such as we'll hear later in *Beautiful Dreamer*. Some of the phrases are repeated fairly regularly and act as a refrain (e.g., "Well, well, well, don't you rise no more"), some are repeated in a varied form, some are never repeated. Toward the end, from the words "Run and call Major," the tempo gets faster, and it sounds like a completely different song, with a much more regular repeated melody. The singing is mostly syllabic (one note for each syllable of the text), but especially at the ends of phrases the words are stretched out, with lots of pitch-bending or pitch-shading. This sort of sliding around and into a note, instead of hitting it squarely and not varying it, is sometimes called "circumlocution"; it's found not only in some African musics, but in some African languages as well, as a speech inflection. To close the whole thing off, Doc Reese goes into a high falsetto, a popular way of singing in Africa, and still used in contemporary R & B (rhythm-and-blues). Like the next two songs, *Ol' Hannah* is functional music, telling the workers' story as they labor and making it easier for them to do and to bear.

➤ *Juliana Johnson.* Sung by Leadbelly (Huddie Ledbetter), accompanying himself on the 12-string guitar.

This is an ax-chopping song, and Leadbelly's vocal *WHA*'s are the ax strokes. It isn't additive, but strophic: the same music is repeated over and over, but each time with new words. There are two chords in each short verse (I and V, if you have some musical training). The verse begins on one chord (I), which is repeated a few times, then changes to the other (V), and then finishes on the chord on which it began (I). So the *form* of the verse, or how it's built, is determined not just by the tune, but by the harmony as well, by the regular and repeated pattern of the chords.

➤ *John Henry.* Sung by Leadbelly; Brownie McGhee, guitar; Sonny Terry, harmonica.

Also a work song—rhythmical, to support the work-rhythm, and additive, so that the singer can keep adding verses as long as the work goes on—but at the same time one of the most famous folk ballads of this country, combining elements from both black and white traditions. John Henry was a terrifically strong steel-driving man, whose woman, Polly Ann, could "handle steel like a man." After John Henry's heart gives out, as he's racing a steam engine to drive the steel, the song asks "Who's going to shoe your pretty little foot," and from there the words go back to seventeenth-century England and to the white folk songs sung in Appalachia and the South.

➤ *Freedom Song.* A spiritual, sung *a cappella* (unaccompanied) by Roberta Flack.

This song is strophic, with three choruses, or strophes. What's gorgeous here, besides the song itself, is the way the singer embellishes and individualizes the melody. Instead of singing it "straight," as one would read it from a page, she bends some of the pitches and adds her own decorations and fillers. One particular kind of decoration is called the "blue" note, where the singer sings a little bit flat, or below pitch, giving the note and the words a new expressive color: at the end of the first chorus, for example, in the lines "And before I'd be a slave, I'd be buried in my grave," the words "slave" and the next "I'd" are the same basic pitch, but "I'd" is flatter, lower, and blue. Listen, too, to how the third chorus is slightly different from the first, even though the words are identical. This sort of musical and emotional invention feeds right into the feelings and colors of jazz.

➤ *Come On Children, Let's Sing*. Gospel, sung by Mahalia Jackson, accompanied by piano and organ.

The form of this song—would you call it sectional or strophic? what's repeated, and how regularly?—is less important to us right now than Mahalia Jackson's delivery of it, with her melodic decorations and improvised phrases. Many black hymns were taken over or derived from the hymns of white Protestant religions, as white slave-owners required their blacks to abandon African religions for Christianity. What is not derived from European-based Christian music is the melodic conception of the song, the improvisation of new melodies, the general vocal delivery, and sometimes the call-and-response among singers or between a singer and a congregation. (The latter isn't in force

Mahalia Jackson. Music Division, The New York Public Library for the Performing Arts, Astor, Lenox and Tilden Foundations.

here, but you may hear some call-and-response between the singer and her keyboard backup.) Listen to Mahalia's (we're not condescending: whenever she was addressed as "Miss Jackson," she always said, "Just Mahalia, baby") phrasing of the words: her diction is absolutely clear, the meaning is always out front and strongly projected to the audience or congregation, and it would be impossible to say in a song like this whether the music or the words were more important, or to say which carried the essential message. This is a trait that carries directly into all jazz.

➤   *Beautiful Dreamer*, Stephen Foster. Leslie Guinn, baritone, accompanied by Gilbert Kalish on a nineteenth-century piano.

This kind of sentimental ballad was very popular with the middle classes—both black and white—in the late nineteenth and early twentieth centuries. Songs like this one were composed (not improvised, not part of an oral tradition) by both whites and blacks, and they were used for home entertainment. Occasionally they also showed up in minstrel shows and other kinds of public, staged productions.

Such tunes are strophic; in this example (two strophes, or choruses), the form of the strophe is aaba-coda. Each of these letters denotes a phrase, a subunit of the strophe as a phrase in language is a subunit of a sentence or of a paragraph. The phrase "Beautiful dreamer, wake unto me . . ." is labeled a, just because it's the first phrase. Then with the words, "Sounds of the rude world," that same melody and the chords underneath it (this is a homophonic texture) are repeated: the second a, since it's the same music. The third phrase is different, in melody, chords, and accompaniment figuration. Since it's new music, it's labeled b: when we get to later popular and jazz tunes, the b phrase will be called the *bridge*. It is also sometimes called the "release" or the "middle 8." The fourth phrase is just like the first two, so it's another a. (If it were a repetition of the third phrase, as the second was of the first, the form would be aabb. If the fourth phrase were new music, the form would be aabc. The system is simple: you just give a phrase or section a letter, beginning with a; if that phrase or section is repeated at any point, you call it a again; each differing phrase or section is labeled b, c, d, and so on, throughout the whole composition. In this book, we will distinguish *phrases* labeled with *lower-case letters* from *SECTIONS* labeled with *UPPER-CASE LETTERS*.) Finally, in *Beautiful Dreamer*, there is a short coda, or concluding section, at the end of the strophe, rounding off the verse and the song.

Notice, again, the singing style. Just as this is a composed, semi-formal song, the singer's tone is cultivated, trained, the kind of timbre sometimes called "sweet." There is no improvisation or decoration of the melody, none of the "rough" or so-called "natural" vocal delivery of the more or less spontaneous embellishments of our earlier work songs and religious music. Both of these kinds of music—the composed songs and the work songs and religious songs of the oral folk traditions—were familiar to prejazz and early jazz musicians.

RAGTIME

Before listening to ragtime, listen to a march; any march by John Philip Sousa will do. Marching or brass bands were among the most popular ensembles in the United States during the last years of the nineteenth century (indeed into the 1950s, and even today in New Orleans and in those universities like the Big 10 where football reigns supreme), and these marches contributed to early jazz in several direct ways. Many of the earliest jazz players in New Orleans, the Midwest, and the Southwest played in such ensembles and even learned their instruments playing marches. The form of the march is *sectional* (a succession of sections that differ from one another, as opposed to a strophic form, which repeats the same music over and over) and *additive* (the composer can just keep adding on new sections and doesn't necessarily have to "round off" the piece by ending where he or she began—for example, ABCD as sectional and additive, ABA as sectional and closed).

This sort of form is transferred almost literally to ragtime, and it is easy to categorize and to hear, at all levels from—so to speak—the ground up. First of all, the meter is duple. *Meter* is the organization of beats into a regular and recurring pattern of strong and weak. The pattern of duple meter is a grouping by 2s: STRONG weak STRONG weak, or 1 2 1 2, LEFT right LEFT right. (Or it could also be 1 2 3 4 1 2 3 4.) Triple meter, which we'll meet rarely in jazz, but have already heard in *Beautiful Dreamer*, is a grouping in 3s, 1 2 3 1 2 3, STRONG weak weak, STRONG weak weak, aka "waltz time."

Each unit of a pattern (1 2 1 2 or 1 2 3 1 2 3 or 1 2 3 4 1 2 3 4) is repeated over and over; and this unit is called the *measure*. The measure is said to be 2 (or 3 or 4 or whatever) beats long. Just as the meter of marches and ragtimes is duple, the measures having 2 or 4 beats, the *phrases* of marches have 4 or 8 measures, and the *sections* usually have 4 phrases. A typical pattern for a march might be:

beat	1 2 1 2 1 2 1 2 1 2 1 2 1 2 1 2
measure	1 2 3 4 5 6 7 8
phrase	a a
section	A

For the present, it's enough to be able to distinguish among the big sections, to recognize a repetition of music you've heard before, or to know that something is new, that you haven't heard it. We'll subdivide these sections later on, in the second version of Jelly Roll Morton's *Grandpa's Spells* and in the units on early jazz.

➤   *Maple Leaf Rag*. Scott Joplin. Three versions.

Ragtime was music originally written for solo piano that came in during the 1890s, derived from marches and from popular contemporary dances such as the cake-walk. (See the section titled "Early Jazz (1)," pp. 25–26, *Cake Walking Babies From Home* by the Red Onion Jazz Babies.) The basic features are: sectional form, duple meter, the *oom-pah* left hand that is referred to as "stride" piano, and the syncopated

Scott Joplin. Music Division, The New York Public Library for the Performing Arts, Astor, Lenox and Tilden Foundations.

melodies in the right hand (again, syncopation refers to the accents coming on weak beats of the measure, or between beats). Three contrasting versions of *Maple Leaf Rag* are a performance by Joplin himself, taken from a 1916 piano roll, an orchestration of the rag for a small ensemble, and a reinterpretation of the piece by another, later pianist, a jazz version of the piece by Jelly Roll Morton, done in 1938 in a style that sounds like the music played by a New Orleans jazz ensemble, but by a single person.

Joplin piano roll. The form is AABBACCDD (sectional and additive). Each section is 16 measures (mm., aka bars) long. Note the absolutely regular, ever-stiff rhythms—no fooling around here. This is a strict performance of a composed and completely notated (written down) piece.

Instrumental version (orchestrated ragtime). Performed by the New England Conservatory Ragtime Ensemble, conducted by Gunther Schuller. This is taken from a collection called *The Red Back Book*, a number of ragtimes orchestrated for a small ensemble (strings, brass, woodwinds, piano, drums) and done during Joplin's lifetime. As with Joplin's solo piano version, there is no improvisation here; this is a note-for-note transcription of his composition, played from the notated music. It would have been performed by a dance orchestra (of the polite persuasion, certainly not in a bar or brothel) and at outdoor concerts.

Jelly Roll Morton version. Form: introduction ABACCDD. This is a reinterpretation of Joplin's work by another great pianist and composer. This transformation of the original rag "swings" a lot more than the Joplin version, and it's closer to jazz than to "classic" ragtime. The left hand isn't restricted to the straight oom-pah figures; there are a lot more syncopations (such as those unexpected rests in the A chorus), as well as little trills and turns that sound like the New Orleans-style clarinet playing we'll hear at the end of this chapter. Morton also improvises his own new material over the basic chords and melodies of the original; and he uses a lot more variety in rhythms, melodies, and register (relative highness or lowness) than Joplin did.

➤ *Grandpa's Spells.* Two versions.

Jelly Roll Morton's original recording of *Grandpa's Spells*, from 1923, was a piano solo. His second, from 1926, was with his group, the Red Hot Peppers. Instead of the solo piano version, it's more interesting to use a transcription for small ensemble; the two of these together will exemplify (again) the transition from ragtime to jazz. The earlier version will sound a lot like the orchestrated ragtime version of *Maple Leaf Rag* (and other Joplin rags), whereas the latter is much closer to New Orleans-style jazz ensemble playing.

The earlier version of *Grandpa's Spells* can be heard performed by Gunther Schuller and The New England Conservatory Ragtime Ensemble. The form is intro-ABBACC. The intro is 4 measures long, the A, B, and C sections are each 16 bars. In the B sections, mm. 7–8 are a piano break. The comments above under the New England Conservatory Ragtime Ensemble's performance of *Maple Leaf Rag* apply here as well.

The performers on the 1926 recording are Jelly Roll Morton, piano; George Mitchell, trumpet; Kid Ory, trombone; Omer Simeon, clarinet; Johnny St. Cyr, guitar and banjo; John Lindsay, bass; Andrew Hilaire, drums. The formal layout is:

intro	4 bars
A	guitar (stop-time), then ensemble (4 + 4); 16 bars
A	trumpet, then ensemble; 16 bars
B	ensemble (mm. 7–8, piano break); 16 bars
B	clarinet (mm. 7–8, clarinet break); 16 bars
A	trombone, bass, ensemble (4 + 4); 16 bars
C	trumpet; 16 bars
C	clarinet; 16 bars
C	piano (1st 8), clarinet (2nd 8)
C	ensemble; 16 bars
coda	guitar (as in intro), ensemble tag chord (2 bars)

The two versions are roughly the same in formal terms, the only differences being that the later performance repeats the C section twice more. Very different, however, are the *textures* (the number of simultaneous melodies and the relationship of melody to accompaniment) and the *kind of melody*. The texture of the first version is primarily *homophonic* (all instruments playing together in block chords), and the melodies are basically orchestrations of the original piano tunes. In the later version, there is more textural variety, and the melodies are new—improvised by the players on top of the basic framework of the original tune.

In the second version, there are solo sections and sections in which the whole ensemble plays. The ensemble sections are *polyphonic*—the trumpet, clarinet, and trombone play independent and equally important, improvised melodies over the basic structure laid down by the rhythm section. This simultaneous group improvisation is a hallmark of the New Orleans jazz style. And we also hear here the stop-time texture (first A chorus and thereafter), in which one melody instrument plays alone, while the rest of the ensemble comes in with chords only on the downbeat (the first beat of a measure) or on every other downbeat.

THE BLUES: EARLY AND CLASSIC

By "blues," I will mean a specific pattern of chords and phrases in a strophic 12-measure form. The 12-bar blues consists of three 4-bar phrases, aab. This is the pattern:

Phrase	a		a		b			
Measure	1 2 3 4		5 6 7 8		9 10 11 12			
Chord	I		IV I		V (IV) I			

What that pattern means in words is that there will be a beginning phrase (a) which last for 4 measures and uses only one basic chord; then the words of that phrase will be repeated, with more or less the same melody, but there will be a change of chord at the beginning of this phrase (measure 5), and another change, back to the first chord, halfway through the phrase (second a); then there will be a third 4-bar phrase, different from the first two in melody, words, and chords (b). The blues is a strophic form, each 12-bar strophe or chorus showing this same aab pattern. The most straightforward examples here are the selections by Ma Rainey and Sippie Wallace, and Bessie Smith's *Lost Your Head Blues*. It pays to listen to these cuts until you can hear, first, the succession of choruses, and then, within those choruses, the three phrases. The phrases are signaled to us by a variety of means, as I'll describe below, so don't panic if you can't hear "chord changes." You will hear *something* happening at regular intervals; and that something will have to do with chorus, phrase, words, melody, as well as with chords. We're starting here with vocal blues for two reasons: first, that's how the form itself began, as far as we know, though the blues "feeling" came out in instrumental music as well; and second, because repetition of words and melody helps one hear the strophic form and the phrase structure of those strophes.

Historians often distinguish among three varieties of vocal blues—country, classic or city, and urban (often electric, and leading into R & B). We'll deal here with the first two of those. *Country* blues comes directly out of the oral folk traditions of the South and the

Southwest and is usually performed by a man accompanying himself on the guitar. Country blues singers were often itinerants who sang for their suppers, literally, or who entertained in bars for payment in beer or liquor. The stories told in country blues are personal, by and about the singer himself, but like all blues they have to do with love—usually unrequited—and with the miseries of being human and mortal. Scrapper Blackwell and Robert Johnson are our examples; others are Mississippi John Hurt, Lightnin' Hopkins, Blind Lemon Jefferson, and such white singers as John Hammond, Jr., and the early Bob Dylan.

Classic or *city* blues were sung by women, backed up by piano and perhaps a small ensemble. They also tell stories of trouble and love gone wrong. But these songs, though still personal and often written by the singer herself, are often more sophisticated than the country blues of the folk tradition, and sometimes tend in the direction of the popular "torch song." They are called "classic" blues not simply because they're classics in the genre, but because of the effect of the so-called "blues craze" that swept the United States from 1920 (Mamie Smith's hit record *Crazy Blues*—which, ironically, was not a blues in form) until 1929 or so. Blues songs have never ridden so high as they did during that decade, though they've been with us ever since, nor has any period been so identified with a single musical form as that era is with the blues. Furthermore, many of the musicians in the classic blues singer's backup group were jazz players; and what people like Fletcher Henderson, Louis Armstrong, and Fats Waller heard from the singers didn't desert them when they cut their own jazz recordings.

Urban blues, which won't be discussed here, is a post-1945 phenomenon. Often electric, it's a product of urban blacks, and the best-known variety comes from Chicago. Chicago-blues players include Muddy Waters, Little Walter, Otis Spann, Willie Dixon, and many others. Urban blues was also the music of a new young generation after 1945, people like Ray Charles and Little Richard, and with them fed directly into rhythm-and-blues (popular since the 1950s), the "soul" music of the 1950s and 1960s, and the blues-rock popular since the 1960s. There are many varieties of urban blues: the Chicago blues just mentioned; the blues played by British rock bands and performers like Eric Clapton; the blues of Southern white bands such as the Allman Brothers; blues of individual artists like Aretha Franklin, Patti LaBelle, or Esther Phillips; or the electric blues of Janis Joplin, who became famous with her cover version of Big Mama Thornton's *Ball and Chain* (as Elvis Presley, in the 1950s, first became famous with Thornton's *Hound Dog*) and her own "classic blues" composition *Turtle Blues.*

What all these types have in common is the earthy, funky feeling, and the phrasing, three 4-bar phrases to the 12-bar chorus; often, especially in the earlier years, each of those 4-bar phrases divided into 2-plus-2, two bars vocal followed by two bars instrumental "break." Instrumental blues such as Basie's may not strike you at first as "blue": but don't be confused by such matters as tempo or good-time feeling. "Blues," after 1930, means a great deal more than what I've described above. It becomes something analogous to the aaba format, or to the sonata or symphony of a classical composer, a model or pattern to work from, a general vehicle for your own individual voice.

➤ *Down South.* Scrapper Blackwell, vocal and guitar.

This is a straightforward 12-bar country blues, in which Blackwell alternates vocal and purely instrumental choruses. (That will be your first landmark in finding your way through the form.) Each strophe follows this basic pattern:

Phrase	a				a				b			
Measure	1	2	3	4	5	6	7	8	9	10	11	12
Chord	I	(IV)	I	I	IV	IV	I	I	V	IV	I	I

➤ *Hellhound on My Trail*, Robert Johnson. Robert Johnson, vocal and guitar. Recorded 1937.

Like the Scrapper Blackwell, this is an example of the country blues, which comes primarily from the South (the Mississippi Delta) and the Southwest. Compare the vocal style here to that of Doc Reese and Leadbelly from the Afro-American section. The lyrics are also a sign of this blues' country origin. "Sweet rider" (or "easy rider") means lover; "hot-foot powder" was also called "goober dust" or "goofer dust," and means peanut shells ground up as part of a voodoo spell, sprinkled around a victim's house to bring him or her bad luck.

Don't worry about the harmonic structure (chord changes) in this example. Notice, the aab structure of the words; and listen to the way Johnson sings his own "breaks" (the last 2 measures of the 4-bar phrase), seeming to answer himself in a sort of solo call-and-response phrasing.

➤ *Countin' the Blues*, Ma Rainey. Ma Rainey, vocal; Louis Armstrong, trumpet; Buster Bailey, clarinet; Charlie Green, trombone; Fletcher Henderson, piano; Charlie Dixon, banjo; Kaiser Marshall, drums. Recorded 1924.

Ma Rainey was a professional singer, touring all over the country, and the first musician to gain a wide reputation as a blues singer. She began to include blues songs in her act around 1902, and she was the first classic or city blues singer. Her only contemporary rival was Bessie Smith.

This is the basic 12-bar blues. Each 4-bar phrase is two bars vocal, two bars break (trumpet or clarinet solo). Again, as with all the other singers in this section, compare the vocal style to that of the Afro-American roots section. Can you hear any similarities between the clarinet and trumpet here and those in the ragtime and early jazz sections? (Armstrong is coming, in all his glory, in the early jazz section, and we'll also hear from Fletcher Henderson again.) How does the texture work here—how do trumpet, clarinet, and voice work together over the rhythm section?

➤ *(I'm a) Mighty Tight Woman*, Sippie Wallace. Sippie Wallace, vocal and piano; Natty Dominique, cornet; Johnny Dodds, clarinet; Honoré Dutrey, trombone. Recorded 1929.

Like Ma Rainey and Bessie Smith (and also Alberta Hunter, whom we'll hear below in *Cake Walking Babies From Home*, and who 50 years later, in her 80s, began to knock 'em dead all over again in New York), Sippie Wallace was a part of the "race-record" blues craze of the 1920s. (These blues were called race records because they were made by black artists for black audiences. The records were usually sold only in stores in black neighborhoods. Although originally intended for blacks, the music quickly became popular with white musicians and audiences as well.) And, like them, she was a city-blues singer backed up by New Orleans/Chicago/New York jazz instrumentalists. In later years, Wallace became a sort of mentor to the singer Bonnie Raitt, who recorded her own cover version of *Mighty Tight Woman* in the early 1970s.

This is another standard 12-bar blues. Once you've got the phrase structure down (three 4-bar phrases in each chorus, aab, the phrases defined by melody and chords), listen to the texture, the backup instrumentalists and their interaction with the vocal. Is this overall sound different from or reminiscent of the music in the ragtime and early jazz sections?

Pay some attention, too, to the lyrics. With the classic blues of the 1920s, lyrics tend to become more forward and brassy—no longer just telling a sad story, they're also now the words of an independent woman telling her man what he can do, where and when he can do it, and to shove off if he doesn't like it. The blues really "grows up" in the 20s; in songs like *Young Woman's Blues* and many others, there is quite a bit of irony in the lyrics, and the songs take on a truly sophisticated adult emotional subtlety.

➤ *Lost Your Head Blues*, Bessie Smith. Bessie Smith, vocal; Joe Smith, cornet; Fletcher Henderson, piano. Recorded 1926.

Bessie Smith was and is known as The Empress of the Blues. This cut and the next are her own compositions, and the perhaps apocryphal story about *Lost Your Head Blues* is that Bessie and company ad-libbed it when they needed another side to fill out a recording session. It may be true: this is a standard 12-bar blues (by 1926, a format that every professional musician could do for days on end), its text a composite of blues conventions. The power here comes from Bessie Smith—the pure sound of her voice, the weight she gives to the words and to their delivery—but she gets a lot of help from Joe Smith's (no relation) hot and distant cornet. Listen to the last chorus: "Days are lonesome, nights are so long." Here Bessie gives up the 2-plus-2 structure (vocal plus cornet break) and sings through all four measures herself. She stretches out the vowels and colors the words: in effect, she takes over from the backup and does it all herself. These long, piercing phrases are a great example of pure blues feeling.

Bessie Smith has probably been the most important influence on jazz singing, though she herself sang primarily blues and not jazz as it has been understood since the 1930s. Billie Holiday, a premiere jazz singer, cited Bessie Smith and Louis Armstrong as the musicians she wanted to sound like. And whether through Billie Holiday (or another singer, Dinah Washington) or through her own recordings, Bessie Smith's style and delivery have colored all jazz/blues singing ever since. Keep her in mind.

➤ *Young Woman's Blues*, Bessie Smith. Bessie Smith, vocal; Joe Smith, cornet; Buster Bailey, clarinet; Fletcher Henderson, piano. Recorded 1926.

Not a standard 12-bar blues, but a blues in its text, its individual 4-bar phrases, its ensemble, its overall power. This is a masterful song, and its subtlety and emotion are supported by the ambiguity of its form.

After an 8-measure introduction and a 2-bar "vamp" (the musicians repeat a short chordal pattern until the singer is ready to come in), Bessie first of all sings a few preliminary phrases that set the scene for the story to come, telling that her lover's left her in the middle of the night, "no time to marry, no time to settle down." Then, with the words "I'm a young woman, I ain't done running 'round," she begins a lament that starts off brassy and defiant and ends up lonely and uncertain.

The 4-bar phrases, beginning with that "I'm a young woman," can be labeled in this way:

a a b a(?) a b x a.

But even though that pattern may *look* like a 12-bar blues, it doesn't *sound* like one. There's no sense of closure, of stopping, after the first b phrase, and the phrases don't fit together in aab choruses. On the contrary, the stop-time b phrase ("Some people call me a hobo . . .") leads without a pause right into the next phrase, without any 2-bar instrumental break, so that the listener thinks, huh, maybe a 16-bar chorus? maybe she's not through yet? But then the next phrase ("I ain't no high yellow . . .") is a straight repetition of the second a phrase above, which had sounded like the second a phrase of a standard 12-bar form. The second b phrase, again stop-time, leads into new music, doesn't stop, carries us directly to the end of the song (which recalls the first "I'm a good woman"). So what's going on?

What happens is this. Every a phrase is the singer's insistence that she's a good woman and that losing her lover is no big deal. But every time she repeats that, it gets a little weaker, a little less certain. When she goes directly from the first b phrase into what I've labeled a(?), the line "I'm as good as any woman in your town" sounds more ironic than assertive. The insinuation is that that doesn't have to be very good. The next b phrase is again brassy, again stop-time and daring, but she's not singing her own words here, she's taken over the words her lover left her with: "I ain't gonna marry, ain't gonna settle down." What he can do, so can she—whether that's really what she wants or not. All she can see now is an empty life ahead. But, she tells herself, I'll get another man. It's a sad, sad song. And what's going on formally—the refusal of the music to stop anywhere, to break up into clear strophes—is exactly what's happening emotionally, the gradual slide from clarion defiance, into reassuring herself, and singing the blues alone.

➤   *St. Louis Blues*, W. C. Handy. Bessie Smith, vocal; Louis Armstrong, cornet; Fred Longshaw, reed organ. Recorded 1925.

W. C. Handy's *St. Louis Blues* (composed in 1914) was for many years the single most famous example of its type, a song that everyone knew and that was performed by singers and instrumentalists of practically every stripe. Bessie Smith's version is definitive, almost stereotypical, classic blues.

The form of *St. Louis Blues* is not strophic, but sectional: AABC. A and C are 12-bar blues (with different melodies), B is 16 measures, although its 4 phrases retain the 2-plus-2 call-and-response of the blues. B is also in the minor mode, which makes a nice contrast to the blues choruses surrounding it—even though it's not a blues form, it certainly has the blues feeling.

Listen, as ever, to the singer's interplay with her backup musicians, the way Louis Armstrong and Fred Longshaw answer her phrases. One interesting little detail is the organist's playing in the A sections. During the vocal phrases, he emphasizes 2 beats to the bar instead of the blues' usual 4; he goes back to the 4-to-the-bar rhythm during the breaks and the later strains. This always makes me imagine that Bessie Smith is playing her own accompaniment; and the effect in the A-section breaks is to bring their intensity up to that of her singing, by intensifying the rhythmic activity.

EARLY JAZZ (I)

➤   *Black Bottom Stomp*, Jelly Roll Morton. Jelly Roll Morton's Red Hot Peppers: Jelly Roll Morton, piano; George Mitchell, trumpet; Kid Ory, trombone; Omer Simeon, clarinet; Johnny St. Cyr, banjo; John Lindsay, bass; Andrew Hilaire, drums. Recorded 1926.

In the section on ragtime, we heard two versions—one by the New England Conservatory Ragtime Ensemble and one by this group—of *Grandpa's Spells*, as an example of the transition from orchestrated rags to jazz. This cut, recorded in the same year as the latter version of *Grandpa's Spells*, throws us into the early jazz of the 1920s. First, notice the ensemble—the typical New Orleans "front line" of clarinet, trumpet, and trombone, and a rhythm section which includes banjo (soon to give way to the guitar) and bass (which has superseded the tuba), as

well as piano and drums. The layout here is sectional, as was that of
Grandpa's Spells, but here there are only two sections or strains, the first
one (A) heard three times and the second (B) seven. There's a great variety of textures here, too: there are sections of New Orleans polyphony,
the group improvisation of melodies from the front line, the contrast of
solo and ensemble choruses, the alternation of ensemble homophonic
chords with solo breaks, the quick alternation of phrases which is
called "trading 4s" (meaning that two instruments, or a solo instrument
and the ensemble, take turns playing 4-bar phrases, in call-and-
response antiphony), stop-time, and so on. Here is the sectional layout:

Section	Instruments	Length (in measures)
Intro	Ensemble	8 (4 + 4)
A^1	Ensemble	16 (homophonic chords, slow then quick, 4 + 4 twice)
A^2	Ensemble	16 (trumpet, others trade 4s)
A^3	Clarinet/banjo	16
Transition	Ensemble	4
B^1	Ensemble	20 (trumpet/trombone break, mm. 7–8)
B^2	Clarinet	20 (solo break, mm. 7–8)
B^3	Piano solo	20
B^4	Trumpet	20 (stop-time)
B^5	Banjo	20 (solo break, mm. 7–8)
B^6	Ensemble	20 (cymbal break, mm. 7–8)
B^7	Ensemble	20 (trombone break, mm. 7–8)

Each A chorus is the same 8-bar phrase, played twice. B is also two 8-
bar phrases which begin similarly; but their ends are different, since the
second phrase has a 4-measure extension at the end. The B choruses are
real, joyful New Orleans polyphony—compare them to the later version of *Grandpa's Spells*, and notice Morton's stride piano. The rhythm
that the ensemble plays in the last two bars of B^2 and B^3, and that
underlies the stop-time chorus (B^4), is the "black bottom" rhythm, a
syncopated pattern associated with the dance called the "black bottom"
and close to the still-famous Charleston rhythmic pattern.

   In passing: Morton worked out the sequence of ensembles, solos,
and kinds of texture for cuts like this and the later ones, in advance.
Much of his work, no matter how immediate and spontaneous it
sounds, was carefully arranged. But the term "arranger" is usually
associated with the men and women who wrote for bigger bands,
beginning in the 1920s. Our first real example of the jazz arranger, in

Jelly Roll Morton. Music Division,
The New York Public Library for the
Performing Arts, Astor, Lenox and
Tilden Foundations.

this sense, will be Fletcher Henderson's *Copenhagen*, arranged by Don
Redman, the first selection in the chapter on big bands and Swing.

➤   *Dead Man Blues*, Jelly Roll Morton. Jelly Roll Morton's Red Hot Pep-
    pers: Jelly Roll Morton, piano; George Mitchell, trumpet; Edward
    "Kid" Ory, trombone; Barney Bigard, Darnell Howard, Omer Simeon,
    clarinet; Johnny St. Cyr, banjo; John Lindsay, bass; Andrew Hilaire,
    drums. Recorded 1926.

   A typical—but still elegant and delightful—blues in the style of
early jazz, Morton's *Dead Man Blues* begins with a quote from Chopin's
"Funeral March" (composed in 1837, then used as the slow movement
of his piano sonata in b♭ minor, op. 35, completed in 1839) that we'll also
hear at the end of Duke Ellington's *East St. Louis Toodle-Oo* (1927), and
which by this time had long been a musical cliché. The fake-lugubrious
trombone lead in the intro tells us not to take it all too seriously. Thereafter, the group plays seven choruses of the 12-bar blues. The first chorus is by the entire group, New Orleans polyphony in an understated
swing. Then there is a solo chorus from Omer Simeon on clarinet, and
two choruses on trumpet. Morton thickens the texture from this point,

with a clarinet trio in tight harmonies and playing a repeated 2-bar phrase or riff for the first 6 bars of their chorus. The sixth chorus is a literal repetition of this clarinet trio, with the added melody of the trombone beneath them, in the same "mournful" mood as the tune's intro. Having moved from solos over the rhythm section to clarinet trio to clarinet trio plus trombone, Morton's arrangement returns to the whole ensemble for the last chorus, and then closes with a 4-bar "tag" coda, the clarinet trio playing the same riff that they had played in fifth and sixth choruses.

➤ *King Porter Stomp*, Jelly Roll Morton. Jelly Roll Morton, piano. Recorded 1939.

Back in the ragtime section we heard Morton's rendition of Scott Joplin's *Maple Leaf Rag*. This performance of his own composition is rhythmically and emotionally less driving than his *Maple Leaf Rag*, but they share a number of general elements. The *King Porter Stomp* is a sectional ragtime composition, with a 4-measure introduction, three 16-bar strains or sections, each repeated, and an interlude between the second and third of these: intro AA BB interlude CCC. (The last C section is cut short, or "elided," to 12 measures.) In this performance, Morton alternates the stride left hand with march-like octaves that sound like a transition between the oom-pah tuba and stride piano of early jazz and what we'll call the walking bass lines of Swing. In the C section, especially, he builds up some of the riffs to the point where he begins to sound almost like a boogie-woogie piano player of the 1920s, a style we'll hear below with Meade Lux Lewis's *Honky Tonk Train Blues*.

The *King Porter Stomp* became a favorite of Swing bands in the 1930s, after Fletcher Henderson's arrangement of it. As with Ellington's *Stompy Jones*, which we'll discuss at the end of the section about his band, it's an early jazz piece that lives on to be a standard in later eras as well.

➤ *Dippermouth Blues*, Joe "King" Oliver. King Oliver's Creole Jazz Band: King Oliver, Louis Armstrong, cornets; Johnny Dodds, clarinet; Honoré Dutrey, trombone; Lil Hardin, piano; Bud Scott, banjo and vocal break; Baby Dodds, drums. Recorded 1923.

A note about this band: Johnny and Baby Dodds were brothers; Lil Hardin and Louis Armstrong were married for some years. This selection has nine choruses of the 12-bar blues. You hear both the dense New Orleans polyphony—simultaneous, group improvisation—and solos from two of the most famous early jazz musicians, Johnny Dodds (clarinet, third and fourth choruses) and King Oliver (cornet, sixth and seventh choruses). Oliver's muted *wa-wa* solo, in particular, was a standard for years, and copied by other cornet players.

➤ *Blue Horizon*, Sidney Bechet. Sidney Bechet and His Blue Note Jazzmen: Sidney Bechet, clarinet; Sidney De Paris, trumpet; Vic Dickenson, trombone; Art Hodes, piano; George "Pops" Foster, bass; Manzie Johnson, drums. Recorded 1944.

Bechet (1897–1959) was a contemporary of Johnny Dodds (1892–1940), Louis Armstrong (1901–1971), and Bix Beiderbecke (1903–1931); and, like them, he helped transform jazz from the early group improvisation to soloist-led music. This cut is anomalous in a couple of ways: first, it's *all* solo, each chorus led by Bechet, with the other musicians just working as a backup group; second, Bechet plays here not his favorite instrument, the soprano sax, but the clarinet (which he'd played before latching onto the sax). Also, it was recorded not in the heyday of New Orleans or post-New Orleans jazz (by which latter term I mean early jazz that emphasizes the solo rather than the improvising ensemble), but in 1944. Still, it's a good example of Bechet's playing and of his contribution to jazz.

Three things to listen to: 1) Bechet's distinctive tone (timbre), mainly a function of his vibrato, very fast and very straight, not a vibrating around the central pitch but a sort of rapid ha-ha-ha *on* that pitch (compare his tone to that of Johnny Dodds on *Dippermouth Blues* or to Benny Goodman in the Swing unit to come); 2) Bechet's use of register to set off choruses and even individual phrases one from another, to shape his overall solo; and 3) the attribution of this standard 12-bar blues to Bechet as his own *composition*. This, like Bessie Smith's *Lost Your Head Blues* and King Oliver's *Dippermouth Blues*, above, or Louis Armstrong's *West End Blues*, yet to come, is an example of individual *melodic* composition, using as its framework a standardized, conventional *harmonic* pattern.

➤ *Cake Walking Babies from Home*, Clarence Williams, Chris Smith, and Henry Troy. The Red Onion Jazz Babies: Louis Armstrong, cornet; Sidney Bechet, soprano sax; Charlie Irvis, trombone; Lil (Hardin) Armstrong, piano; Buddy Christian, banjo; Alberta Hunter and Clarence Todd (listed as "Beatty and Todd"), vocal. Recorded 1924.

In the late nineteenth century, the "cake-walk" was a dance so named because the best dancers won a cake as their prize—they take the cake. (Note the lyrics here: "The only way to win is to cheat 'em. You may tie 'em, but you'll never beat 'em.") And who wouldn't want to dance to this? The tune is strophic, with (rather unusually) a 40-bar chorus, 16 bars plus 16 bars plus an 8-measure extension. (We've already heard a 20-bar strain in Morton's *Black Bottom Stomp*, another dance, and we'll hear yet another in the Eddie Lang/Joe Venuti *After You've Gone*, below.)

Like ragtime, this cake-walk emphasizes 2-to-the-bar meter and syncopated melodies. All the instrumental choruses are ensemble ones, unflagging New Orleans polyphony. After the first chorus there is a 16-bar "verse" section, then the vocal chorus, where the ensemble torques back a little, but still keeps up the energy and the texture of New Orleans polyphony. (Clarence Todd, the male singer, even sings his own "filler" breaks at the beginning, repeating "Oh here they come!") The vocal chorus is followed by two ensemble choruses, but these now including standard breaks in mm. 15–16 (by Sidney Bechet on clarinet in the first of the two and Charlie Irvis's trombone in the second) and an 8-bar stop-time phrase (mm. 25–32 of each chorus), Louis Armstrong leading the charge on cornet in the first and Sidney Bechet again in the second.

EARLY JAZZ (II): LOUIS ARMSTRONG (1901–1971)

Louis Armstrong's place is at the top of the pantheon of jazz. He is the first of only a few musicians to whom we'll devote an entire section in this book. (The later ones will include Duke Ellington, Count Basie, Billie Holiday, Charlie Parker, Miles Davis, and John Coltrane.) In the previous sections he's appeared behind Bessie Smith in *St. Louis Blues*, on King Oliver's *Dippermouth Blues* and, as a soloist, the Red Onion Jazz Babies' *Cake Walking Babies from Home*. In the first section of the chapter on big bands and Swing, we'll hear him again as a soloist on Fletcher Henderson's *Copenhagen* (1924, the same year as *Cake Walking Babies* and the year after *Dippermouth Blues*).

In this section, we'll hear Armstrong's work as a soloist and leader in the late 1920s and an early example of a more "pop" kind of music, from 1933, the kind of music he played and sang from the early 1930s until the late 1940s, when he formed a "New Orleans-revival" sort of group that he led—with continued forays into pop tunes such as *Mack the Knife*, *Hello Dolly*, and *What a Wonderful World*—until his death. Whatever style he was playing, Armstrong was a musician without a chink in his armor. Every aspect of his playing—his brassy and invigorating tone, his extraordinary rhythmic mastery, his endless melodic inventiveness, his complete ease in every register of the trumpet from lowest to highest, his evident deep joy in and through music and the way he made all his listeners equally joyful—every aspect is seemingly at the top of the humanly possible. Rare, and more probably nonexistent, is the jazz musician who does not owe a great debt to Louis Armstrong.

➤ *West End Blues*, King Oliver, Clarence Williams. Louis Armstrong and His Hot Five: Louis Armstrong, trumpet and vocal; Fred Robinson, trombone; Jimmy Strong, clarinet; Earl "Fatha" Hines, piano; Mancy Cara, banjo; Zutty Singleton, drums. Recorded 1928.

Armstrong's short solo intro is one of the most famous moments in jazz history; and, as with the rhythmic work in *Weather Bird* (see below), we're not going to hear anything like it until we get to bop in the 1940s. (An equally famous moment, and an analogous one, is Charlie Parker's "Famous Alto Break" in his 1946 recording of *Night in Tunisia*; see Chapter Three.) This intro is a free-tempo cadenza (virtuoso solo section) and a spectacularly dramatic opening gesture, making us all sit up and take notice. There are two main phrases: the first is the bold and brassy swoop down and up again to a long high note, where the physical effort of starting high, playing fast and loud and tricky, makes the listener breathe along with the player; the second phrase begins high and gradually circles down, gradually relaxes into the music to come.

When we get to the tune proper, its contrast in mood to Armstrong's intro makes us sit up and listen again. This is a straightforward, uncomplicated 12-bar blues, simply harmonized and laid out. There are five choruses: trumpet solo (notice how Armstrong ends with that same upward arpeggio as at the end of the first phrase of his intro); trombone; clarinet/vocal call-and-response duet; piano; and the final ensemble chorus, with Armstrong being the equal partner who's more equal than others.

➤ *Weather Bird*, Joe "King" Oliver. Louis Armstrong, trumpet; Earl "Fatha" Hines, piano. Recorded 1928.

This is another sectional tune, a succession of different strains. Formally, this is closer to orchestrated ragtime and the earliest jazz; later jazz tends to be strophic. But there is nothing "early" or "formative" about the music that Armstrong and Hines lay down in the course of those sections. The form is:

$$\text{intro } A^1 \ B^1 \ B^2 \ A^2 \ \text{interlude } C^1 \ C^2 \ C^3 \ \text{coda.}$$

Each lettered section is 16 measures long. The intro and the interlude (which is the polymetric section where you'll lose the beat) are both 4 measures. The coda is 12. Both B^2 and C^1 are piano solos. (This is simply guidance to help you keep your place.)

This stomps, but it all transpires in phrases of 4 or 8 bars, and in the 16-measure sections; work on being able to hear that. Listen especially to the rhythmic interplay between Armstrong and Hines, to the cross-accents and the polyrhythms. Listen, too, to the way that the lines are built up out of small motives that the musicians toss around. And listen, finally, to the way the alternation between trumpet and piano becomes more frenetic in the course of the tune (in the coda we hear 2 measures of each, then 1). This is competition as well as cooperation, Armstrong and Hines driving each other on and up.

Armstrong's playing is a lot warmer in tone and hotter in rhythm than was Oliver's on *Dippermouth Blues* or Bix Beiderbecke's on *Singin' the Blues* (pages 33–34). By the end of these sections on early jazz, the individual voices of these three great players should be familiar to you. Listen just as carefully to Hines's piano work—there are still some traces of stride, here and there, but his left hand does a lot more than just oom-pah along. His right hand often plays melodies that sound more like Armstrong's than like, say, Scott Joplin's piano lines. (One runs into descriptions of Hines's playing that call it "trumpet style," because of the long, single-note lines, the avoidance of simple punched-out chords.) It's also important here that Hines is not just an accompanist, a one-man rhythm section backing up the soloist; on the contrary, he's an equal partner.

➤ *Hotter Than That*. Lil Hardin Armstrong. Louis Armstrong and His Hot Five: Louis Armstrong, trumpet and vocal; Kid Ory, trombone; Johnny

Dodds, clarinet; Lil Hardin Armstrong, piano; Johnny St. Cyr, banjo; Lonnie Johnson, guitar. Recorded 1927.

And it *is* hotter than that, hotter than any sustained effort we've heard yet from Satchmo. Rhythmically, Armstrong's singing is of a piece with his playing. Try to sing along in the chorus where his scat is working *against* the backup rhythm, where he's singing (or syncopating) in $\underline{3}$ (1 $\underline{2}$ 3 1 $\underline{2}$ 3) against their $\underline{4}$ ($\underline{1}$ 2 3 4 $\underline{1}$ 2 3 4). Louis comes out at the right place at the right time, and had a good time doing it, thank you; can you follow it?

The formal layout of this cut is:

intro	8 measures
trumpet chorus	32 measures
clarinet	32 measures
scat-singing	32 measures (plus extension, a vocal/guitar duet)
trombone, then	16 measures
trumpet/ensemble	16 measures
coda	trumpet/guitar, echoing the end of the scat chorus

You might also notice that in this cut the solo breaks come in the *middle* of the chorus (bars 15–16 out of the 32), as they did in some of our earlier ragtime pieces (*Grandpa's Spells, Cake Walking Babies*), and that at the end of each chorus, the next soloist comes in to pick up where the last has left off (these are transitions, not pure breaks). One result of this is a particular balance of variety (solo break in mid-chorus) and unity (chorus-to-chorus transitions), and the real forward drive that this creates.

➤ *Big Butter and Egg Man from the West*, Louis Armstrong and Percy Venable. Louis Armstrong and His Hot Five: Louis Armstrong, cornet; Kid Ory, trombone; Johnny Dodds, clarinet; Lil Hardin Armstrong, piano; Johnny St. Cyr, banjo. Recorded 1926. [The version on the *Smithsonian Revised Collection* is abridged.]

A "big butter and egg man" was, in derogatory slang of the 1920s, a rube from the sticks who came through the city and tried to impress the "sophisticates" by throwing money around on the high life. If any of that survives in this music—and if it does, I can't hear it myself—it might be in the lesser heat generated by Armstrong and the ensemble here than in our surrounding cuts.

Be that as it may, what we hear here is two 32-bar choruses and a 6-bar tag ending. Armstrong leads the ensemble in the first chorus and solos over the rhythm section in the second. In this tune he stays in the cornet's middle range, and his tone is less brassy than in other things we're listening to. You might also notice the melodic continuity of his playing, how one thing leads directly into the next by repetition, extension, or varied repetition. It's a gently swinging reinterpretation of the song's original melody; but, as ever with Armstrong, the rhythms are tricky and delightful, even when they seem at their most laid back.

➤   *Potato Head Blues*, Louis Armstrong. Louis Armstrong and His Hot Seven: Louis Armstrong, cornet; John Thomas, trombone; Johnny

Louis Armstrong. Music Division, The New York Public Library for the Performing Arts, Astor, Lenox and Tilden Foundations.

Dodds, clarinet; Lil Hardin Armstrong, piano; Johnny St. Cyr, banjo; Pete Briggs, tuba; Baby Dodds, drums. Recorded 1927.

Despite its name, this is a 32-bar tune with a 16-measure verse (Armstrong's first solo) and a 4-bar banjo break between the second and third choruses of the main strophe. As with *Big Butter and Egg Man,* Armstrong stays in his middle register here (this also has something to do with his playing the cornet in this recording, and not the trumpet), and the tempo and overall effect are less hot than some of his other music. The layout of the tune is standard: a first chorus from the whole ensemble, with Armstrong the main musician, and the last two measures a cornet break that leads Armstrong into his solo on the tune's verse. This is followed by Johnny Dodds's solo chorus, complete with the 2-bar break in mm. 15–16 and stop-time at the beginning of the fourth phrase, mm. 25–28. Then comes the banjo interjection and Armstrong's stop-time chorus, the ensemble coming in on every other downbeat, and with a break exactly where Dodds's had been (mm. 15–16). Finally the whole ensemble joins in for a final 16 bars.

➤ *Struttin' with Some Barbecue,* Lil Hardin Armstrong. Louis Armstrong and His Hot Five: Louis Armstrong, cornet; Kid Ory, trombone; Johnny Dodds, clarinet; Lil Hardin Armstrong, piano; Johnny St. Cyr, banjo. Recorded 1927.

We return to a quicker tempo, Armstrong playing higher in the cornet's range, and a hotter effect than in the last two numbers: the group is indeed "struttin'." This is a 32-bar abac tune. The recording begins with a 12-bar introduction. Then we hear Armstrong, as the most important of the horn players (this has to do with the nature of the New Orleans front line, the cornet staying closest to the original tune, and with Armstrong's prominence in 1927, his fronting the ensemble), leading the New Orleans polyphony for the thematic chorus. The last 2 measures are a banjo break that set off this first ensemble chorus from the solos to come. The second chorus is split between a clarinet solo (with a break in mm. 15–16) and a trombone solo (break, mm. 31–32). Then Armstrong takes his solo, with his patented complex-but-sound-easy rhythms, and the expected solo break in mm. 15–16. In the last two measures of this chorus, we get a little break from the horns in tight harmonies, reminiscent of Jelly Roll Morton's New Orleans arrangements (and exactly contemporaneous with them). These bars lead us into the final ensemble chorus—again a break (banjo) in mm. 15–16 and stop-time in the last 8-bar phrase—and then a 4-bar tag coda with those horns again in tight harmony. The ending is a good-natured little "strut," a little flaunting and amused grin.

➤   *Sweethearts on Parade*, Carmen Lombardo and Charles Newman. Louis Armstrong and His Orchestra: Louis Armstrong, trumpet and vocal; George Orendorff, Harold Scott, trumpet; Luther Graven, trombone; Les Hite, alto sax, baritone sax, and leader; Marvin Johnson, alto sax; Charlie Jones, clarinet and tenor sax; Henry Prince, piano; Bill Perkins, banjo and guitar; Joe Bailey, bass; Lionel Hampton, drums. Recorded 1930.

➤   *I Gotta Right to Sing the Blues*, Harold Arlen, Ted Koehler. Louis Armstrong and His Orchestra: Louis Armstrong, trumpet and vocal; Elmer Whitlock, Zilmer Randolph, trumpet; Keg Johnson, trombone; Scoville Brown, George Oldham, clarinet and alto sax; "Budd" Johnson, clarinet and tenor sax; Teddy Wilson, piano; Mike McKendrick, banjo and guitar; Bill Oldham, bass; Yank Porter, drums. Recorded 1933.

These two cuts represent what was, for the purist, Armstrong's "pop" phase, from ca. 1930 until he formed his "All-Star" small groups in the late 1940s, again playing New Orleans jazz, many of the same tunes and in the same format as in the late 1920s. For those who are less tied to external labels, this is still Louis Armstrong, now doing more middle-of-the-road material but still with his usual elegance, inventiveness, and generosity of feeling. What is different here from what we've heard earlier in this unit, besides the large ensemble, is the rhythmic framework. Both these arrangements use the 4-to-the-bar meter that is a hallmark of the Swing era which began in the late 1920s. In the next chapter we'll follow the development of the big-band format and the Swing style (two different things, but which did occur at the same time) in the music of Fletcher Henderson, Duke Ellington, and others. If you review all the recordings in which we've heard Louis Armstrong so far—with King Oliver, Fletcher Henderson, his own small groups, and here with an "orchestra"—you'll trace that same development.

Sweethearts on Parade is a 32-bar aaba form. After a 4-measure introduction, we hear the first Armstrong chorus, on muted trumpet, and then his vocal chorus. Following a short sax break, Armstrong plays a chorus on open (i.e., unmuted) trumpet, with the by-now standard break in mm. 15–16 and 23–24. This last chorus is extended with Armstrong playing the military "reveille."

In *I Gotta Right to Sing the Blues,* listen especially to the final trumpet chorus. Try to remember the tune from the vocal chorus, and compare it to what Armstrong plays here: notice that the latter melody is actually simpler, easier, a sort of paring-down of the tune. There are fewer notes, held longer and embellished differently, and the trumpet seems to ride over the band, not to punch so much as the vocal did. But the horn sound is still warm and full: can you connect it with the sound of Armstrong's singing? (Can you connect his playing and singing in *all* the cuts we've heard where he's done both?)

EARLY JAZZ (III)

Louis Armstrong is usually remembered as the first great jazz horn player and singer, and with Jelly Roll Morton on piano, the first great jazz soloist. He is also held up as the prime example of the jazz musician of the 1920s. He was all of that. But Armstrong didn't do it alone, any more than anyone ever does in any field. What we'll now hear from Bix Beiderbecke, Jack Teagarden, James P. Johnson, and other soloists from New York and around the country is also a part of "early" jazz in the 1920s.

➤   *Singin' the Blues,* Dorothy Fields, Jimmy McHugh. Frankie Trumbauer and His Orchestra: Bix Beiderbecke, cornet; Frankie Trumbauer, C-melody sax; Bill Rank, trombone; Jimmy Dorsey, clarinet and alto sax; Itzy Riskin, piano; Eddie Lang, guitar; Chauncey Morehouse, drums. Recorded 1927.

Don't be misled by the word "orchestra": except for the two saxes (and guitar instead of a banjo), this is the same ensemble as the contemporaneous Morton and Oliver groups. And don't be misled, either, by the title of the cut; this is not a 12-bar blues, but a 32-bar song, aba'c. We hear three choruses: the first, after a 4-bar intro, is a sax solo (Trumbauer), the second a cornet solo (Bix), and the third an ensemble chorus, with some solo phrases. Notice how often the 8-measure phrases end with a 2-bar break. And try to compare the solos—timbre, drive, use of register, and range—with those in the other selections in the unit.

Beiderbecke, for example, swings; but his playing—rhythm, tone, and even elements like the use of vibrato—isn't so "hot" as Louis Armstrong's. Yet because of both Armstrong and Beiderbecke (and others, of course, including Johnny Dodds with Armstrong and the musicians we'll hear on *After You've Gone* and other 1920s cuts), jazz in this decade

The Jean Goldkette Orchestra while on tour in New England. Top row, left to right: Don Murray, Howdy Quicksell, Frank Trumbauer. Bottom row, left to right: Ray Ludwig, Itzy Riskin, Spiegle Willcox, Doc Ryker, Bill Rank, Chauncy Morehourse, Bix Beiderbecke, Bill Challis, Steve Brown, Fuzzy Farrar. Music Division, The New York Public Library for the Performing Arts, Astor, Lenox and Tilden Foundations.

became more of a soloist's art, and headed away from the polyphonic group improvisation of the earlier New Orleans style. The soloists are listening to each other and, so to speak, conversing: in the sax solo, there is a "rip" upward at the beginning of the second and third phrases, which Beiderbecke echoes at the beginning of his third phrase. In the sax solo, again, there is a downward-spiraling arpeggio which the guitar answers (with a downward scale) in the third phrase. In the fourth phrase, the guitar repeats that same figuration, but moves upward with it; in the cornet chorus, the guitar moves up again, similarly, as the cornet moves down. This sort of call-and-response is for many the heart and soul of jazz group work. And it's a different conception of improvisation and of music-making than that of the group polyphony of the earlier New Orleans style.

➤   *Riverboat Shuffle*, Hoagy Carmichael, Irving Mills, and Mitchell Paris. Frankie Trumbauer and His Orchestra: Bix Beiderbecke, cornet; Bill Rank, trombone; Don Murray, clarinet and baritone sax; Frankie Trumbauer, C-melody sax; Doc Ryder, alto sax; Itzy Riskin, piano; Eddie Lang, guitar; Chauncey Morehouse, drums. Recorded 1927.

It's hard to put together the sound of this cut with that of *Singin'
the Blues*, but they were in fact done by the same basic group in the
same year. Because of its ensemble, fast tempo, constant breaks, and
other factors, *Riverboat Shuffle* will sound to some people like early car-
toon music. Get over it.

In the 20-bar introduction, as with the 16-bar section that comes
after Bix Beiderbecke's solo, there are absolutely unpredictable breaks
by soloists or small units. These give the tune its speeded-up effect.
Moreover, in the first ensemble chorus, there are breaks by the guitar
(mm. 3–4, 7–8), piano (mm. 15–16), clarinet (mm. 19–20), and cornet
(mm. 31–32); and in the last chorus, there are again 2-bar breaks by the
cornet (mm. 3–4), sax (mm. 7–8), guitar (mm. 15–16), and sax again
(mm. 19–20). In between these, we hear solo choruses from Bix on cornet (with the standard break in mm. 15–16) and Don Murray on clarinet
(ditto). Finally, there's a little tag from the whole group.

Another reason this is hard to hear as being from the same players as *Singin' the Blues* is the tone colors of the players. Bix, especially,
plays with a hot timbre; and he plays not only the same time of "rip"
he used in the earlier cut, but also a very sexy little break in his solo
chorus. Bix and Tram (i.e., Trumbauer) also played with Paul White-
man's orchestra in the 1920s; but rarely does their work get so hot as in
this cut. Compare it to the next one for the same sort of combined
"lazy," laid-back music and straight-ahead drive.

➤ *After You've Gone*, Henry Creamer, Turner Layton. Eddie Lang-Joe
  Venuti and Their All Star Orchestra: Charlie Teagarden, trumpet;
  Benny Goodman, clarinet; Jack Teagarden, trombone and vocal; Joe
  Venuti, violin; Frank Signorelli, piano; Eddie Lang, guitar; Harry Good-
  man, bass; Ray Baduc, drums. Recorded 1931.

This was in fact, as they billed themselves, an all-star group. The
Teagardens were brothers, as were the Goodmans (we'll hear Benny
again, repeatedly). Jack Teagarden worked with Louis Armstrong in
the late 1940s in the New Orleans-revival group that Satchmo took
around the world. Lang and Venuti had been a famous duo for some
few years, and Lang had recorded with black musicians (unusually for
the era) under the "black-sounding" name Blind Willie Dunn. Like the
Trumbauer/Beiderbecke band, this group of white musicians came
mostly from Chicago (the Teagarden brothers were from Texas), and
they played the New Orleans/Chicago/New York kind of jazz that had
become a national—if not universal—musical language by the late

1920s. There were, of course, local dialects, some of which we'll discuss later. But by and large, this sort of musical mix of solo and ensemble, polyphonic improvisation and other textures, and the sort of tune you hear—and have heard from Armstrong's groups, too—were what most people in the late 1920s understood "jazz" to mean.

After You've Gone was a popular tune of the 1910s and 1920s, sung by people like Sophie Tucker and Mae West (vaudeville "red-hot mamas," as they were called) as well as by jazz musicians. (Remember how jazz musicians also learned from blues singers in the same era.) It's a 20-bar song with an unusual phrase structure of 8 bars plus 12 bars (the latter sometimes 4 plus 8, sometimes 4 plus 4 plus 4). We hear four choruses here. The first begins with a clarinet solo (Benny Goodman) for 8 measures, then a 4-bar solo from the guitar (Eddie Lang), and a final 8 measures from Benny Goodman. The second chorus starts with Jack Teagarden on trombone (8 bars), and then Charlie Teagarden on trumpet (12 bars). The third chorus is Jack Teagarden's vocal. The last, hot, double-time chorus features Joe Venuti on violin for the first 12 bars (listen to that 2-bar solo break in mm. 7–8!) and then the whole ensemble to close.

You'll hear that this is primarily the soloists' music. Only the last part of the last chorus is in the New Orleans polyphonic style, and all the rest is homophonic. The rhythm section here does little except keep time and lay down the basic chords; they swing, and give the cut a lot of its rhythmic drive, but they're not featured in any way. The solos are all based on the original tune—you can sing along with the whole cut and never get lost—but the players are all very inventive in carving new melodies out of that original one, using range and rhythms and rests to create their own new lines. Listen to Teagarden's vocal: like Armstrong, he sang in the same way he played, and in some of the phrases here Teagarden even sounds to me like Armstrong. After his work in Armstrong's small group in the 1940s, he formed a similar group (similar to this one and to Armstrong's) and toured with that for many years.

➤   *Carolina Shout*, James P. Johnson. James P. Johnson, solo piano. Recorded 1921.

Johnson was the "Father of Stride Piano," a performing and compositional style that came out of ragtime and was centered in New York in the 1920s. Other stride pianists include Willie "The Lion" Smith, Fats Waller, and—at a stylistic remove or two—Art Tatum and Duke Ellington. You should also go back here and listen to Scott Joplin and Jelly

Roll Morton. There are still stride pianists working the keys today: some, like Dick Wellstood and Judy Carmichael, play mainly stride; Dave McKenna uses stride as a major part of his style; others, like the late Jaki Byard, include stride as just one of the styles of which they are masters.

Carolina Shout became a "test piece" for any pianist coming through New York in the 1920s: if you couldn't cut it, you got off the stand. It consists of three strains or sections, plus a 4-bar intro and a 4-bar tag coda: intro AABCCCCC coda. Each lettered section is 16 meas-`ures long, and each of these is subdivided aa'ab in form. (Remember Joplin's *Maple Leaf Rag*: same format.) The groupings, as with Joplin and Jelly Roll Morton, are duple from the ground up, 2-plus-2 into 4-bar phrases, these combining into 16-bar sections. But listen to the way Johnson plays with the beat, especially in the second A chorus, when the "oom" of the oom-pah left hand seems to work in patterns *against* the 1-2 beat. In the 2-plus-2 phrases, can you hear anything of the earlier 2-plus-2s discussed (e.g., the call-and-response we talked about in the blues)?

➤ *Honky Tonk Train Blues,* Meade Lux Lewis. Meade Lux Lewis, piano. Recorded 1937.

This is your basic boogie-woogie: 12-bar blues progression, left-hand *ostinato* pattern (*ostinato* means a rhythmic/harmonic pattern repeated over and over without a break, like a riff; the English cognate is *obstinate*), and that left-hand ostinato being <u>8</u> to the bar, not 4. Boogie-woogie was a craze that began around 1920, in the same place and at the same time as New York stride, and eventually survived into MGM movie musicals and such groups as the Andrews Sisters in the 1940s. It also descended to levels that are now described as "pure 30s" and remembered as either nostalgia or camp: one of the Andrews Sisters' hits was called "Beat Me, Daddy, Eight to the Bar"; and Martin Williams mentions a song, "Scrub Me, Mama, With A Boogie Beat." There's also Bette Midler's cover of "The Boogie-Woogie Bugle Boy of Company B" from the 1970s, when she was in her "camp" phase. Boogie-woogie's basic format—the blues progression with that distinctive left-hand bass—still shows up in some rock music, especially the kind called rockabilly, and in music by people like Jerry Lee Lewis.

The blues progression and the left-hand pattern will, I hope, be immediately obvious to you. What you should listen for, in addition, is the drive and the variety in the pianist's right hand.

➤   *Four or Five Times*, Byron Gay, Marco H. Hellman. Jimmie Noone's
    Apex Club Orchestra: Jimmie Noone, clarinet and vocal; Joe Poston,
    alto sax and vocal; Earl "Fatha" Hines, piano; Bud Scott, banjo and gui-
    tar; Johnny Wells, drums. Recorded 1928.

This is a good-time tune, strophic, with a 16-bar chorus aa (8 plus
8). It differs from most of what we've heard above, and is on the way
to Swing music, in its 4-to-the-bar beat. We've heard "Fatha" Hines
with Louis Armstrong, especially in *Weather Bird*, recorded the same
year as this tune; here, as in that tune, listen to his syncopations, especially in his solo chorus, when the "downbeats" come in early, as syncopations against himself. The last two ensemble choruses are still New
Orleans-style, led by the band leader Noone on clarinet. (There's a nice,
if raunchy, sax lick in the first of these last two "out" choruses.) The
vocal duet should remind you of that in the Red Onion Jazz Babies'
Cake Walking Babies from Home, above. And the title of the cut, *Four or
Five Times*, is of the same suggestive ilk as the first title of Basie's *One
O'Clock Jump, 6 or 7 Times* (see Chapter Two): cf. the lyrics, "I like doing
things right 4 or 5 times." The lay-out of the recording is: piano intro,
ensemble chorus, Hines's chorus (piano), vocal duet (2 choruses), and
2 ensemble choruses to end.

➤ Chapter 2

Big Bands, Small Combos, and Swing
(Swing, Brother, Swing!)

Although big bands and Swing music began and developed in the same years—from the mid-1920s through the late 1930s—the two terms don't always involve the same sort of music. The big-band *format* (the instruments in the group and, to some extent, the ways in which they're used) has remained more or less constant since the 1930s, with some exceptions such as Stan Kenton, Gil Evans and Miles Davis, groups that come out of the "free" jazz of the 1960s and later, and some new groups in the 1990s. But Swing, which is a *style* of music, has been followed by many other styles since the mid-1940s. Some of these later styles have also used the big-band format, but the music isn't in the Swing style. (We'll hear examples of the latter: big bands of Dizzy Gillespie, Woody Herman, Gil Evans, Lester Bowie, and others.) During the Swing era itself, there were big bands that some are regarded not as jazz groups but as dance bands that played commercial entertainment music, even if they did use a few tricks and traits of the real jazz organizations. (The same sort of distinction holds today with various sorts of rock, country, and "commercial" bands.) As is always the case, there are no absolute and distinct boundaries among these various categories, and sometimes the label attached to a group depends more on the listener than on the group itself. But distinctions between format and style can be made, and you need to keep them in mind as you listen to this music.

The big band is a group of more than ten players, divided into three sections: rhythm, brass, and reeds. The rhythm section is the same as it had been for New Orleans-style groups: piano, guitar, bass, and drums. (Notice that the banjo and tuba of the early New Orleans years are now—after a few last licks—gone, until the 1980s.) Occasionally, and later (in the late 1930s and 1940s), there is also the vibraharp or vibraphone, colloquially known as the "vibes." The horn sections are an expansion of the New Orleans "front line," now subdivided by instrumental family. In the big band, there is now a reed section, also called a reed "choir," consisting of three to five saxophones, normally alto (1 or 2), tenor (1 or 2), and baritone (1). Depending on the band and on the era, you may also find bass sax, clarinet, soprano sax, and/or flute. Although reed players usually specialize on one or maybe two of these instruments, most are professionally competent on more than two, and that will be a factor in the particular kind of arrangement a given band favors. The brass section (or, again, "choir") still consists of trumpets and trombones: three to five trumpets (sometimes fluegel-horn) and normally two or three trombones (for example, two tenor trombones and one bass trombone). These numbers can be expanded: many stage bands have five saxophones (two alto, two tenor, one bari), five trombones, and six trumpets. A standard seating arrangement is the rhythm section on stage right (the audience's left as you face the stage), the saxes seated stage center, trombones behind them, and the trumpets behind the trombones.

The big band sound is characterized by the playing-off of these sections against one another. The rhythm section is the busiest, since it almost always plays behind and supports the others, laying down the basic chords and beat, just as it had in earlier jazz. The rhythm section also often plays by itself, the reed and brass choirs laying out. The horn sections are contrasted in a variety of ways. One of the sections, reeds or brass, may take a chorus of a tune while the other is silent. The two may be used together, but in a call-and-response pattern: for example, in a 12-bar blues chart, each 4-bar phrase may be subdivided into 2 bars saxes, 2 bars brass (or vice versa). If the sections play at the same time, one choir will be given the melody and the other will play a back-ground accompaniment. If there is a soloist, a sax soloist will typically play over a brass accompaniment, a trumpet or trombone over the saxes. This may also involve the kind of call-and-response just men-tioned between whole sections. The entire band plays together—with-out this sort of melody/accompaniment arrangement—usually just in the first (thematic) chorus, to get things rolling, or more often in the final (out) ones, when everything comes screaming to a conclusion.

With all these people involved, and sometimes playing for hours at a time, often playing too much music for anyone to remember or learn by heart, it is necessary for big bands to have an arranger, someone who works out the music in advance and who supplies the players with written parts. Our only real arranger in the first chapter was Jelly Roll Morton. The function of the arranger is not simply to decide on the order of things, to keep people straight on what they're doing (first chorus everybody, second chorus saxes, third chorus sax solo over trombones, for example), but to write the individual parts for all this, to show off the musicians at their best advantage, whether as a section or as soloists, and to arrive at some sort of satisfying variety of design in the course of a tune. (Thirty-two continuous choruses from the sax section, for example, would be extraordinarily tiring for the players and fairly tedious for the listeners.) In this chapter we'll emphasize the arranger for the first selections discussed as introductory examples (Fletcher Henderson), and for all the music of Duke Ellington. But you should pay attention to this throughout the chapter, even if the discussions of selections don't concentrate on it. The kind of arrangement that a band uses is often that band's real signature, that which sets it apart from other groups. And the arrangement is the aspect of this music that gives it its overall structure, its overall drive to a climactic final chorus (for example, *Moten Swing*) or the play of tension and release that keeps us on the edge of our seats, hardly willing to breathe (as in Goodman's *Sing, Sing, Sing*).

Big bands were a product of the cities during the 1920s and 1930s, since that's where the money for music was and where the musicians went: the more money, the more people, the bigger the possible group. And in the cities there were ballrooms which by sheer size alone demanded a large group to fill the space with sound. There were also night clubs that featured floor shows as well as music for dancing, such as the Cotton Club in Harlem (New York). There were also many cabarets and clubs that were big enough to support live music for listening. Swing music began as *entertainment* music—for dancing or, in Ellington's notable case, as background music for floor shows—and only later became "concert" music, music that you listened to for its own sake. This has a great deal to do with the development of the Swing style.

That style is a function of several things. (NB: we are here getting into the difference between the big-band *format* and the musical Swing *style*.) The Swing style includes what is sometimes called the "emancipation," or increased importance, of the rhythm section—the "hot," 4-to-the-bar beat, insistent and driving, the rhythmic surprises over that

4-to-the-bar framework, coming as syncopations, sudden drum shots, whatever; riffs, which are as important rhythmically as they are melodically, and which also keep the music driving forward; call-and-response among the sections; hot, up-front tone colors; and straightforward melodies that are easily remembered because of their balance and regularity and because they're easy for the nonmusician to sing. (One might do a comparison between the Charlie Parker tune *Ornithology* and the Swing standard on which it's based, *How High the Moon*, to emphasize Swing's regularity and memorability in contrast to bop's asymmetry and immediate vividness. In a scat chorus of *How High the Moon*, as the great example, Ella Fitzgerald sings the melody of *Ornithology*, but phrases it in 8-bar units, as if it were a Swing tune, ironing out the cross-phrasing. See Chapter Three.) Many of these Swing traits will also be found in bop, which was a direct outgrowth of Swing and not entirely a revolt against it. But such specific traits will show up in different contexts when we get to later jazz. For the present, it's enough to trace some of these characteristics and their development through specific examples. We begin the first section of this chapter with three charts by the Fletcher Henderson organization, to trace (in one way) the development of both the big-band format and the Swing style; and we end the section with a tune of Jimmie Lunceford, in a classic arrangement. In between, we hear early Ellington, the 1930s Moten orchestra, an early Basie tune, and an early Goodman cut.

We'll then concentrate on individual ensembles. The Ellington section is long, since few people—as we'll see—agree on what's "essential" in the Ellington repertory. After Ellington, we'll turn our attention to Basie's band(s) and then to Goodman, band and small groups. Following other Swing bands, we'll look at some soloists, and end this section with a longer section about Billie Holiday, the "Voice of Jazz"—even today, some 40 years after her death.

INTRODUCTION TO BIG BANDS AND SWING

➤   *Copenhagen*, Charles Davis, Walter Melrose. Fletcher Henderson and His Orchestra: Fletcher Henderson, piano; Howard Scott, Elmer Chambers, Louis Armstrong, trumpets; Charlie Green, trombone; Buster Bailey, clarinet, alto and soprano saxes; Don Redman, alto sax, clarinet, and arranger; Coleman Hawkins, tenor sax and clarinet; Charlie Dixon, banjo; Bob Escudero, tuba; Kaiser Marshall, drums. Recorded 1924.

With the advent of the bands, we have to consider not just the soloists, but the art of the jazz arranger as well. This cut was arranged by Don Redman. It's a sectional piece with three strains, each strain built up in 4-bar phrases. But listen to the way Redman achieves a balance of unity and variety by contrasting the clarinet trio and the trumpet trio (a reed "choir" and a brass "choir"); by alternating these trios with the full ensemble and with the two solos; and by alternating notated homophony, whether in the trio or ensemble sections, with improvised polyphony in the solos and ensembles. Compare this cut, on all counts, with Jelly Roll Morton's 1926 *Black Bottom Stomp* and other tunes. Although *Copenhagen* is reminiscent of the general sound of the New Orleans-style *Black Bottom Stomp*, using the same families of instruments in the same ways (reeds, brass, and rhythm) and recalling the sound of New Orleans-style polyphonic improvisation, there is actually much less improvisation here than in the Morton arrangement. Improvisation is restricted to the solo choruses and to the solo passages in the ensembles, for example when one of the clarinets plays alone and not as a member of the clarinet trio. Also, the rhythms here are less varied, less hot, than in the Morton, and the swing of the cut comes mainly from the banjo's off-beats. The overall focus here is on the group and its possibilities, and less on the work of individual soloists. This will be the case for virtually all the music in this first section.

Notice how many of these musicians also played behind Bessie Smith in the mid-1920s: Fletcher Henderson, Charlie Green, Buster Bailey, and Don Redman were among her most frequent accompanists in the recording studio; Louis Armstrong, Coleman Hawkins, and Charlie Dixon also worked with her. Such recruitment of a backup group or small instrumental combo from a single big band is very common, and this particular one is an example of the close relationship of instrumental jazz and classic blues in the Swing era.

The formal arrangement:

Section	Instruments	Length (measures)
A	Trumpet trio, ensemble	8
A	Clarinet trio, ensemble	8
B	Clarinet trio (12-bar blues)	12 (repeated)
B	Armstrong solo	12
A	Ensemble	8 (repeated)
C	Trumpets—clarinets—trumpets	16
A	Clarinet trio, ensemble	8
A	Clarinet trio, ensemble	8
B	Trombone, ensemble	12 (repeated)
C	Brass, Bailey solo	16

A   Alternating trios/ensembles   7 (!)
                                                      10

Coda   Ensemble   4

➤   *The Stampede*, Fletcher Henderson. Fletcher Henderson and His
    Orchestra: Fletcher Henderson, piano; Russell Smith, trumpet; Joe
    Smith, Rex Stewart, cornet; Benny Morton, trombone; Buster Bailey,
    Don Redman clarinet and alto sax; Coleman Hawkins, clarinet and
    tenor sax; Charlie Dixon, banjo; Ralph Escudero, tuba; Kaiser Marshall,
    drums. Recorded 1926.

We hear again here the beginnings of a big-band style formulated
by Fletcher Henderson and his arranger in the mid-1920s, Don Redman. Many of the remarks made under *Copenhagen*, above, will apply
to *The Stampede* as well. There are more solos in this particular cut, but
the same idea of balance among sections and between sections and
soloists still holds. What begins to sound more like the Swing music to
come is the hotter timbres of the soloists, particularly the cornetists,
and the increasing regularity of their phrasing, one of the things that
makes the music swing. The thickness of the texture, the use of banjo
and tuba, and the clarinet trios still mark this as early big-band jazz of
the 1920s.

The tune is a nice mix of strophic and sectional, things returning
but not in a heavy-handed and predictable way. It begins with a 16-bar
intro, Rex Stewart (cornet) and the ensemble trading 4s. This is followed by a 32-bar ensemble chorus, a solo chorus from Coleman
Hawkins, whom we heard with the Red Onion Jazz Babies and in the
Henderson band playing *Copenhagen*, and whom we will hear again as
a soloist; this chorus, like the later solo one, has the by now inevitable
break in mm. 15–16. After Hawkins's solo is a 4-bar interlude from the
saxes, and then a 32-bar cornet solo (Joe Smith, whom we heard backing up Bessie Smith on *Lost Your Head Blues* and *Young Woman's Blues*).
Finally we hear a chorus led by the clarinet trio, and a last chorus introduced by Rex Stewart on cornet (as in the intro), yielding to the whole
ensemble.

➤   *Wrapping It Up*, Fletcher Henderson. Fletcher Henderson and His
    Orchestra: Russell Smith, Irving Randolph, Henry "Red" Allen, trum-
    pet; Keg Johnson, Claude Jones, trombone; Buster Bailey, Hilton Jeffer-
    son, Russell Procope, clarinet and alto sax; Ben Webster, tenor sax;

Horace Henderson, piano; Lawrence Lucie, guitar; Elmer James, bass; Walter Johnson, drums. Recorded 1934.

Our first example of full-blown big band Swing, this is Henderson's arrangement of his own composition, eight years after *The Stampede* and ten after *Copenhagen*. The ensemble is slightly larger—one more trombone, one more reed man—and we have now moved definitively to guitar and bass in the rhythm section. The arrangement, like others from the Henderson book, was also recorded by Benny Goodman's organization. And with *Wrapping It Up* we're a long way from the vestiges of post-New Orleans jazz that we heard in *Copenhagen* or the later Louis Armstrong.

After an 8-bar introduction (call-and-response, brass and saxes), there are four choruses of the 32-measure theme, abab'; the 8-bar phrases are clearly articulated in each chorus. The first chorus begins with the sax choir (with brass interjections), then we hear the whole group. The second chorus is an alto sax solo (Hilton Jefferson) over soft, sustained brass chords. The third chorus is a trumpet solo (Red Allen) over an active sax section; their rhythms, especially, recall the music of the first chorus. The final chorus combines the whole ensemble (brass and clarinets, a clarinet solo, then saxes and brass) in a variation of the first chorus. Underneath it all is the hot 4-to-the-bar swing of the double bass. The playing-off of sections (brass vs. reeds) was mentioned in *Copenhagen*, and it is a hallmark of the big band. A second standard technique demonstrated here is using a soloist from one group (alto sax) against the background of the contrasting section (brasses).

➤ *East St. Louis Toodle-Oo*, Bubber Miley, Duke Ellington. Duke Ellington and His Orchestra: Duke Ellington, piano; Bubber Miley, Louis Metcalf, trumpet; Joe "Tricky Sam" Nanton, trombone; Otto Hardwicke, saxes; Harry Carney, clarinet and saxes; Rudy Jackson, clarinet and tenor sax; Fred Guy, banjo; Wellman Braud, bass; Sonny Greer, drums. Recorded 1927.

This is an early example of Duke Ellington. For many people, Ellington is the United States' greatest composer, and it seems beyond question that Ellington's work, during a fifty-year career as a composer/arranger/bandleader/pianist, has been of the highest musical and historical importance to this country. He did it all, as they say. One of the central elements of Ellington's work—and one thing that makes

Duke Ellington and His Cotton Club Orchestra. Left to right: Freddy Jenkins, Sam
Nanton, Cootie Williams, Harry White, Arthur Whetsol, Sonny Greer, Duke Ellington, Harry Carney, Fred Guy, Johnny Hodges, Wellman Braud, Barney Bigard. Courtesy of the Rutgers Institute of Jazz Studies.

that work so striking, as well as so unmistakably "Ellington"—is that
for him, melody, texture, and color were factors of *equal* musical importance, inseparable in his musical conceptions. Ellington was a genius at
cultivating his players' individual sounds and at combining those various colors into his own ensemble. *East St. Louis Toodle-Oo* marks a
beginning, and in the next section, we'll follow the Ellington band into
the 1930s and the 1940s, their full and lengthy maturity, with even a
taste of later music.

The last word in the title of this tune is pronounced "Toad-Low."
Bubber Miley once saw, in East St. Louis, Illinois, a man so bent and
crumpled with age that he walked "toad-low" to the ground. As we'll
see later, Ellington often gave his compositions descriptive titles, connecting his music to scenes (as here), emotions (*Mood Indigo* or *Prelude
to a Kiss*), or people (*The Clothed Woman* or the musical "portraits" he
wrote).

East St. Louis Toodle-Oo is a 32-bar aaba song form, with an 18-
measure "trio" C, two 8-bar phrases plus a 2-measure extension at the
end. We are calling this latter section a "trio" not because it's played by
three instruments (it's a solo over the rhythm section the first two times
we hear it), but after the terminology of marches, where contrasting C
sections are called "trios." This, in turn, derives from earlier European
stylized dance music, such as the minuet and trio.)

intro	8 bars	Low saxes, *bowed* (not plucked) bass, etc.; the backup harmonies for the a̲ phrases of the main chorus
aaba	32 bars	Miley, "growl" trumpet solo with plunger mute
C	18 bars	Carney, baritone sax solo
C	18 bars	Nanton, trombone solo
aa̲C̲a	42 bars	16 bars (aa), Rudy Jackson, clarinet
		18 bars (C), ensemble (especially brass)
		8 bars (a), Miley, as above

The final cadence is an echo of Chopin's "Funeral March" (1835), which had become a cliché in jazz as well as in European "classical" music. It opened Jelly Roll Morton's 1926 *Dead Man Blues* (above), and we'll hear it again as the tag for Ellington's 1927 *Black and Tan Fantasy* and on other charts. When you've listened to this cut, you may want to skip ahead to hear Ellington's later *New East St. Louis Toodle-Oo* (1937), or try to find the 1970s cover version of the tune by the band Steely Dan.

➤   *Moten Swing*, Buster and Benny Moten. Benny Moten's Kansas City Orchestra: Hot Lips Page, Joe Keys, Dee Stewart, trumpet; Dan Minor, trombone; Eddie Durham, trombone, guitar, alto sax; Eddie Barefield, clarinet and alto sax; Jack Washington, alto and baritone sax; Ben Webster, tenor sax; Count Basie, piano; Leroy Berry, guitar; Walter Page, bass; Willie McWashington, drums. Recorded 1932.

A great Kansas City band in full cry, playing a chart that's a succession of 32-bar riff choruses. A *riff* is a short—usually just two measures—rhythmic, melodic, and/or harmonic figure that serves as the basic musical material of a given phrase or chorus. The riff is derived from the call-and-response patterning which we first mentioned in connection with African and Afro-American musics. For the clearest example here, listen to the bridge (the b̲ phrase) of the first chorus, where the 2-chord brass figure trades off with the saxes playing in unison.

1st chorus: basically an introductory section, although it's a 32-bar aaba form, like all the choruses to come. Piano takes the a̲ phrases, the bridge is the call-and-response riffs mentioned above.
2nd chorus: a̲ phrases, saxes in harmony. The bridge is given to the rhythm section, especially to the guitar.

3rd chorus: in the first two a̲ phrases, brass section in harmony and a tenor sax solo (again, a contrast of sections with a reed solo over a brass background); bridge is a sax solo continued over the rhythm section; the final a̲ phrase (the "last 8") is a repetition of the brass riff, sax now laying out.

4th chorus: the three a̲ phrases are a trumpet solo (Hot Lips Page), the bridge another sax solo. Notice how the bridge is distinguished from the a̲ phrases not just by its music, the melody and harmony, but often by the instruments playing as well.

5th chorus: sax section all the way. The band here is really working—you can hear them calling musical encouragement to each other, really exhorting one another on in this chorus.

Coda: 4 bars.

Moten Swing is thus a series of five choruses over the same harmonies (chords and chord progressions), but in every chorus the riffs, the basic material, the rhythms and tunes you hear, are different. The chords are those of a contemporary popular song, *You're Driving Me Crazy*. This is a standard procedure that we've already seen in the blues—new melodies over the conventional chord- and phrase-structure—and which is still with us. We'll see it again in many bop tunes which use the chord progression of the old George and Ira Gershwin standard *I Got Rhythm* or other Swing-era jazz and pop tunes.

Finally, notice the remnants of stride piano in Basie's work. He was influenced in his early days by the stride pianist James P. Johnson and even got some instruction, albeit on organ, from Fats Waller. Listen also to Walter Page's 4-to-the-bar playing on bass: this hot rhythmic activity gives the cut a lot of its drive, and it's one of the important elements of the Swing style.

➤ *Shout and Feel It,* Count Basie. Count Basie and His Orchestra: Ed Lewis, Buck Clayton, Bobby Moore, trumpet; George Hunt, Dan Minor, trombone; Earle Warren, alto sax; Herschel Evans, Lester Young, clarinet and tenor sax; Jack Washington, alto and baritone sax; Count Basie, piano; Freddie Green, guitar; Walter Page, bass; Jo Jones, drums. Recorded 1937, as an "air-check"—i.e., a live radio broadcast—at the Savoy Ballroom in New York (see the next cut, Goodman's *Stompin' At The Savoy*).

Like the Moten cut, this is a succession of 32-bar aaba riff choruses. After Moten died in 1935, Basie reunited the nucleus of the

Moten band, and the new group stuck largely with the Kansas City-style riff arrangements at which they had become such experts.

The layout is as follows:

intro	4 measures
1st chorus	Ensemble
Transition	4 measures
2nd chorus	Buck Clayton, trumpet solo, aa; ensemble bridge; Herschel Evans, tenor sax, final a
3rd chorus	Basie, piano solo, a phrases (the voice shouting encouragement in the background is Billie Holiday's)
4th chorus	Ensemble a phrases; trumpet solo by Bobby Moore in the bridge

By now you should be able to tell the difference between the Kansas Citians, Moten and Basie, on the one hand, and the New Yorkers, Henderson and Ellington, on the other. We'll follow this up and reinforce it in the two sections to come.

➤ *Dinah*, Henry Akst, Sam M. Lewis, Joe Young. Red Nichols and His Five Pennies: Red Nichols, Manny Klein, Leo McConville, trumpet; Jack Teagarden, Bill Trone or Herb Taylor, trombone; Benny Goodman, clarinet; Babe Russin, tenor sax; Arthur Schutt, piano; Carl Kress, guitar; Art Miller, bass; Gene Krupa, drums. Recorded 1929.

Compare this cut to *After You've Gone* from Chapter One. It shares some of the same musicians, especially Jack Teagarden (who doesn't sing here), and it's a sort of way-station between the early jazz of that music and the Swing era to come. The tune was a standard ("Dinah, is there anyone finer?") for both pop and jazz musicians of the era, and we'll hear it again later in this chapter from the great Belgian electric guitarist, Django Reinhardt, and his group.

The tune is a 32-bar aaba. After a 2-bar intro led by Teagarden on trombone, we hear a thematic chorus that stays very close to the original melody. Teagarden plays the a phrases and Nichols the bridge. In the second chorus, following a 2-bar interlude, Benny Goodman plays the first 2 a phrases, over the banjo sounds of the rhythm section. Babe Russin, tenor sax (whom we'll also hear again, with Goodman's own band) plays the bridge, and then Goodman returns for the last phrase. In the last chorus, Teagarden plays the first 24 bars, aab, and the whole band comes in for the final a, in collective improvisation. Two things especially prevent this cut from falling completely into the category of Swing: first, the rhythm section is playing 4-to-the-bar, but not yet in the Swing way. Instead of getting 4 equal bars from the rhythm section (especially bass, drums, and pianist's left hand), the bass and piano emphasize 1 and 3, and the drums accent 2 and 4. It's still a little clunky, like 1920s jazz, and not so smooth as Swing will be. Second, the soloists also reflect this lack of rhythmic continuity, and they don't seem to be thinking in the regular, satiny 8-bar phrases that soloists of the 1930s will.

➤ *Stompin' at the Savoy*, Edgar Sampson, Benny Goodman, Chick Webb. Benny Goodman and His Orchestra: Benny Goodman, clarinet; Nate Kazebier, Harry Geller, Ralph Muzzillo, trumpet; Vernon Brown, Joe Harris, trombone; Herman Schertzer, William Depew, Arthur Rollini, Dick Clark, sax; Jess Stacy, piano; Allan Reuss, guitar; Gene Krupa, drums; Harry Goodman, bass. Recorded 1936

The Savoy was a ballroom in New York, one of the biggest and most popular places for dancing and listening to Swing, and this tune is one of the standards of that era. Goodman, in fact, was known, at least to some people, as the "King of Swing," after he and his group became an overnight sensation as a result of a gig at the Palomar Ballroom in Los Angeles in 1935. Goodman's sense of Swing is different from that of other bands in this section; he emphasized precision in ensemble work (the sections or the whole band playing *together*), in rhythms and rhythmic attacks (beginning and ending precisely together, no oozing into or out of the lines), and in playing in tune (no circumlocution, no fooling around with the pitch). So the Goodman organization falls somewhere between, on the one hand, the black groups such as Ellington's, Basie's, Moten's, and Lunceford's (different as those four are from one another), and, on the other hand, the "sweet" dance bands such as the Dorsey brothers' or Glenn Miller. And Goodman combines black and white in another, and even more important way, as well: with his hiring of Teddy Wilson, piano, and later Charlie Christian, guitar, and Lionel Hampton on vibes, first to work with his small groups and then as part of his big band, Goodman opened the way to *public* integration of the races in jazz groups. By "public," I mean that there had been some instances of integrated groups before the mid-1930s. Goodman himself, and other white musicians, had played on Billie Holiday's first recordings in 1933. The white guitarist Eddie Lang, for instance, had recorded with black musicians in the 1920s. But Lang used a name that "sounded" black, "Blind Willie Dunn," instead of his own; and neither the public—at least the white public—nor the managers and booking agents at the time were prepared to accept groups that included both black and white musicians. Goodman helped open the path to integration, but the situation held, at least in popular entertainment, in television and the movies, into the 1960s.

Stompin' at the Savoy is another succession of riff choruses in a 32-bar aaba song form; compare it to the Basie Shout and Feel It, discussed previously. There is a 4-bar intro, then three choruses, then a final elided (cut short) chorus, aba. The first chorus features the saxes in unison, with interjections from the brass (like the bridge of Moten Swing, first chorus). The second chorus turns that around—longer brass phrases, with 2-note sax riffs—and Goodman takes a solo in the bridge. Then in the elided final chorus, the brass section leads the first a phrase, Goodman solos again in the b, and the final a is as above, with unison saxes and brass interjections. Notice that although the rhythm section is here still working 4-to-the-bar, the tempo is slower than in the Moten or Basie cuts; this particular selection may "swing," but it isn't particularly "hot." Goodman bought charts from the black bands (especially Henderson and Basie) and used black arrangers, but his band's performance of those same charts is much different from a performance by the Henderson or Basie bands. Compare the sound of this cut with the selections from Goodman's 1938 Carnegie Hall concert, below, with Basie and others sitting in.

➤ Lunceford Special, Eddie Durham. Jimmie Lunceford and His Orchestra: Eugene "Snooky" Young, Gerald Wilson, Paul Webster, trumpet; Elmer Crumbley, Russell Bowles, Trummy Young, trombone; Willie Smith, Earl Carruthers, Ted Buckner, Dan Grissom, alto saxes; Joe Thomas, tenor sax; Edwin Wilcox, piano; Al Morris, guitar; Moses Allen, bass; Jimmy Crawford, drums. Recorded 1939.

We have here a big hit for the Lunceford band, and a straight-ahead Swing chart. By now, you should be able to find your way through a number like Lunceford Special without much outside guidance. The harmonies are simple and repetitive (listen to the bass), and it exemplifies virtually all the Swing characteristics we've noted thus far. The layout, in the sketchiest of terms, is: 4-bar intro, 8-bar phrase, 4-bar transition. Then come four aaba 32-bar choruses: first chorus, ensemble (saxes in the a phrases, brass in the bridge); second chorus, trumpet solo (first 16 bars), alto sax solo (second 16 bars); third chorus, trombone (first 16), tenor sax (second 16); fourth chorus, ensemble, with trumpet solo in the last 8 (the final a phrase); 16-bar coda, featuring the trumpet solo.

Does the playing here sound to you like any of the bands you've heard so far in this chapter? Which bands? Why?

DUKE ELLINGTON (1899–1974)

For many musicians and listeners, Duke Ellington stands at the very top of musical achievement in the United States. He created a huge catalog of compositions in a wide variety of formats and styles, including 32-bar standards, blues, extended compositions (both single-movement tone poems and multimovement suites), the film score for the 1959 movie *Anatomy of a Murder* (it is perhaps worth noting that this is music by a great black composer and his musicians for a story that has no racial elements at all), ballet, work on an opera, and at the end of his life, three Sacred Concerts that were mixed-media works combining Ellington's music with dance and theatrical elements. His performing career lasted for some 50 years, and he worked continually for all that time. He received many honorary doctorates and some of this country's highest honors.

Yet no two listeners will ever agree on the "greatest" Ellington. The first edition of this book included eight Ellington recordings, only one of which also appeared in the first version of the *Smithsonian Collection of Classic Jazz* (the 1927 *East St. Louis Toodle-Oo*); that earlier edition shares with the *Revised Smithsonian Collection* both the *East St. Louis Toodle-Oo* and the 1940 *Cotton Tail*. A 1990 French CBS compilation, *The Essential Duke Ellington*, has 17 items, but only four compositions in common with the present book (*Mood Indigo*, *Take the "A" Train*, *In A Mellow Tone*, and *Black and Tan Fantasy*) and none of these in the same recorded version. Other greatest-hits anthologies show the same diversity.

Given this inexhaustible embarrassment of riches, the present book includes fifteen Duke Ellington compositions or performances, eight from the *Revised Smithsonian Collection*, and seven from before and after the years emphasized by that anthology. We have already

Duke Ellington. Music Division, the New York Public Library for the Performing Arts, Astor, Lenox and Tilden Foundations.

heard the 1927 *East St. Louis Toodle-Oo*; other cuts from the 1920s and early 1930s (Ellington's years at the Cotton Club in Harlem) include *Black and Tan Fantasy, Mood Indigo*, and *Daybreak Express*. The *Smithsonian* emphasizes the late 1930s and early 1940s, which for a great many listeners is the greatest Ellington era and band. Eight of our selections come from these years. Finally, I include a number from Ellington's 1947 Carnegie Hall concert, as an example of his solo piano playing, and two tunes from the late 1950s, a famous Johnny Hodges vehicle (*Prelude to a Kiss*), and a small-group version of an early jazz tune (*Stompy Jones*). Even this large an infusion of Ellington's music will still remain just a beginning; there will always be much, much more to listen to and enjoy.

➤   *Black and Tan Fantasy*, Duke Ellington, Bubber Miley. Duke Ellington and His Orchestra: Bubber Miley, Louis Metcalf, trumpet; Joe "Tricky Sam" Nanton, trombone; Otto Hardwicke, Rudy Jackson, Harry Carney, sax; Fred Guy, banjo; Wellman Braud, bass; Sonny Greer, drums; Duke Ellington, piano and arranger. Recorded 1927.

Black and Tan Fantasy, one of Ellington's earliest compositions, alternates 12-bars blues choruses with sections not based on the blues. The layout:

A	ensemble (12-bar blues)
B	sax (16 bars: two 8-bar, 6-plus-2, phrases)
A	Miley solo
A	Miley solo
C	Ellington piano solo (12 measures; note stride style)
A	Nanton solo
A	Miley solo
	tag ending from Chopin's "Funeral March" (cf. *East St. Louis Toodle-Oo* and Jelly Roll Morton's *Dead Man Blues*)

The blues-chorus solos use Ellington's so-called "jungle style," which most notably employs unusual or "exotic" timbres. Ellington and his band, particularly with the impetus of Bubber Miley, developed this sound during their stay at the Cotton Club in Harlem from 1927 to 1932, when Ellington was responsible not just for dance music, but for background music for floor shows as well. Ellington was able to give full play to his predilection for composing with timbres and colors, for writing descriptive or pictorial music at this, the start of his career. He did this all his life, but the "jungle" style—one has to swallow the epithet, or at least put it in the context of its time—was a first success and a first trademark, the earliest of the recognizably "Ellington" sounds. To produce these colors, the soloists, Bubber Miley on trumpet and Tricky Sam Nanton on trombone, covered the bells of their horns with rubber plungers to produce a "growl" sound and to try to imitate the sound of the human voice. On another tune from the same period, *Creole Love Call*, Ellington did a sort of twist on this device: he gave his singer, Adelaide Hall, a wordless melody to sing. Her tone sounds uncannily like a voice, like a violin, like a sax, even like a trumpet. And Ellington plays off her with the instrumentalists, whose timbres approach the vocal.

Compare *Black and Tan Fantasy* with *East St. Louis Toodle-Oo*, in the previous section, for style, sound, and for the use of that "Funeral March" tag. And notice that although Ellington is already composing and arranging with timbres as well as with chords and melodies, he doesn't yet have his mature style down. The sound of the band is big, even though there are only ten players. But the sax solo is completely out of character, and doesn't fit at all with the brass choruses; the rhythm section is heavy and draggy, and Ellington's piano solo still has a lot of the stride/ragtime in it; and, unlike later Ellington, it doesn't swing.

➤ *Mood Indigo*, Duke Ellington, Irving Mills, Barney Bigard. Duke Ellington and His Cotton Club Orchestra: Arthur Whetsol, Freddie Jenkins, Cootie Williams, trumpet; Tricky Sam Nanton, Juan Tizol, trombone; Harry Carney, Johnny Hodges, Barney Bigard, sax; Fred Guy, banjo; Wellman Braud, bass; Sonny Greer, drums; Duke Ellington, piano. Recorded 1930.

Since its composition, *Mood Indigo* (indigo is a deep, deep *blue*) has been one of Ellington's most popular tunes, perhaps second only to *"A" Train* (below), the band's theme song. The first thing to listen for is the unusual instrumentation (such unusual writing being the usual with Ellington, and one of his outstanding characteristics): the soloists playing the theme are muted trumpet (highest), muted trombone (middle), and clarinet (lowest). Not only is this a rare example of cross-voicing (mixing the different families of instruments, so that their colors are combined, as opposed to the contrasting of reeds and brass that we've heard so far), but it's an even rarer example of mixing high and low. The trombone is playing *above* the clarinet, although the latter's overall range is higher than that of the trombone.

The cut is a 16-bar aaba. How many choruses are there? (There is also a 4-measure piano interlude after the first, thematic, chorus.) What instruments solo? Notice that the last chorus is just like the first, but the instrument playing out front this time is the *middle* sibling, the trombone, not the trumpet on top.

Again, this *Mood Indigo* doesn't really swing, and there's very little improvisation. So is it really jazz? The answer is: absolutely yes. But why?

➤ *Daybreak Express*, Duke Ellington. Duke Ellington and His Famous Orchestra: Arthur Whetsol, Freddie Jenkins, Cootie Williams, Louis Bacon, trumpet; Tricky Sam Nanton, Juan Tizol, Lawrence Brown, trombone; Harry Carney, Otto Hardwicke, Barney Bigard, Johnny Hodges, sax; Fred Guy, guitar (*not* banjo); Wellman Braud, bass; Sonny Greer, drums. Recorded 1933.

Here at last is a piece that *swings*. This is one of Ellington's descriptive pieces, the portrayal of a train trip. Listen to the "naturalistic" writing—the whistles, the wheels spinning faster, etc. And listen to the sound of the big band, especially the sax choruses when the train is at full speed: four players working absolutely together in rhythmic unison. How long are the choruses, once the train gets going?

It's important that the choruses *aren't* so clearly articulated as they were in *Mood Indigo* or the other earlier cuts. The point of this piece, like the action of a train, is that when it hits full speed it seems unstoppable, its energy self-perpetuating. But there are in fact choruses, there is an underlying form, and you should try to pick it out.

➤   *The New East St. Louis Toodle-Oo*, Bubber Miley, Duke Ellington. Duke Ellington and His Famous Orchestra: Duke Ellington, piano; Wallace Jones, Cootie Williams, trumpet; Rex Stewart, cornet; Joe "Tricky Sam" Nanton, Lawrence Brown, trombone; Juan Tizol, valve trombone; Barney Bigard, clarinet and tenor sax; Johnny Hodges, clarinet, alto sax, and tenor sax; Harry Carney, clarinet and baritone sax; Otto Hardwicke, alto sax; Fred Guy, guitar; Hayes Alvis, Billy Taylor, bass; Sonny Greer, drums; Freddie Jenkins, chimes. Recorded 1937.

Compare this on all counts with the first, 1927, *East St. Louis Toodle-Oo*; this version regularizes some of the elements of the earlier recording, as one would expect during the Swing era, but at the same time it enriches almost every aspect of the tune. First, the ensemble is larger: 16 men instead of the earlier 10. The texture, the general sound, is much thicker than the earlier version, and the saxes in particular are much smoother and much more suave. This becomes most important (or at least most noticeable) in the last two phrases, which not even Ellington could have done in the 1920s. This smoothness also stems from the fact—if to a lesser degree—that the music is now in a Swing 4-to-the-bar, not in the earlier and clunkier 2.

The structure of the tune is also simpler and more regular than the original *East St. Louis Toodle-Oo*. That, as you'll recall, was a strophic tune (aaba) with an additional C section. In this rendition, the C is discarded, and we hear two choruses of the aaba, with the same 8-bar intro as in the original. This intro uses the same harmonies as the a phrase of the main chorus, and it introduces the smooth, heavy sounds of the music to come. Even more, it introduces the "growl" trumpet—Cootie Williams, the trumpet player, comes in in the 6th measure of the intro, as if he can't wait to strut it out, and his sound is immediately echoed by the trombone section. (This is also going to happen again at the very end of the cut.)

In the first chorus, the <u>a</u> phrases are played by Cootie Williams over the full sax section, with brass interjections. The bridge melody is carried by the saxes, with response from the trumpets. In the second section, the trombones get the tune in the <u>aa</u> phrases, over a more active bass line. These trombone phrases get a response first from the trumpet section, then from a clarinet soloist, Barney Bigard. In the bridge, Bigard plays over the full texture of the band, and in the final <u>a</u> phrase, *everybody* plays in an amazingly rich texture. Separate out every element you can distinguish—all the sections are doing different things, but everything is derived from something we've heard before, and it all fits together without a flaw. If we traced the development of the big band and the Swing style through three tunes of Fletcher Henderson, we could do the same thing again here, with the two versions of *East St. Louis Toodle-Oo* and *Mood Indigo* and *Daybreak Express* in between. But at the same time, this would be even more specific than the Henderson series. You can hear Fletcher Henderson's band as representative of Swing big bands in general; but Ellington was and is the *only* Ellington.

➤ *Diminuendo in Blue* and *Crescendo in Blue*, Duke Ellington. Duke Ellington and His Famous Orchestra: Duke Ellington, piano; Wallace Jones, Cootie Williams, trumpet; Rex Stewart, cornet; Joe "Tricky Sam" Nanton, Lawrence Brown, trombone; Barney Bigard, clarinet; Johnny Hodges, clarinet, soprano sax, and alto sax; Harry Carney, clarinet, alto sax, and baritone sax; Otto Hardwicke, alto sax and bass sax; Fred Guy, guitar; Billy Taylor, bass; Sonny Greer, drums. Recorded 1937.

Decrescendo is the musical term for growing softer, *crescendo* for growing louder. Originally two sides of a single 78-rpm disc, these two numbers were sometimes combined by Ellington into a single extended composition (the most famous instance being a 1957 performance at the Newport Jazz Festival, with a blazing Paul Gonsalves as tenor solo, playing 27 consecutive choruses), but sometimes played independently. This back-to-back juxtaposition may be the best of both worlds.

Both these tunes are blues, but both also use *extended* choruses, longer than the standard 12 bars. The way to listen for this is to listen for the instrumentation and the texture; Ellington still distinguishes one chorus from the last in this way, and continues the standard blues (or 30s jazz blues) by doing so, and keeping up the musical interest and drive in this fashion.

The *Diminuendo in Blue* begins with the whole ensemble, then features the brass section in the next two choruses, then moves to a separation of the choirs, and finally (this is the "diminuendo" part) to a single growl trumpet over the sax section, then a combination of trombones and baritone sax (the music is also getting lower in register as well as lower in dynamic level) and finally to Ellington alone as the soloist. *Crescendo in Blue* reverses the process. It begins with two choruses of contrasting and competing saxes and brass, and then begins to move up in register as well as to get louder and fuller in sound. In the fourth chorus we hear a solo clarinet. In the next two choruses we get the reed choir against the brasses, successively higher. After a trumpet chorus and another high reed chorus, the tune ends with the full band playing at top volume, riffing like crazy and setting up a tremendous amount of sound and swing. The piece then ends with a tag coda.

➤   *Ko-Ko*, Duke Ellington. Duke Ellington and His Famous Orchestra: Duke Ellington, piano; Wallace Jones, Cootie Williams, trumpet; Rex Stewart, cornet; Joe "Tricky Sam" Nanton, Lawrence Brown, trombone; Juan Tizol, valve trombone; Barney Bigard, clarinet, tenor sax; Otto Hardwicke, Johnny Hodges, alto sax; Ben Webster, tenor sax; Harry Carney, baritone sax; Fred Guy, guitar; Jimmy Blanton, bass; Sonny Greer. Recorded 1940.

This cut and the next five come from 1940 and 1941, examples of the so-called "Blanton-Webster" Ellington band, the group that lasted from 1939 to 1942 and which is for some people the greatest of all the Ellington assemblages. *Ko-Ko* is a blues. There are an intro and a coda built up from "tom-tom" sounds reinforced by the baritone sax, and in between seven choruses of Ellington's progressively building arrangement. (This is in contrast to many blues by, say, the Basie band, which are often a succession of solos between choruses by the full band, and don't use this kind of increasing texture and volume.) The first chorus is by Juan Tizol on valve trombone, in a 2-plus-2 call-and-response with the sax section. Then Tricky Sam Nanton plays two choruses over distant sax riffs. At this point the arrangement begins its drive toward the end. Ellington plays a cascading and often percussive solo over the sax and brass section. In the fifth chorus we hear a 3-way call-and-response among the trombones, the reeds, and the trumpets. In the sixth chorus, the horns and the solo bass trade 2s. The last chorus features the full band in a 2-plus-2 call-and-response. Like the *Diminuendo in Blue* and the *Crescendo in Blue* above, *Ko-Ko* combines two features of blues charts that aren't always found in the same arrangement, the sequence of new material, new licks, and at the same time the recycling and enrichment of riffs from one chorus to the next, as part of the increasing texture and the buildup to the conclusion.

➤ *Concerto for Cootie*, Duke Ellington. Duke Ellington and His Famous Orchestra: Duke Ellington, piano; Wallace Jones, Cootie Williams, trumpet; Rex Stewart, cornet; Joe "Tricky Sam" Nanton, Lawrence Brown, trombone; Juan Tizol, valve trombone; Barney Bigard, clarinet and tenor sax; Otto Hardwicke, Johnny Hodges, alto sax; Ben Webster, tenor sax; Harry Carney, baritone sax; Fred Guy, guitar; Jimmy Blanton, bass; Sonny Greer, drums. Recorded 1940.

This is our first example of Ellington's featuring a soloist for the whole of a single composition. (A "concerto" is a piece for soloist and larger ensemble.) The soloist here is Cootie Williams, the trumpet player who replaced Bubber Miley in the band, taking over his growl solos and adding some new specialties of his own. The *Concerto for Cootie* is a return to earlier formal structures, but it's very unusual in its phrase structure. After a 7-bar intro, there is an aaba chorus; but the first 2 a phrases are 10 bars long, while the b and the final a are 8 bars each. Then there is a 4-bar orchestral transition and a 16-bar C section (as in *East St. Louis Toodle-Oo* of 1927). Finally the a phrase returns and runs without break into a short coda that echoes the intro.

What you want to notice here is the variety in Williams's solo—color, especially, but also melodic and rhythmic variations on the main tune. Williams plays the second a phrase muted, the bridge in a growl style, other phrases open, the coda again muted. This muting of the trumpet is not just for making the brassy sound quieter and more distant, as it would be in most "classical" arrangements, but equally for the *color* of the sound. (Since a soloist normally has a microphone, anyway, volume isn't really a question.) Similarly, the basic tune itself is a single motive repeated three times in each a phrase, the third time extended so that it's twice as long as each time before, and actually reaches a cadence. Each of these phrases, within each a phrase, emphasizes the soloist; the rest of the band exists more or less as a backdrop for him. So Williams gets quite an opportunity to do his stuff, and he demonstrates what a quintessential Ellington trumpet player likes to do.

Ellington modified this *Concerto for Cootie* into the more popular vocal standard *Do Nothin' Till You Hear from Me*. He did this by lopping off the end (the orchestral part) of the 10-bar a phrases so that the tune becomes a standard 32-bar aaba, and by dropping the C section. *Do Nothin' Till You Hear from Me* now shows up in almost everybody's Ellington medleys.

➤ *Take the "A" Train*, Billy Strayhorn. Duke Ellington and His Famous Orchestra: Ray Nance, Wardell Jones, Rex Stewart, trumpet; Tricky Sam Nanton, Lawrence Brown, Juan Tizol, trombone; Harry Carney, Otto Hardwicke, Barney Bigard, Johnny Hodges, Ben Webster, sax; Fred Guy, guitar; Jimmy Blanton, bass; Sonny Greer, drums; Duke Ellington, piano. Recorded 1940.

This was Ellington's theme song, and probably his most famous recording. But he didn't write it: *"A" Train* was composed and arranged by Billy Strayhorn, Ellington's alter ego for some 30 years, who also wrote such famous Ellington standards as *Satin Doll*. This is another "train" piece, like *Daybreak Express*, but this train is the 8th Avenue express of the IND subway in New York. As the lyrics say, "You must take the 'A' train if you want to get to Harlem," where the action was.

You should be able to find your way through the form of this cut: after a 4-measure piano intro, there are three choruses of a 32-bar aaba, with a 4-bar interlude between the second and third choruses, and an extension, an extra aa, at the end. Pay attention to who plays which phrases and choruses, how the sections are combined or contrasted, and so on. Listen carefully, too, to that interlude between the second and third choruses. Writers sometimes make a big deal about the group's going into a meter of three here, but that ain't necessarily so. The chart stays in 4, but uses cross-accents, accents on the normally weak beats of the measure:

1 2 3 4 1 2 3 4 1 2 3 4 1 2 3 4.

The point, as it was with Armstrong's *Hotter Than That*, is to hear the meters of 3 and of 4 at the same time. Work on it: get the meter of 4 solidly in your ears, and then try to register the rhythms of that 4-bar interlude. Do both meters at the same time, and you've got it all.

➤ *Cotton Tail*, Duke Ellington. Duke Ellington and His Famous Orchestra: Wallace Jones, Cootie Williams, trumpet; Rex Stewart, cornet; all other personnel as on *"A" Train*. Recorded 1940.

The form of *Cotton Tail* is conventional—six choruses of a 32-bar aaba tune—but its arrangement and melodies are not. The layout first:

1st chorus: elided (cut short), aab, plus a 4-measure transition into the next chorus. The melody is stated in unison by the saxes and trumpets over the rhythm section (aa). The bridge is a call-and-response between the sax section and a solo muted trumpet (Cootie Williams).

2nd, 3rd choruses: a great and famous solo by the tenor sax man, Ben Webster, over the rhythm section in the a phrases and using rifflike figures in a call-and-response with the brass in the bridge.

4th chorus: brass section in the aa; baritone sax solo (Harry Carney) in the bridge; Ellington (piano) solo in the final a. Notice the traces of stride style in his playing.

5th chorus: saxes all the way.

6th chorus: brass riffs in the aa, call-and-response with the sax section; brass in the bridge; in the final a, the only direct repetition of the first two a phrases of the first chorus, to round out the chart.

Now, this is a typical jazz chart in many ways: the form, the pitting of brass and saxes against each other, the overall design of solo versus whole group, the call-and-response, the occasional riffs. But it's less typical in that it's *all* very highly arranged, each chorus being different in melody and in instrumentation. The fifth chorus is especially remarkable: all those saxes playing together as one person, phrasing as a group, seeming to think with one mind. This sort of ensemble work is possible only in groups like Ellington's, where the players worked together for years and knew one another's playing inside out. Basie's band was also capable of such tight playing, as we'll see, but for different reasons. Finally, the basic melody of *Cotton Tail* is not typical of its era. It doesn't sound like the smooth, singable tunes we've heard elsewhere; on the contrary, it's jumpier, not very singable, conceived directly for instruments, in other words idiomatic. The way it jumps around the range, with ever-changing rhythms and accents, prefigures the sort of melodies that the bop players will begin to improvise and to write a little later in the 1940s.

Listen especially to three players here: Ben Webster, whose solo in the second and third choruses made him famous overnight; Jimmy Blanton, the first great modern bassist, a man who was a primary mover of the bass into an independent, even a solo, instrument (as in *Ko-Ko*, above), and who really makes *Cotton Tail* swing; and Ellington himself, who directs the group very subtly and then stomps out in the one phrase he allows himself.

➤   *In a Mellotone,* Duke Ellington. Duke Ellington and His Famous Orchestra: personnel as in *Cotton Tail.* Recorded 1940.

➤   *Blue Serge,* Mercer Ellington. Duke Ellington and His Famous Orchestra: personnel as in *Cotton Tail,* but with Ray Nance replacing Cootie Williams, trumpet. Recorded 1941.

These last two cuts from the "Blanton-Webster" Ellington band are in a more relaxed mood than what we've heard earlier, as might be guessed from their titles. *In a Mellotone* (sometimes written *In a Mellow Tone*) is a 32-bar aa'ab, the end of the <u>b</u> phrase using the riff that is the main <u>a</u>-phrase tune. After an orchestral first chorus, there are solos by Cootie Williams, over the sax section, and then Johnny Hodges.

Blue Serge was written by Ellington's son, who worked with the band for many years, and fronted it after Duke's death. The tune is an <u>8</u>-bar blues. After a 6-measure introduction, with high reeds for four bars and then the low brasses coming in yet again with that motive from Chopin's "Funeral March" (cf. *Dead Man Blues,* and the *East St. Louis Toodle-Oo*). There are, in order, choruses by Ray Nance on trumpet; the full orchestra (this chorus extended to ten bars); Tricky Sam Nanton on trombone; the brass section, over the saxes; Ellington on piano; Ben Webster on tenor sax over the brasses (this chorus extended to twelve bars); and a final chorus from the whole orchestra. Unlike *Ko-Ko* or the *Diminuendo* and *Crescendo in Blue,* this chart doesn't build its blues or its tunes to a climax at the end. Like *In A Mellotone,* it is relaxed and understated. In this instance, that quietness gives the chart an air of melancholy that we haven't heard elsewhere in Ellington's music (although it exists in tunes we haven't covered, such as the standard *Solitude*).

➤   *The Clothed Woman,* Duke Ellington. Duke Ellington, piano, with a little backup from his orchestra. Recorded live in Carnegie Hall, 1947.

Although the band plays a little in the background, this is basically a solo "impressionist" piece. Listen to the variety of colors and sounds that Ellington gets out of the supposedly black-and-white piano: his keyboard work is as much about timbre as are his band charts. Listen, too, to all the different kinds of music that are packed into these five minutes, including those elliptical solos that anticipate

Thelonious Monk (a bop composer and pianist whom we'll hear later).

➤ *Prelude to a Kiss*, I. Gordon, Irving Mills, Duke Ellington. Duke Ellington and His Orchestra: Duke Ellington, piano; Clark Terry, Willie Cook, Shorty Baker, Cat Anderson, Ray Nance, trumpet; Quentin Jackson, Britt Woodman, trombone; John Sanders, bass trombone; Paul Gonsalves, tenor sax; Jimmy Hamilton, tenor sax and clarinet; Johnny Hodges, alto sax; Russell Procope, alto sax and clarinet; Harry Carney, baritone sax; Jimmy Woode, bass; Sam Woodyard, drums. Recorded 1957.

A heart-stopping vehicle for Johnny Hodges, this is one of the most romantic recordings in jazz. Think first about the title itself: this is the musical evocation of a moment that can seem timeless, and the music seems to prolong that timeless moment for its full 4 minutes-plus.

The song is very simple structurally, a 32-bar aaba chorus, with here a repeated <u>ba</u>. The focus is entirely on Johnny Hodge's gorgeous playing, his tone, his phrasing, the way it takes him forever to slide up to those high notes, the combination of forward motion and holding back. This is the kind of music Ellington used to refer to as "excruciating ecstasy"; he was not wrong. After Ellington's solo introduction, Hodges plays the <u>a</u> phrase first over brass, and then over the whole orchestra. This use of the whole band to cushion and support his playing will carry through the rest of the cut. The only real variety is the second <u>b</u> phrase, where Hodges picks up and intensifies the melodic activity, but without giving up an iota of the romantic intensity of his sound.

➤ *Stompy Jones*, Duke Ellington. Johnny Hodges, alto sax; Duke Ellington, piano; Harry "Sweets" Edison, trumpet; Al Hall, bass; Les Spann, guitar; Jo Jones, drums. Recorded 1959.

Small-group Ellington, for the first time we've heard it since 1927, and 6 minutes of pure joy. *Stompy Jones* is a composition from Ellington's early years, and here he and his small group, co-led by Johnny Hodges, do it with a combination of Swing and early jazz elements. The tune itself is a 16-bar chorus, and the series of choruses builds to a terrific climax at the end of the cut. The layout is equally straightforward. The intro is Ellington, 8 bars. The first three choruses are by Johnny Hodges over the rhythm section. The next three choruses are by Harry "Sweets" Edison and the rhythm; listen to the little cat-and-mouse call-and-response between Ellington and Edison in the first of these choruses. Then there are three choruses—by this time you should have noticed the equal time given to all the soloists so far—by Les Spann, guitar. In the third chorus, Spann plays his solo in octaves. The last solo is five choruses from Ellington. In his first chorus, he picks up again (briefly) the little riff figure from the call-and-response duet with Edison; in the second chorus, he uses the rhythmic riff we've already heard (if only subliminally) underneath earlier solos and which will become the main material of the last choruses; and in his last three choruses, he does an enormous buildup in dynamics, register (getting higher), and rhythmic intensity. This spins us forward into the last four choruses, by the whole small group, Edison in the lead, the rest playing riffs behind, like the texture of early jazz and 1930s Swing; the rhythmic riffs parallel those in Ellington's second solo chorus, but here they're played by the whole group, and the propulsive swing is absolutely irresistible.

COUNT BASIE (1904–1984)

➤ *One O'Clock Jump*, Count Basie. Count Basie and His Orchestra: Count Basie, piano; Buck Clayton, Ed Lewis, Bobby Moore, trumpet; Dan Minor, George Hunt, trombone; Earle Warren, alto sax; Jack Washington, alto and baritone sax; Herschel Evans, Lester Young, tenor sax; Freddie Green, guitar; Walter Page, bass; Jo Jones, drums. Recorded 1937.

This is a riffed 12-bar blues. *One O'Clock Jump* was Basie's signature tune from 1935 onward. Its "composition" was gradual: according to Ross Russell (*Jazz Style in Kansas City and the Southwest*; see the Bibliography), a key phrase came originally from Fats Waller. Waller's tune was reworked in 1929 and recorded by Don Redman, sometime arranger for Fletcher Henderson and others, under the title *6 or 7 Times*. When Basie's group began to use its riffs as a head arrangement, it went through another title or two, ended up with the present one, and is now attributed to Basie himself.

This is typical Basie and typical Kansas City-style jazz. After an 8-

bar intro (Basie) and two solo Basie choruses, we hear solos in turn by Herschel Evans (tenor sax, over brass riffs), George Hunt (trombone, over sax riffs), Lester Young (tenor, again over the brass), Buck Clayton (trumpet, again over the saxes), Basie and the rest of the rhythm section, and then three final choruses from the whole ensemble, with additional riffs in each chorus.

▶   *Doggin' Around*, Herschel Evans, Edgar W. Battle. Count Basie and His Orchestra: personnel as for *One O'Clock Jump*, except for Harry "Sweets" Edison on trumpet, instead of Bobby Moore; Eddie Durham on trombone and guitar; Benny Morton instead of George Hunt, trombone. Arranged by Herschel Evans. Recorded 1938.

This tune has an 8-bar intro, six 32-bar aaba riff choruses, drum tag, and coda. The first chorus is by the whole band, with a sax solo

Count Basie. Courtesy of the Rutgers Institute of Jazz Studies.

(Earle Warren) in the bridge. The second chorus is a sax (Herschel Evans) solo. The third chorus has Harry "Sweets" Edison, trumpet, on the aa and Jack Washington, alto sax, on the ba. The fourth chorus is a Basie solo, the fifth a tenor solo by Lester Young, and the last chorus from Jo Jones on drums and the whole band.

Listen especially to Lester Young's solo. "Prez" (the affectionate and admiring nickname came from his fellow Kansas City musicians, who saw that we already had a "Duke" and a "Count" but needed a "President") worked with Basie until 1940 and formed a great musical partnership with the singer Billie Holiday. ("Lady Day" was the name he gave her.) His most important hallmarks included his timbre, *very* light and reedy for a tenor sax, and his inventive sense of musical time and of phrasing, which was listened to very closely by the boppers of the next generation. (He shared that light timbre and the supple phrasing with Holiday.) In the solo here, listen to the way he plays with the basic rhythms of the 2- and 4-bar phrases, starting early or lapping over, even staying silent for a measure or so. Young and Coleman Hawkins (below) were the two most important tenor men of the 1930s; and we'll hear Prez throughout this section and again in the section devoted to Billie Holiday.

➤ *Taxi War Dance*, Lester Young, Count Basie. Count Basie and His Orchestra: as above, plus Shad Collins, trumpet; Dickie Wells, trombone; Buddy Tate, tenor sax, instead of Herschel Evans. Arranged by Buck Clayton. Recorded 1939.

This is another 32-bar aaba riff tune, although the form might not be clear until the third chorus. There's an intro; Lester Young solo; Dickie Wells (trombone) solo; then two choruses during which the band and Prez trade 4s in the a phrases and Basie takes the solo bridges. As with *Doggin' Around*, pay special attention to Lester's first chorus and to the kind of solo melody he plays. We've moved into what, again, is called "idiomatic" instrumental music—that is, melodies that really could not be easily sung (as they might have been with *Dippermouth Blues*, *West End Blues*, *I Gotta Right to Sing the Blues*), but are conceived directly on and for the instrument. This also gives us a contrast between solos and background riffs, since many of the latter *could* be sung, and between solos on different instruments. How do the solos of Young and Wells differ in elements like rhythms, melodic contour, pitch-bending, and so on?

➤ *Sent for You Yesterday*, Count Basie, Eddie Durham, Jimmy Rushing. Jimmy Rushing, vocal; Buck Clayton, Ed Lewis, Harry "Sweets" Edison, trumpet; Dan Minor, Benny Morton, Eddie Durham, trombone; Earl Warren, alto sax; Jack Washington, alto and baritone sax; Herschel Evans, Lester Young, tenor sax; Count Basie, piano; Freddie Green, guitar; Walter Page, bass; Jo Jones, drums. Recorded 1938.

This is a more highly arranged blues than you might expect, and features Basie's male blues-shouter Jimmy Rushing (aka "Mr. 5-by-5"). Rushing as blues-shouter was part of a great Kansas City tradition, including Big Joe Turner, the pianist/bandleader Jay McShann, Joe Williams, and the young Kevin Mahogany in the recent Robert Altman movie *Kansas City*.

The tune begins with an intro from Basie and then the band that will return as an interlude between choruses and as the coda. Otherwise this cut is a succession of 12-bar blues choruses, its 4-bar phrases all 2-plus-2 call-and-response between sections of the band, or between a soloist (Herschel Evans, "Sweets" Edison, Rushing) and the larger group. Listen, as ever, to the riffs, the interaction between solo and group, and the patented (if understated) Kansas City swing of the rhythm section and the whole ensemble.

➤ *Jumpin' at the Woodside*, Count Basie. Buck Clayton, Ed Lewis, Harry "Sweets" Edison, trumpet; Dan Minor, Dicky Wells, Benny Morton, trombone; Earl Warren, alto sax; Jack Washington, alto and baritone sax; Herschel Evans, Lester Young, tenor sax; Count Basie, piano; Freddie Green, guitar; Walter Page, bass; Jo Jones, drums. Recorded 1938.

The Woodside was a hotel and musicians' hangout in Harlem. This cut, another of Basie's signature tunes, begins with a piano intro and then swings (literally) into a series of <u>aaba</u> riffed choruses. All the energy here comes from the rhythm and the drive of the riffs; there are only two chords in each <u>a</u> phrase, and that singularity keeps your ear and your feet focused on the rhythm. Earl Warren solos on the bridge of the first chorus, Basie in the second. Then we hear solo choruses from Buck Clayton, Lester Young, and Herschel Evans on clarinet. Listen here to how these soloists work over the riffs from the rest of the band. It's call-and-response, but it's also a mutual driving each other forward.

➤   *Lester Leaps In,* Lester Young. Count Basie's Kansas City Seven: Count
     Basie, piano; Buck Clayton, trumpet; Dickie Wells, trombone; Lester
     Young, alto sax; Freddie Green, guitar; Walter Page, bass; Jo Jones,
     drums. Recorded 1939.

This is similar to 1920s instrumentation, but it's a small group
made up of men from the big band. This 32-bar riff tune is structurally
identical to the big-band charts, contrasting soloists, and contrasting
those solos with ensemble sections. After the intro, there's an ensemble
chorus, then two solo choruses by Young (in the second of these, listen
to the Young/Basie duet in the last a phrase and the stop-time in the
last 8), a chorus in which Basie and Young trade 4s, and two final choruses contrasting the group with individual solos in 4-bar choruses.

➤   *Shiny Stockings,* Frank Foster. Count Basie and His Orchestra: Wendell
     Culley, Reunald Jones, Jr., Thad Jones, Joe Newman, trumpet; Henry
     Coker, Bill Hughes, Benny Powell, trombone; Bill Graham, Marshall
     Royal, alto sax; Frank Foster, Frank Wess, tenor sax; Charlie Fowlkes,
     baritone sax; Count Basie, piano; Freddie Green, guitar; Eddie Jones,
     bass; Sonny Payne, drums. Arranged by Frank Foster. Recorded 1956.

Count Basie's band from the early 1950s was less of a Kansas City-
riff oriented group such as we've heard to this point, and more of a
mainstream Swing/bop group, but always with hot brass players and
Basie's great rhythm section. The music they played tended to be more
highly arranged than the earlier riff charts, as well as sometimes more
complicated in tunes and harmonies. But, again, the Basie band always
swung, irrepressibly.
    Shiny Stockings is an example of all of this. The composer and
arranger was Frank Foster, one of the "Two Franks" who arranged and
played in the tenor section. (The other was Frank Wess. They also led
the band for a time after Basie's death in 1984.) The tune is a 32-bar
abab, the theme in the first chorus played by the muted trumpet section. (The b phrase is signaled by all the repeated rising figures in the
melody.) The arrangement is full of delights. The first thing we hear is
a quintessential Basie/rhythm intro. In the last phrase of the thematic
chorus, the low brass and rhythm section make a wonderful surprise
entry, louder than the rest of the band, and accented. This throws us
into an 8-bar interlude, the last two measures of which are a break for

the trumpet soloist, Thad Jones (and this break, in turn, throws us forward into his solo).

Jones's solo is interesting. He plays boppish kinds of lines—lots of quick notes, with cross-phrasing, cross-accents at the beginning of the second 16 bars, with a muted timbre. But at the same time this solo doesn't have the hyperdrive of, say, Dizzy Gillespie's bop solos, as we'll hear in the next chapter, or the tense propulsion we'll hear from a lot of bop musicians. This solo may use some bop techniques, but by the mid-1950s bop had become the mainstream musical language, and some of its initial emotional characteristics had worn off. The emotional effect of Jones's solo here is like that of trumpet players in the Swing era, even if some of what he does doesn't use specific Swing techniques.

After Jones's solo, Basie takes a solo 16 bars (ab). Then we get two choruses from the full band, the second suddenly louder in a drive to the conclusion, with a drum break in mm. 15–16. These are followed by a short coda—Basie, then the saxes, then the whole band again.

Shiny Stockings has become a standard for big bands and school stage bands for the last 30 years or so, and other tunes from the Basie book have done so, too. (The other best example is Neil Hefti's *Li'l Darlin'*.) Basie maintained the popularity of his group uninterruptedly until his death, and the band has gone on (still under his name) since then. The band was unusual for having two such different styles in its 50-year existence, as only the Ellington band did. But what was constant to all the Basie bands was, not surprisingly, the leader with his penchant for swinging and for his great and solid rhythm sections.

BENNY GOODMAN (1909–1986) AND OTHERS

➤ *Don't Be That Way*, Benny Goodman, Edgar Sampson, Mitchell Parish. The Benny Goodman Orchestra: Benny Goodman, clarinet; Hymie Schertzer, George Koenig, alto sax; Babe Russin, Arthur Rollini, tenor sax; Harry James, Ziggy Elman, Gordon Griffin, trumpet; Verson Brown, Red Ballard, trombone; Gene Krupa, drums; Allan Reuss, guitar; Jess Stacy, piano; Harry Goodman, bass. Recorded 1938.

This cut and the next were recorded at Goodman's landmark concert at Carnegie Hall, which until then had been a bastion of "classical" music only. There had been earlier concerts of nonclassical music there,

Benny Goodman. Music Division, The New York Public Library for the Performing Arts, Astor, Lenox and Tilden Foundation.

but they were very special events, and aimed at a mix of light classical and popular music and always aimed at decorum and respectability. Dancing in the aisles, as happened at the 1938 Goodman concert, was not to be allowed. Great hoo-hah and foofarah all around, but the concert was an unimaginable success in every way. Goodman's band was itself a white group at this point (although there were blacks in his small groups); but for this concert, Goodman also brought in musicians from the Ellington and Basie organizations, including the Count himself. The racial barriers in jazz organizations had begun to break down.

This is an aaba riff tune, but notice the big size of the band and the clean precision with which they play. The latter is a mark of the white Swing bands, in its way (Ellington's *Cotton Tail* was incredibly precise, but the group work also played around a lot more with rhythms and accents than did most of the Swing white groups). Solos are (in order) from Goodman (clarinet), Russin (tenor sax; listen to those drum shots from Krupa), Harry James (trumpet), drum break (wildly applauded) from Krupa, and Brown (trombone), then Goodman again. Then comes a terrific succession of a phrases, softer and softer, to another Krupa break and a shouting ensemble final phrase.

Krupa and James were the real matinee idols of the Swing era, like Frank Sinatra in the 1940s, and later nonjazz musicians like Elvis Presley in the 1950s and the Beatles in the 1960s. Bobby-soxers swooned, young men were appreciative but jealous.

➤   *Sing, Sing, Sing.* Louis Prima. The Benny Goodman Orchestra: as above. In this chart, the band adds to Prima's tune a song by Fletcher Henderson, *Christopher Columbus.*

This song starts with a Krupa opening, riffs from the saxes, and then goes into the tune—aaba (surprise, surprise). Solos are from Goodman, Krupa, Russin, James, Goodman, and Krupa again, and a wonderful, quiet, sort of "afterglow" solo from Jess Stacy. The second part of the cut almost abandons both basic tunes, *Sing, Sing, Sing* and *Christopher Columbus,* in favor of a succession of 8-bar phrases that serves as solos for one or another of the band's stars. This is the Goodman band at its hottest. For many people (whites, usually), this cut epitomized the Swing era.

➤   *Body and Soul,* Robert Sour, John Green, Frank Eyton, Edward Heyman. The Benny Goodman Trio: Benny Goodman, clarinet; Teddy Wilson, piano; Gene Krupa, drums. Recorded 1935.

Another 32-bar aaba song form, this tune is a standard both for jazz musicians (see Coleman Hawkins' version of it, below) and for pop singers as well. In the first chorus, Goodman takes the a phrases and Wilson the bridge, second chorus is the other way around, and the third chorus is like the first. The music here is an example of *thematic* improvisation, not harmonic. Instead of making up new melodies over the basic chords, Goodman and Wilson are improvising variants on the original tune. Billie Holiday, the premiere singer of her time, who worked with both Goodman and Wilson (and also with Basie and Lester Young; see below), was also a masterful thematic improviser. Wilson, by the way, should sound much different to you from either Ellington, Basie, Jess Stacy, or Earl Hines (section I-II with Louis Armstrong). Wilson's highly ornamented melodies and easygoing left-hand work were taken over in part by pop musicians, *greatly* watered down, and turned into what is now called "cocktail piano." But please note: Wilson himself never sank so low.

➤ *I Found a New Baby*, Jack Palmer, Spencer Williams. Benny Goodman Sextet: Benny Goodman, clarinet; Cootie Williams, trumpet; George Auld, tenor sax; Count Basie, piano; Charlie Christian, electric guitar; Artie Bernstein, bass; Jo Jones, drums. Recorded 1941.

➤ *Breakfast Feud*, Benny Goodman. (Composite recording.) Benny Goodman Sextet: Benny Goodman, clarinet; Cootie Williams, trumpet; George Auld, tenor sax; Count Basie or Ken Kersey, piano; Charlie Christian, electric guitar; Artie Bernstein, bass; Jo Jones or Harry Jaeger, drums. Recorded 1940 and 1941.

Charlie Christian (1919–1942) was not the first to add electric amplification to the guitar, but he did pioneer that, and he was also one of the first famous jazz soloists on the instrument. It's primarily for this reason that we've included these two cuts. The first cut features the whole ensemble, the second emphasizes Christian.

Charlie Christian and Gene Krupa. Music Division, The New York Public Library for the Performing Arts, Astor, Lenox and Tilden Foundation.

I Found a New Baby is a 32-bar riff tune. Christian does long, full lines, reminiscent of Lester Young's work with Basie, improvising new melodies on the basic chords of a song. The boppers-to-be listened to Christian as carefully as they did to Prez, as have guitarists ever since. Compare those extended, single-note melodies to the more chordal work we've heard to date; the guitar is now primarily a melody instrument. (We also heard this on Lester Spann's work on Ellington's *Stompy Jones*, but that was recorded in 1959.) Like the pianist's right hand, like the bass (since Ellington's Jimmy Blanton), like the drums after Max Roach (to come with the chapter on bop), this is an example of the rhythm section's "crossing over" into the front line, into the melodic part of a group. And listen to the last ("out") choruses as well as to the solos—the spirit of collective improvisation lives on.

Breakfast Feud is a blues, and almost all solo Christian. We hear ten choruses and then a fade-out. The chart works in two-chorus units: in each unit, the rest of the group plays a 4-bar lick that sounds like a fanfare, as if to set the tone and introduce the soloist; then Christian plays the last 8 bars of that chorus and the whole of the next. Again, his lines are long and swinging, a legacy of his work as a Texas-blues player. Again like Lester Young, his melodies are endlessly inventive. No more 2-plus-2 here, but Christian playing all the way through and beyond the regular 4-bar phrases. And as with music we heard from Basie, this is a "blues," but it may not sound "blue" to you—it's energetic, swinging, propulsive. Yet the earthiness and the assertiveness of the blues are here, combined with the regularity and long rhythmic phrases of Swing.

➤ *Rockin' Chair*, Hoagy Carmichael. Gene Krupa and His Orchestra: Roy Eldridge, Graham Young, Torg Halten, Norman Murphy, trumpet; Babe Wagner, Jay Kelliher, John Grassi, trombone; Mascagni Ruffo, Sam Listengart, alto sax; Sam Musiker, clarinet and tenor sax; Walter Bates, tenor sax; Milton Raskin, piano; Ray Biondi, guitar; Ed Mihelich, bass; Gene Krupa, drums. Recorded 1941.

➤ *I Can't Believe that You're in Love with Me*, Jimmy McHugh, Clarence Gaskill. The Chocolate Dandies, Featuring Roy Eldridge and Benny Carter: Roy Eldridge, trumpet; Benny Carter, alto sax; Coleman Hawkins, tenor sax; Bernard Addison, guitar; John Kirby, bass; Sidney Catlett, drums. Recorded 1940.

For our present purposes, these two recordings serve as examples of the great trumpet player Roy Eldridge, underrated except to musicians and to some of the fans of the Swing style. Eldridge was the link between Louis Armstrong and Dizzy Gillespie, and he was also a terrific and inventive soloist in his own right.

Rockin' Chair was a standard by Hoagy Carmichael, who also composed *Star Dust* and many other major songs. It was a great hit for the singer Mildred Bailey, whom some people held up as the only contemporary rival to Billie Holiday. In this version we hear an 8-measure introduction from Eldridge over the whole band, and then a chorus and a half (aaba ba) from Eldridge over the saxes. Listen to Eldridge's extraordinary variety in every aspect—the different colors of his tone, including a little "growl," the way that his phrasing is lyrical but swinging, the way he plays with a lot of rhythmic heat over the laid-back sax section, how he can raise the temperature of the music as he plays higher. We'll hear this sort of thing again, although without the intense rhythmic swing, in Dizzy's *I Can't Get Started*. After the repeated ba phrases, there's an out-of-tempo coda, call-and-response between Eldridge and the clarinet player, and then he shoots back to the top for the very end, maybe reminding you of Louis Armstrong on *Hotter Than That*.

As we turn to *I Can't Believe that You're in Love with Me*, note for a minute the name of the group: The Chocolate Dandies. Such a name was a relic of the 1920s and before, when black artists were popularly seen (and sometimes seen by management and theater or club owners as well) as less than human. But artists sometimes submitted to such epithets (remember Ellington's "jungle style" in his Cotton Club years) and sometimes adopted them ironically as a way of mocking those who belittled them.

At any rate, the version of *I Can't Believe* . . . (abridged in the *Revised Smithsonian Collection*, with no thematic chorus to begin) starts with two burning solo choruses from Eldridge, picking up nicely from what we heard on *Rockin' Chair*. He plays over just the rhythm (no piano!), dishing out blue and bent notes, swinging with driving rhythms, moving all over the trumpet's range, the sort of thing he was doing at the climax of his solo on *Rockin' Chair*. This is followed by two choruses from Benny Carter on alto sax. Carter does many of the same things as Eldridge, but at the same time his solo is more continuous, one idea leading directly to the next, or one melodic figure repeated and extended, though never in predictable ways. Carter here also uses the range of the sax as Eldridge did of the trumpet, and swings masterfully, if in a less blazing fashion. The last chorus of this cut is played by the whole ensemble (note that we have Coleman Hawkins here again, as we did above and as we shall again in the next section of this chapter)—collective improvisation in the Swing style.

➤ *When Lights Are Low*, Benny Carter, Spencer Williams. Lionel Hampton
and His Orchestra: Dizzy Gillespie, trumpet; Benny Carter, alto sax and
arranger; Coleman Hawkins, Ben Webster, Chu Berry, tenor sax; Clyde
Hart, piano; Charlie Christian, guitar; Milt Hinton, bass; Cozy Cole,
drums; Lionel Hampton, vibes. Recorded 1939.

Hamp was the first great vibes soloist, and also worked with
Benny Goodman in the late 1930s. This cut resembles the softer Swing
style we've heard from Goodman in *Savoy* and *Don't Be That Way*. The
tune is a 32-bar aaba. In the first chorus, the whole group plays the first
a͟a͟, Hampton solos on the bridge, and Benny Carter on the last a͟. The
second chorus is a Hampton solo. Compare his melodic playing to
Charlie Christian—long melodies, swinging rhythms, but less aggressive than you might expect from a "rhythm" player. Again, rhythm-
section work is primarily *melodic*. After the second chorus, there are
4-bar solo breaks from Hampton and then from "Hawk," (Coleman
Hawkins, also called "Bean"), as a sort of transition from Hamp's solo
over the rest of the group to Hawkins's. Hawkins plays the first two a͟
phrases of the third chorus, with a more burning rhythm and timbre
than Hampton uses. Clyde Hart, on piano, takes the bridge, and then
the whole ensemble returns for the final a͟.

➤ *In the Mood*, Joe Garland, Andy Razaf. Glenn Miller and His Orchestra:
Hal McIntyre, Tex Beneke, Al Klink, Harold Tennyson, Wilbur
Schwartz, sax; Glenn Miller, Al Mastren, Paul Tanner, trombone; Clyde
Hurley, Lee Knowles, R. McMickle, trumpet; Richard Fisher, guitar; C.
MacGregor, piano; Rowland Bundock, bass; Maurice Purtell, drums.
Recorded 1939.

Some jazz critics say that Miller's band swung, but was still, or
should still be classed as a "sweet" dance band. Be that as it may, this
cut was perhaps the biggest-selling record in the Swing era, and the
chart is still a standard with stage bands everywhere. After the intro
(saxes, then brass) comes a riffed blues that frames 16-bar solo
choruses, also riffed. The end of this cut—repeated choruses, gradually
softer, and then out in a loud final blow—is like the end of Goodman's
Don't Be That Way, discussed previously.

➤ *Opus One* (aka *Opus No. One*), Sy Oliver, Sid Garris. Tommy Dorsey and
His Orchestra: Sid Cooper, Gail Curtis, Al Klink, Buddy DeFranco,
Bruce Branson, sax; George Seaberg, Vito Mangano, Dale Pearce, Roger

Ellick, trumpet; Nelson Riddle, Jr., Tommy Dorsey, Walter Benson, Collon Sutterwhite, trombone; Robert Bain, guitar; Milton Golden, piano; Sidney Block, bass; Buddy Rich, drums; Joseph Park, tuba; Alex Beller, Leon Atkins, Bernard Tinterow, Peter Dimitriades, Manny Fiddler, Joseph Goodman, Ruth Goodman, violin; Milton Thomas, David Uchitel, viola; Fred Cmalia, cello; Reba Robinson, harp. Recorded 1944.

One difference in this 32-bar aaba riff tune is the addition of the string section (violins et al.) playing sustained chords in the background, which removes it somewhat from the "jazz band" idea. Solos are by de Franco on clarinet. Even more than the Miller cut, much less the Goodman ones, this exemplifies the hybrid of "Swing" and popular "sweet" dance music: it's hot, it swings, but there are *all* those people up there playing a written arrangement, not improvising a thing. The emphasis is rather on swinging, on the attractive, tight, overall sound, on entertaining.

SOME SOLOISTS FROM THE 1930S

➤   *'Round Midnight*, Thelonious Monk, Bernie Hanighen, Cootie Williams. Ella Fitzgerald, vocal; Lou Levy, piano; Herb Ellis, guitar; Joe Mondragon, bass. Recorded 1962.

The inclusion of this cut in this section is anachronistic—it was written by Monk, one of the major composers and pianists of bop (although he wrote it in 1939), and the recording was done in 1962. Similarly, the two other recordings by Ella Fitzgerald were done in 1964 and 1958. Nevertheless, Fitzgerald (1917–1996; "Ella" to all her fans) began her career in the 1930s after winning an amateur contest at the Apollo Theater in Harlem, and "got her chops," "paid her dues" (choose your term) as a singer with a Swing big band, that of the drummer Chick Webb. She also went on to front the band for some three years after Webb died.

   Although she learned from later kinds of jazz, as well as from pop, and with time expanded her resources and her depth, Ella Fitzgerald never radically changed either her repertory or her style. Her tone is light (some critics use the words "girlish" or "innocent," which work fine until they also often go on to say that her *singing*, her message, is also naive, which is rarely the case); her range is huge, exceeded in the music in this book only by Sarah Vaughan; and with her incredible ear for true pitch, she can jump from the bottom to the top and hit all the notes straight on, dead-center. She likes long, lyrical phrases when singing ballads, long tricky ones when singing up-tempo numbers. She tends to ornament the tune with melismas (several notes on the same syllable of the lyric), thematic improvisation like Benny Goodman, using blue notes or slides only occasionally. Ella is also famous for her scat singing, as we'll hear in the last of these three cuts.

The form of this song is aaba-coda. The focus is all on Ella, from her solo beginning through the solo cadenza at the end. She stays close to Monk's original tune here, but listen to the way that her delivery conveys both the middle-of-the-night loneliness of the lyrics and also the ambiguity of the words and music: what's the history here? does she want him back or not? can we make a connection with Ellington's *Mood Indigo*?

➤ *You'd Be So Nice to Come Home to*, Cole Porter. Ella Fitzgerald, vocal; Roy Eldridge, trumpet; Tommy Flanagan, piano; Bill Yancey, bass; Gus Johnson, drums. Recorded 1964.

This is a typically insinuating or insidious tune of Cole Porter—all inviting, but it's in the minor mode, which makes it a little unsure, a little uneasy about love's vagaries. (Note the lyrics: "You *would be* so nice to come home to. . . .") The form of the tune is 32-bar abab. Ella sings the first chorus more or less straight, very close to Porter's written melody, in her mid-range and in a jazz/pop style. In the second and third choruses, she gets progressively more "jazzy," letting Eldridge (see the previous section) help her along, and moving further away from the given tune. She still sticks with the given lyrics, however. This cut is the most typical Ella of the three discussed here, aimed at both her jazz and her pop audiences. She sings a gorgeous song, but doesn't stretch either as she did in *'Round Midnight* or as she does in *St. Louis Blues*.

➤ *St. Louis Blues*, W. C. Handy. Ella Fitzgerald, vocal; Lou Levy, piano; Max Bennett, bass; Gus Johnson, drums. Recorded 1958.

Go back to Bessie Smith's *St. Louis Blues* in Chapter 1, and listen to that again. It's as close to received knowledge as one gets in jazz; but here Ella *assumes* that it's received knowledge, that the entire audience (and this was recorded in Rome, Italy) knows the whole tune, and she proceeds to make it into something of her own era. The idea of the blues, or more especially of blues standards, has changed in the 30 years between Bessie Smith's recording and Ella Fitzgerald's; in the latter, we're no longer hearing an original lament, but ringing changes on a favorite tune. This is a jazz procedure since Day 2 (whenever that was) of the music, akin to taking funeral marches and turning them into celebratory dances on the way home: let's take our blues, let's take our old songs, but let's make 'em *happy*, make 'em *dance!*

Ella sticks with the three main strains of the original *St. Louis Blues*. The A sections are at a blues tempo, but already she's improvising the melody (she can assume, as I've said, that any audience in the world will know the original) and doing wonderful work over and against the rhythm section. She also amuses the audience and herself by quoting—already in the first chorus—a popular hit of the day, Peggy Lee's *Fever*. The second A strain begins with a sort of "reveille" figure and then continues to improvise away from W. C. Handy's original tune.

Now the surprises set in. The B strain ("St. Louis woman, with all your diamond rings") picks up the tempo and emphasizes the "tango" flavor that has since its earliest incarnations been the flavor of this section. But then in the C section ("Got the St. Louis Blues"), the tempo gets even faster, and from here on Fitzgerald takes off. The C strain is again in blues form (the B isn't). In the first chorus of this, Ella sings the original lyrics. In the second and third, she sings new ones, albeit completely traditional ones. She then sings 19 scat choruses, and no one is better at this Swing scat-singing than Ella Fitzgerald. She's a trumpet player for these 19 choruses. Not without reason did she once put out a recording called *Rhythm Is My Business*. But she also injects her typical and personal humor into what she's doing. In her eighth scat chorus, she begins singing words again, but these are just to assure the audience (as if we didn't know) what tune she's still doing. Then, that done, back to scatting. In the sixteenth chorus, she brings in the tune *Friendship,* and in the seventeenth, the hoary standard *Only You.* The nineteenth chorus takes her back to the lyrics of the original *St. Louis Blues,* in the twewntieth she and the trio go into a stop-time chorus to wind it all up, and she returns to where she began. Not a long, strange trip, but an exhilarating one.

➤ *I Ain't Got Nobody,* Spencer Williams, Roger Graham. Fats Waller, piano. Recorded 1937.

Fats Waller. Music Division, The New York Public Library for the Performing Arts, Astor, Lenox and Tilden Foundation.

Waller is best known for three things—his wit ("One never knows . . . DO ONE?"), his compositions (most recently showcased in the revue *Ain't Misbehavin'*), and his piano playing. We isolate the last one here. This version of a Swing-era standard is a storehouse of almost everything he did. After a 4-bar intro, we hear two 32-bar aaba choruses of the tune, seemingly straightforward but increasingly slippery as you listen to what Waller does. In the first two phrases (aa) of the first chorus, the melody is indeed on the top, but all the interest seems to be in his left hand. After that, Waller goes into some two-fisted stride playing, and in the second chorus, into boogie-woogie as well. His technical virtuosity here is beyond question, but at the same time it doesn't hit you, as it will with Art Tatum, or as it did in the last chapter with James P. Johnson or Jelly Roll Morton: he just tosses off those scales, for example, as if anyone could do it. This is also a hallmark of the Swing era: let's do something serious, but let's pretend it's not.

➤ *Willow Weep for Me*, Ann Ronell. Art Tatum, piano. Recorded 1949.

➤ *Too Marvelous for Words*, Richard Whiting, Johnny Mercer. Art Tatum, piano. Recorded 1955.

➤ *Tiger Rag*, The Original Dixieland Jazz Band. Art Tatum, piano. Recorded 1933.

Tatum was another pianist, like Waller, whose playing derives—here at more than one remove—from stride. He was also a *towering* virtuoso. "Classical" pianists like Vladimir Horowitz used to go listen to him play in clubs. There's a wonderful story, told by Fats Waller: Waller was playing in a club and Tatum came in to listen. (Tatum had studied with, been inspired by, Waller.) Fats was no shrinking violet, but he saw Tatum, stood up from the piano bench, and said "*I* play the piano, but *God* is in the house!" He then sat down to hear Tatum play.

The cut *Willow Weep for Me* is a jewel: an introductory vamp, two choruses (aaba, 32 bars) with a recall of the vamp at the end of the <u>a</u> phrases, and coda recalling same. Notice that only in the bridge phrases does Tatum lay down a steady rhythm; in the <u>a</u> phrases, the meter is not so up-front. Notice also that in some phrases, Tatum decorates the original melody with scales and "filigree" ornaments, but that in others (for example, the beginning of the second chorus) he improvises completely new music (and, in those measures, very blues-y). Tatum's facile technique and his melodic variations are the most easily heard aspects of his playing, but those who have had some training in harmony should listen to his harmonies, too. Tatum was a master, even a pioneer, at what are called "substitute chords": chords which are substituted for, or added to, the original chords of a tune, and which are more complex than those original chords. Fluency in such chord substitutions has become central in jazz since bop, and, like Tatum's rippling melodic lines, it's a lot tougher than it may sound. (For those of you without experience or training in hearing chord changes: you should still know intellectually about substitute chords. And you ought to be able to hear that there are just more chords—that there is more activity and that the notes down in the chords, not in the melody, change faster in this piece than in something like *Lost Your Head Blues* or *Taxi War Dance* or *In the Mood*.)

Too Marvelous for Words is another Swing-era standard, a 32-bar aaba. Tatum does 3-1/2 choruses. Notice here what seems to be the disjunction of his left and right hands, even more so than we heard in James P. Johnson's *Carolina Shout* in Chapter One (p. 36–37). You'll also remark Tatum's extraordinary virtuosity, his use of stride techniques, and so on. At the end of the cut, he goes into a lyrical, out-of-tempo section; but again, as in earlier tunes we've heard, this seems to be not entirely serious, at least in a musical or emotional way.

Tiger Rag is breathtaking virtuosity. There is not much left here of the old New Orleans style (the source of the original composition), or of the original *Tiger Rag*, if it comes to that. After the introduction, where the chords are very unusual and very complex for a 1930s piano solo, we hear the rag itself: the sectional form is still there, and some quotations from the original, but this is almost entirely a new improvisation on that older framework. And it's much further away from that framework than was Jelly Roll Morton's *Grandpa's Spells* of 1926, or his piano version of *Maple Leaf Rag*. This may have something to do with Tatum's background—he was born in Toledo, spent most of his life in New York and California, and played for such singers as Adelaide Hall and the Kansas City blues shouter Joe Turner, and therefore had virtually no contact with the pure New Orleans performance. In style, this is closer to the New York-based stride piano, with the oom-pah left hand and all the emphasis on melodic cascades and on rhythm. But at the core, it's original Tatum.

➤   *Dinah*, Henry Akst, Sam M. Lewis, Joe Young. The Quintette of the Hot Club Of France: Stéphane Grappelli, violin; Django Reinhardt, Roger Chaput, Joseph Reinhardt, guitar; Louis Vola, bass. Recorded 1934.

The same tune we've recently heard from Red Nichols and his group, and our only real example of European jazz. (Joe Zawinul and Miroslav Vitous, whom we'll meet in Chapter Four, won't count for us: they work in the United States, with American musicians, and have done so since their breaking into the ranks.) Django Reinhardt was a Belgian-born, French-speaking gypsy; he played gypsy music, jazz, "folk," and pop tunes. He learned jazz initially from recordings and from American expatriate musicians in Paris; he also played briefly in this country. This group, the Quintette du Hot Club de France, is the format he's most remembered for.

This is the same 32-bar aaba we heard above. Django takes the first two choruses in a Swing style with swirling lines like Tatum's (not so much like Charlie Christian's). He also likes to quote other tunes in his solo. Then Grappelli takes two choruses, with the guitars as his backup. A "multicultural" question: if you didn't know who was playing this, would you assume it was "American," "Afro-American," or what?

➤   *Body and Soul.* Robert Sour, Frank Eyton, John Green, Edward Heyman. Coleman Hawkins and His Orchestra: Coleman Hawkins, tenor sax; Tommy Lindsay, Joe Guy, trumpet; Earl Hardy, trombone; Jackie Fields, Eustis Moore, alto sax; Gene Rodgers, piano; William Oscar Smith, bass; Arthur Herbert, drums. Recorded 1939.

This is another landmark in jazz history, like Louis Armstrong's *West End Blues* intro, Bix and Tram on *Singin' The Blues*, Bobby Hackett on *String of Pearls*, Ben Webster on *Cotton Tail*, and Lester Young on *Doggin' Around* or *Taxi War Dance*. This cut was not only a great influence on other musicians, it was a huge popular success as well. Compare this version to the Goodman trio's, above: whereas the latter was

Lester ("Prez") Young, left, and Coleman Hawkins, right. Courtesy of the Rutgers Institute of Jazz Studies.

an example of thematic improvisation, consisting mainly of ornamentations of the original melody, Hawk's reading is primarily harmonic. He arpeggiates the chords of the chart and makes new lines out of those notes rather than out of the melody. This practice is not standard in 1930s jazz, but will be of utmost importance when we get to bop. This version is *similar* to the Goodman in that both are understated, "laid back." It swings, both because of Hawk's rhythms and because of the drummer's steady 4-to-the-bar playing.

Compare Hawk's timbre to Lester Young's, too. Hawk's big, rich sound was the model before Prez came along, and sax players thereafter modeled themselves on one or the other. The timbres were the primary difference between the two, though. Both Hawk and Prez came out of the Midwest and Southwest, were born in Missouri, and played in Kansas City bands (Hawkins also with Bessie Smith), and both were harmonic improvisers, players who turned chord changes into melodies.

➤   *The Man I Love*, George Gershwin, Ira Gershwin. Coleman Hawkins Quartet: Coleman Hawkins, tenor sax; Eddie Heywood, piano; Oscar Pettiford, bass; Shelly Manne, drums. Recorded 1943.

This tune was originally a real torch song, done by people like Judy Garland, and also by such jazz singers as Billie Holiday and Ella Fitzgerald. This version, though, is double-time and swings like your best. The comments for Hawks' *Body and Soul*, on timbre, swing, and harmonic improvisation, apply here, too.

BILLIE HOLIDAY—LADY DAY (1915–1959)

➤   *Miss Brown to You*, Leo Robin, Richard A. Whiting, Ralph Rainger. The Teddy Wilson Orchestra: Roy Eldridge, trumpet; Benny Goodman, clarinet; Ben Webster, tenor sax; Teddy Wilson, piano; John Trueheart, guitar; John Kirby, bass; Cozy Cole, drums; Billie Holiday, vocal. Recorded 1935.

Billie Holiday's first recording (*Your Mother's Son-in-Law*, 1933) had been with Benny Goodman and was produced by John Hammond (who worked with artists from Bessie Smith to Bob Dylan, Janis Joplin,

Billie Holiday. Courtesy of
the Rutgers Institute of Jazz
Studies.

and Bruce Springsteen). Goodman's small-group pianist after 1935 was
Teddy Wilson, one of Billie's favorite accompanists. They're all here,
plus Roy Eldridge (whom we heard extensively in the last section of
this chapter, and who worked with Fletcher Henderson, Gene Krupa,
and others), Ben Webster (the tenor soloist on Ellington's *Cotton Tail*),
and Cozy Cole (who first recorded with Jelly Roll Morton, 1930, and
went on to be as influential a Swing drummer as Jo Jones, from Basie's
rhythm section, or "Big Sid" Catlett, whom we heard on *I Can't Believe
that You're in Love with Me*). In other words, from her start at the age of
18, Billie Holiday commanded the cooperation of the greatest instrumentalists of her time.

This cut is a 32-bar aaba; choruses are by Goodman, Holiday, Wilson, with an ensemble coda. In this era the vocalist, called the "girl
singer" or the "boy singer," usually did just one chorus in the course of
a tune. But listen to the way Holiday sidles into that first line and
makes the song hers. As someone once said, Billie just couldn't sing
anything *straight*; she had to make it hers, somehow. And, as she said
herself in *Lady Sings the Blues* (the book, not the movie), if you didn't do
that, it wasn't music, it was close-order drill.

Note, also, two clichés of the Swing era: again, that the title of the
song is often the final lyric of the a phrases, and that cuts often end
with the drum shot. There are also here the beginnings of a particular
Holiday vocal signature or mannerism—she fades at the end of a

phrase, without cutting the line off precisely. In the cuts to come, this turns into a downward glissando (slide) at the ends of phrases, usually to emphasize the final word of the line as well as the end of the musical phrase.

Listen especially in this cut and the ones to come to Holiday's timbre, to her delivery, and to her command of phrasing. She could ride any tempo and make it sound either effortless or hot, as she wanted. She had an unbeatable sense of rhythm, though less explosive than Louis Armstrong's or Ella Fitzgerald's scat work. Her interplay with the instrumentalists in the group was real jazz give-and-take, and her sense of phrasing, or placement of the lines, was the equal of anyone's. The first truly great jazz singer—at least, the first truly great jazz singer who didn't play an instrument (her only predecessor or contemporary was Louis Armstrong)—Billie Holiday has since her lifetime been called "The Voice Of Jazz," and you can hear her influence in all the great jazz singers working today.

➤ *These Foolish Things (Remind Me of You)*, Holt Marvell, Jack Strachey, Harry Link. Teddy Wilson and His Orchestra: Jonah Jones, trumpet; Johnny Hodges, alto sax; Harry Carney, baritone sax and clarinet; Teddy Wilson, piano; Lawrence Lucie, guitar; John Kirby, bass; Cozy Cole, drums; Billie Holiday, vocal. Recorded 1936.

The form here is 32-bar aaba, with choruses by Wilson (*great* entrance to the bridge by Carney), Holiday (with *obbligato* melody from Hodges), and Jones (basically playing the tune). This song is also a good example of typical 1930s lyrics in two ways: it is a sort of sophisticated juxtaposition of the mundane with the really deeply felt ("A tinkling piano in the next apartment, / Those stumbling words that told you what my heart meant"), and the words that can be read as either innocent or adult ("You came, you saw, you conquered me," a literary reference, sort of, to Shakespeare's *Julius Caesar*, followed by "When you did *that* to me. . . ."). This is the song we'll finish this chapter with, another version by Holiday from 1952.

➤ *Billie's Blues*, Billie Holiday. Billie Holiday and Her Orchestra: Bunny Berigan, trumpet; Artie Shaw, clarinet; Joe Pushkin, piano; Dick McDonough, guitar; Pete Peterson, bass; Cozy Cole, drums; Billie Holiday, vocal. Recorded 1936.

This is one of the first of Billie's cuts recorded under her own name as leader. It's a racially mixed group—Billy and Cozy Cole were black, the rest white (Berigan also sang, and did a recording of the standard *I Can't Get Started* that rivaled Holiday's and shows up as background music in one scene of the movie *Chinatown*). One of the great things about this cut is that last chorus: you try to put together the meaning of the lyrics, the barrelhouse tempo, and Cozy Cole's drumshots. This is as uptown a blues as Bessie Smith's *Young Woman's Blues*.

➤   *Swing, Brother, Swing!*, Lewis Raymond, Walter Bishop, Clarence Williams. Count Basie and His Orchestra: Ed Lewis, Bobby Moore, Buck Clayton, trumpet; Dan Minor, George Hunt, trombone; Earle Warren, Jack Washington, Herschel Evans, Lester Young, sax; Count Basie, piano; Freddie Green, guitar; Walter Page, bass; Jo Jones, drums; Billie Holiday, vocal. Recorded 1937.

Like Basie's *Shout and Feel It*, discussed earlier, this was an air-check done during the few months that Lady Day worked with the Basie band. The form is aaba (two choruses), and it's riffed. Listen to the rhythm work and to Billie's hot singing over that. You can interpret the lyrics for yourself, but listen to the joyous sound of her voice in this cut and the way she can ride a tempo.

➤   *He's Funny That Way*, Richard A. Whiting, Neil Moret. Billie Holiday and Her Orchestra: Buck Clayton, trumpet; Buster Bailey, clarinet; Lester Young, tenor sax; Claude Thornhill, piano; Freddie Green, guitar; Walter Page, bass; Jo Jones, drums; Billie Holiday, vocal. Recorded 1937.

Here's Billie working with a small group culled from the Basie band. Listen especially to her duets with Lester Young—they were partners, mutual influences, and it was he who first called her "Lady Day." And listen, as ever, to Holiday's singing of the lyrics. She was not just a singer who could find her way through a set of words, but a *musician* who *delivered* them. It's even possible for some people (not for me) to forget that she's singing, since the single words and phrases are uttered with such conviction; but (despite what she said herself) you cannot

separate the way she sang lines from the words that she was pro-
nouncing. She was like Prez in this: he knew the lyrics to all the songs
he played and heard them in his mind as he soloed. The emotional
import of the words was, for these two, the central factor in the music
they improvised around those words.

➤   *All of Me*, Seymour Simons, Gerald Marks. Billie Holiday and Eddie
     Heywood and His Orchestra: Shad Collins, trumpet; Leslie Johnakins,
     Eddie Barefield, alto sax; Lester Young, tenor sax; Eddie Heywood,
     piano; John Collins, guitar; Ted Sturgis, bass; Kenny Clarke, drums; Bil-
     lie Holiday, vocal. Recorded 1941.

Another Holiday/Young collaboration. Here she uses blue notes
and sings a pop song in the same way that she had *Billie's Blues*, above.
Unlike Ella Fitzgerald or Sarah Vaughan, Billie Holiday likes narrow
melodic ranges and singing a song *almost*—but never quite—straight.
She also sings the word "baby" (here and in other cuts) quite unlike any
other singer.

➤   *God Bless the Child*, Billie Holiday, Arthur Herzog, Jr. Billie Holiday and
     Her Orchestra: Roy Eldridge, trumpet; Jimmy Powell, Ernie Powell,
     alto sax; Lester Boone, tenor sax; Eddie Heywood, piano; Paul Chap-
     man, guitar; Grachan Moncur, bass; Herbert Cowans, drums; Billie
     Holiday, vocal. Recorded 1941.

There are a number of songs indelibly associated with Lady Day:
Am I Blue?, *Miss Brown To You*, *Fine and Mellow*, *Don't Explain*, *Georgia
On My Mind*, *I Cried For You*, and *Strange Fruit* (see below), to name only
a few. Singers still do, some 40 years after her death, entire medleys or
sets of "Billie Holiday songs." *God Bless the Child* stands at the forefront
of these. I leave form and delivery up to you. Holiday sings this as a
universal, and wrote the lyrics when she was almost 30, not for many
years anybody's little girl. What is she singing about?

➤   *Strange Fruit*, Lewis Allen. Billie Holiday, vocal; Charlie Shavers, trum-
     pet; Wynton Kelly, piano; Kenny Burrell, guitar; Aaron Bell, bass;
     Lenny McBrowne, drums. Recorded 1956.

Holiday first sang *Strange Fruit* in 1939 at Café Society, the racially integrated New York cabaret/nightclub which attracted a left-leaning clientele as well as music lovers, and she recorded it in that year as well. Initially she didn't want to do the tune, since it was so far away from her usual material and since she didn't consider herself to be any sort of activist. Once she included it in her sets, however, it became as closely identified with her as any of her other songs, and her delivery of it was shattering. She continued to sing it for the rest of her career. This recording, made in 1956, is also an example of the state of her voice in her last years, and of the depth and immediacy of her performances; we're a long way from *Miss Brown to You*.

A historical note: "Lewis Allen," the song's author, was in reality named Abel Meeropol. It was he who adopted the two sons of Julius and Ethel Rosenberg in the 1950s, after they were arrested and executed on charges of spying for the Soviet Union.

➤ *These Foolish Things*, as above. Billie Holiday and Her Orchestra: Billie Holiday, vocal; Oscar Peterson, piano; Barney Kessel, guitar; Ray Brown, bass; Alvin Stoller, drums. Recorded 1952.

What you want to do here is immediately go back and listen to the Billie Holiday recording of this song from 1936, above. In this small-group recording of the 32-bar aaba, Billie sings a <u>ba</u> that hadn't been here before. The tempo is also significantly slower. The added lyrics may change the meaning of the tune for you; the tempo and the texture certainly should. How did we get here from 1936? Is there life after adolescence?

▶ Chapter 3

From Bird to Trane
(Things To Come)

The years from the mid-1940s to the early 1960s were perhaps the richest and most varied of jazz's 90-year history (with the possible exception of today's variety). The styles discussed so far in this book—New Orleans jazz, post-New Orleans, the Kansas City/Southwest tradition, Swing, and the individual playing of such musicians as Tatum and Billie Holiday—all continued. In addition, there was an exhilarating proliferation of new styles developing from and cross-feeding one another, almost like a chain reaction. And there was a change in musicians' and society's attitudes toward jazz. If it had once been widely regarded as entertainment music, jazz now began to demand recognition for its validity as a musical expression, for its seriousness of purpose (that is, as concert music to listen to for its own sake), and for the professionalism of the musicians. The new developments are summarized in the chart on the following page, to which you should refer from here on. We'll begin this chapter with *bebop* or *bop*, move on to *cool jazz* and *hard bop*, spend a little time on a few soloists and bands of the 1950s, and finish with the two most important of the late 1950s and early 1960s, Miles Davis and John Coltrane.

When it began in the early 1940s, bebop was such a startling development that it seemed to many people like a revolution against everything that jazz had ever been and a real threat to the music's existence. (Most new music, of any type, gets the same reaction—for exam-

A GENERALIZED CHART OF JAZZ STYLES

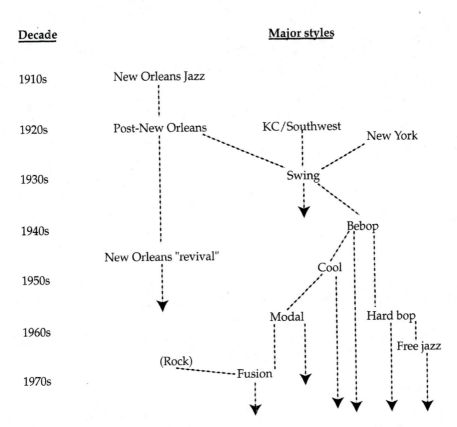

A generalized chart of jazz styles. This sketch indicates when various kinds of jazz entered the scene and traces the major lines of development. Arrows (↓) mean that the style continues, regardless of its placement on the horizontal data plan.

ple, the Beatles in 1963–1964, Bob Dylan when he "went electric," free jazz, fusion, and hip-hop music.) In a 1948 *Down Beat* article ominously titled "Bop will Kill Business Unless It Kills Itself First," Louis Armstrong said:

> [the boppers] want to carve everyone else because they're full of malice, and all they want to do is show you up, and any old way will do as long as it's different form the way you played it before. So you get all them weird chords which don't mean nothing, and first people get curious about it just because it's new, but soon they get tired of it because it's really no

good and you got no melody to remember and no beat to dance to. So they're all poor again and nobody is working, and that's what that modern malice done for you.[1]

Armstrong here summarized all the complaints about bop: "weird chords," "no melody," "no beat," and nothing but "malice" on the part of the musicians. But he was wrong. As people got used to the sound of bop and could hear what the musicians were doing, they grew to understand the new chords, they could hear the tunes and the terrific rhythmic inventions, and they realized that bop was saying a lot that hadn't been heard in music before. Bebop began as the music of a small group of people exploring together, but it became the mainstream language of jazz and the source of all jazz styles to come.

Bop has some specific characteristics or techniques in common with Swing, especially with the Kansas City/Southwest branch of that tradition, and the boppers listened carefully to players such as Lester Young and Charlie Christian. The principal bop innovators—Charlie Parker (alto sax), Dizzy Gillespie (trumpet), Max Roach and Kenny Clarke (drums), Thelonious Monk (pianist and composer), and others—are discussed in the following sections. Before we turn to that music, though, or survey the other styles that came after bop, we need to go over some of the characteristic style traits of bebop, the treatment of texture (in both the specific and general senses of the word), instruments, rhythm, harmony, and so on.

Texture. Remember that the term "texture" has two meanings in music: the first is specific, the number and relationship of various instruments or voices (for example, one principal melody and accompaniment, which is called homophony, or simultaneous melodies of equal importance, called polyphony); the second meaning of texture is general and nontechnical, simply referring to the relative thickness or sparseness of sound, analogous to the texture of a fabric. In the first of these senses of texture, bop is a multilayered music, with more than one thing going on at a time; despite this, the general texture of bop, in the second sense, is lighter and clearer than that of earlier music.

The multilayered nature of bop has to do mainly with rhythm, but to some degree with phrasing as well. That is to say, we're not dealing

---

[1] "'Bop Will Kill Business Unless It Kills Itself First'—Louis Armstrong." *Down Beat*, April 7, 1948, p. 2. Also quoted in Marshall W. Stearns, *The Story of Jazz* (New York: Oxford University Press, 1956), p. 219. The *Down Beat* article is a conversation among Armstrong, the Chicago clarinet player Mezz Mezzrow, and Barney Bigard, the clarinetist who worked with both Duke Ellington and Louis Armstrong.

here just with solo over rhythm section, or the solo/accompanying riffs/rhythm framework. In bop, the basic meter is laid down by the bass and the drummer's ride cymbal, played with brushes, not by the entire rhythm section as in Swing. On top of this, and more to the forefront, you hear cross-accents, "punctuations," polyrhythms from the piano and from the rest of the drummer's equipment. The soloist adds yet another layer to this, or, if there is more than one soloist working, as happens occasionally, each line is another layer.

Bop soloists also use cross-phrasing a great deal more than had the majority of Swing players, although we mentioned cross-phrasing particularly in connection with Lester Young and Charlie Christian, who are often regarded as transitional figures between Swing and bop. The basic 4- or 8-measure phrase is still defined, more or less clearly, by the rhythm section. But the soloists' melodies fall across these divisions, and often break up the 4- or 8-bar units into smaller, asymmetrical sections. This lack of symmetry also shows up in the rhythms and melodic shapes (see below) and was one of the new factors which made bop hard to understand at first for people accustomed to the balance and regularity of Swing tunes.

But if bop is a multilayered music, it is still quite clear and transparent in general overall sound. This is due in part to bop's origins as music for small combo, for a group of soloists rather than for big band. The spare texture is also a function of the timbres of the individual players, who tended to use a much lighter sound than had most Swing players. (Remember again the distinction we made between Lester Young and Coleman Hawkins in this regard.) Finally, it was necessary to keep the sound and the texture light so that the layers and the polyrhythms could be heard clearly; more instruments would muddy up the sound. This may also be a function of bop's origins in small clubs rather than in grand ballrooms: you need less volume to fill the space, and the visceral excitement of the music can rely on more intricate rhythmic interplay than on riffs and danceable regularity.

Instruments. Since bop was the creation of a very small number of musicians working in a close-knit group, it makes sense that, at least at the beginning, the style coalesced in the small-combo format, not that of the big band. But the relationship of the few instruments in the combo is different from that of the Swing ensemble. Again, the bop format is not just solo over rhythm, but a layered combination. Each musician enjoys greater independence and more individuality, and each displays more virtuosity than any but the greatest of earlier soloists.

The most important factor here is the so-called emancipation of the rhythm section, by which the pianist, bassist, and drummer moved out of the background and into the ranks of soloists. We saw this begin in the previous chapter, but it achieves real force only here with the boppers. The rhythm section no longer just puts down the basic chords and meter; in addition to that, they add a great deal of rhythmic interplay with the horns and take extended solos on their own. So when you listen to bop, you don't want just to register the rhythm section on some subconscious level; you need to pay close attention to them as well as to the front line, sometimes even ignore the horns in favor of the drummer or the pianist.

Rhythm. I've mentioned the polyrhythms that are a hallmark of the bop style, the layering of rhythms in bass/ride cymbal, drums and piano, and horns. In addition to that change in rhythmic texture, the rhythmic patterns themselves are different in bop from the patterns of Swing. The emphasis moves away from the balance and regularity of earlier jazz in the direction of greater variety. Whether in a melody or in the purely rhythmic layer, accents often come in surprising places, or they come in different places (on strong beats, weak beats, between beats) in different measures. Players like Charlie Parker like to juxtapose lines of short, fast notes with lines of longer, more sustained ones. A favorite technique, which we'll see in detail with the Dizzy Gillespie composition *Salt Peanuts*, is the repetition of a little pattern over and over, but with the accent coming on a different note each time. This sort of "off-balance" rhythm was jarring to listeners at the beginning (Armstrong, for instance), but it's one of the joys of the music, giving to bop an exciting forward drive and a range of possibilities new to jazz.

Harmony. The boppers' innovations in harmony were in two areas, the sort of chord they used and the new ways in which those chords were connected. First, they began to use "extended" chords, chords with more notes than earlier jazz had employed. Those earlier chords had been made up of three or four notes; boppers added more notes to these chords (*extended* them) and often emphasized the notes they'd added over the notes of the original. This affected not only the harmonies played by the piano, but also the melodies of the soloists, since they now had more notes available to them to play over any given chord. As with the rhythmic innovations, the move here is toward greater variety, with greater possibilities open to the musician.

The new chord progressions, or the ways to move from one chord to the next, were partly a continuation of the substitute chords we mentioned above, particularly with the music of Art Tatum, which had become fairly common coin from the late 1930s. But they were also a result of conscious exploration and study. Dizzy Gillespie, for example, spent long hours at the piano trying out chords and listening to new combinations, new successions. He then figured out how he could use these new progressions as the framework for his trumpet improvisations, and he showed his discoveries to the pianists he worked with.

Since the chords themselves were much more complex than those of earlier jazz, and since they tended to change more quickly than the chords of earlier compositions, it was at first very difficult for musicians to keep up with the boppers. This was one of the sources for complaints like Armstrong's that bop was music full of malice and "weirdness" for its own sake, not for musical reasons. And, at the beginning, the ability to handle these difficulties really did work as a kind of self-defense for the boppers. They were well aware of the hostility and willful incomprehension that other musicians harbored for them. They were proud of their new music, if also defensive about it, and proud of their aspirations as musicians and artists. Being able to navigate through the new harmonies was a key to membership in the club, a sign of being one of "us" and not one of "them." This is secondary, however, as is the whole cultist attitude of bop's early years. What is important is the expansion of the range of harmonic possibilities which very soon became the jazz norm, and which testifies to the boppers' view of themselves as serious artists, concert musicians, exponents of an important and extraordinary tradition, and not simply as paid entertainers.

Melody. Bop tunes share all the general traits noted so far, from the variety and frequent asymmetry of rhythms and phrases to new possibilities opened up by the new chords, and they also reflect the greater virtuosity of the players. We can distinguish between bop melodies and earlier ones, and between bop "themes," the tunes of given compositions, and the improvised solos, by looking at a Charlie Parker classic, *Ornithology*. The tune is based on the chord progression of an older standard, Morgan Lewis's *How High The Moon*. Parker's melody uses the same chords in the same order, and you could play or sing the melodies at the same time without any great, jarring discord. But beyond the chord progression, *Ornithology* and *How High The Moon* have almost nothing in common.

First of all, there are simply a lot more notes in *Ornithology* than in *How High The Moon*, and the bop tune is neither so smooth nor so regular as the older melody. *How High The Moon* has a short, 2-measure pattern that is repeated four times for the first a phrase. Most of its notes are very close together, and the overall range is fairly restricted. In *Ornithology*, by contrast, no two phrases are the same length, there is no repeated pattern, and there's a big variety in the direction of the phrases (whether the notes to up or down). The range is bigger than that of *How High The Moon*, the tune is jumpier, and there are a lot of syncopations, off-beat accents, and other funny rhythmic "corners."

These inventive asymmetries were carried on and extended in the improvised solos that follow a tune's theme. Remember that the boppers improvised new melodies on top of the chord progressions, and didn't just decorate the melody of the thematic chorus. Many bop compositions were in fact originally improvised choruses over the chords of a tune which the musician then wrote down and used as the given melody of his own, new composition. (We've already seen this happen in musicians' treating blues as original compositions, even though they all have virtually identical chord changes.) The wealth of ideas in bop is astounding; the musicians don't just decorate existing melodies, but improvise their own, new ones, each chorus of a solo constituting a whole new set of musical ideas based on a single harmonic framework.

The inventiveness of bop led almost immediately to new inventions: it was such a fertile, open-ended kind of music that as soon as it had achieved a solid measure of acceptance and understanding, bop gave rise to new musical developments. Some of these, notably "cool" jazz, were seen as reactions against bop, just as bop had been seen as a reaction or revolution against Swing. Some, such as hard bop, were continuations. The battle lines between "cool" jazz and bop or hard bop were hard and fast during the 1950s, but they seem less so today. The various streams that came out of bop—"cool," hard bop, modal jazz, the beginnings of free jazz—not only established themselves as new dialects of the jazz language, they also continued to feed back into the mainstream of the music. And this jazz of the 1940s and 1950s, out of bop and from other branches back into bop, continues to be the most widely spread and widely played jazz.

"Cool" jazz arrived in the later 1940s, the creation of a number of musicians working in at least two groups, who took elements from both Swing and bop and combined these with their own predilections. The principal distinctions between bop and "cool" jazz have to do with timbre and texture: the tone-colors of "cool" jazz are lighter and softer than those of bop, avoiding the intensity and the sharpness of the boppers' timbres for sounds that are more relaxed, less pointed. In some groups, as we'll see below when we discuss individual musicians and ensembles, there was a real interest in using new timbres and in mixing timbres in new ways. (See especially the section on Miles Davis's nonet and the recordings called *The Birth of the Cool*.) Finally, the emphasis in "cool" jazz is primarily on melody and melodic flow. The tunes, whether the given ones of a composition or the improvised solos, are long and smooth, the cross-phrasing is very supple, and the rhythmic complexity of bop is avoided, again for smoothness and for more balance and regularity than one hears in bop's explosions. In addition, the emphasis on melody and the melodic lines puts the melodic instruments (the horns and the pianist's right hand) at the forefront of the ensembles, at the expense of the rhythm section. In much "cool" music, the drums and bass aren't so active as they are in bop, but rather keep time and act as a background support for the soloists, like the rhythm sections of Swing. They're necessary, but not paramount. (Like all the general characteristics discussed in these introductory essays, this secondary role of the rhythm section will be qualified in some of the music to come. Max Roach, for example, one of the earliest and most important of bop drummers, also played frequently with "cool" groups. As you listen to the various selections, you should compare his work with bop ensembles to his work with the "cool.")

All these various style traits combine to give this sort of jazz its particular flavor, more relaxed and less aggressive than that of bop, the "laid-back" sound that is summarized in the epithet "cool." But don't assume, because of that, that this music is unemotional, empty, or soulless. Within its particular limits, "cool" jazz has as much variety and as many subtleties as any other kind of jazz. The playing of Lee Konitz, just to choose one example, is full of joys. I've so far put the term "cool" in quotation marks to get a little distance from the word, to deemphasize its connotations of being "uninvolved." With that caveat and for the sake of simplicity, we can now drop the quotation marks.

Hard bop is usually contrasted with cool jazz, since it developed at about the same time or a few years later and because its sound is much different from that of cool's. The characteristics of hard bop include rawer, "funkier" timbres than those of cool, a more assertive drive, perhaps a hotter emotional pitch. Many hard bop players came from the big cities of the North—Detroit, Philadelphia, New York—and they heard not only the bop of the late 1940s, but the post-1945 blues and the R & B (rhythm and blues) that were everywhere in clubs and on the radio in the later 1940s and the 1950s. Their music was a direct continuation of bop—one could say just like bop, except more so—with the addition of the "funk" of R & B. Hard bop isn't really emphasized as a separate style in this book, although it's covered in the section *Bopping On—Soloists of the 1950s*, in the selections from Charles Mingus, and in the first cuts of the sections on Miles Davis and John Coltrane. Compare it to the earlier bop and to the contemporary cool style. And keep it in mind when we get into free jazz in the next chapter: many of the hard boppers moved, or could move when they wanted to, into free jazz, and if those styles in general don't seem to have a great deal to do with each other, the intense melodic lines and the hot emotional pitch of both are similar.

We'll hear one further new kind of music in this chapter, a music once again introduced and championed by Miles Davis, who was deeply involved with every kind of jazz except free jazz from 1945 until his death in 1991. This is modal jazz. It is not a new style as such, since it doesn't involve the same sort of new conceptions of melody, rhythm, and texture that we've seen in other style developments. Rather, modal jazz is a new sort of *composition*, a new way of making tunes and of creating the basic framework for improvising. Modal jazz is explained in detail in the Miles Davis section (under the tune *So What*) and in the Glossary.

This covers the major stylistic developments of jazz during the twenty years from the early 1940s through the early 1960s. But we need, before we go on to the music itself, to stop for a moment and look at another development in the jazz world during those years. This has to do with jazz musicians' attitudes toward their music and themselves, and with the position of jazz and of black people in United States society.

As we've seen, jazz was regarded during the first half of this century as entertainment music—music to dance to or to relax by. The boppers began to change this. They saw themselves not as entertainers, but as serious professional musicians, as artists. And they worked hard to support that view. They studied music theory, they listened to many different kinds of music, they practiced incredibly hard in order to achieve a technical virtuosity on their instruments that was new to jazz and was the equal of any other kind of music. Some musicians even went to "classical" conservatories to study—Cecil Taylor at the New England Conservatory of Music and Miles Davis at the Juilliard School are two examples—and others, like Charlie Parker and John Coltrane, listened carefully to modern "classical" composers such as Bartók, Stravinsky, and Varèse.

But jazz after 1945 was not accorded the popularity that it had enjoyed during the big band Swing era, nor the respect which the boppers felt, rightly, that it deserved as an art music. This went hand in hand with the social attitudes in this country, the ingrained and established patterns of racial prejudice and the refusal of basic civil rights to blacks. Many blacks were "allowed" to fight for the United States during World War II but still couldn't make a decent salary, buy a house, or even vote in some sections of the country.

We'll ignore in this book the effect that this situation may have had on the music. It's easy to say, for example, that the rage these musicians felt was translated into the aggressiveness of their playing, the "malice" that Armstrong heard in bop, but a sweeping generalization like that is also impossible to prove. Those interested in the relations between society and music should read LeRoi Jones's (Amiri Baraka) *Blues People*, an extraordinary statement.

What this situation *did* engender, however, which had a direct and important effect on music, was the growth of a new and outspoken black pride. On the social side, there was the beginning of the civil rights movement, which exploded in the 1960s and which is still working toward its goals. Within music, this pride consisted of a new awareness and new respect for the tradition of jazz, for its roots in black music, and for its leaders as heroes (the word is not too strong). We'll see this again and again in the music of this chapter. Musicians like Dizzy Gillespie turned to Afro-Cuban sounds. The hard boppers, as I've mentioned, brought in the "funk" of black popular music and the "soul" of the black church. There were loving tributes to Duke Ellington (himself a pioneer in this sort of deep respect and love for jazz traditions and its roots in black culture) and Lester Young, among others, as musicians and as men; and there were scathing musical attacks on white segregationists such as Mingus's *Fables of Faubus*. And beginning in the late 1950s, but especially in the 1960s with free jazz, there was renewed interest in the musics of Africa, in their instruments, textures, and rhythms. This last goes straight back to the interest and love for prejazz American black folk musics, such as we heard in the very first sections of this book, on the part of musicians like Ellington and Mingus.

Nothing like this had happened before in jazz's history. Songs such as Jimmy Rushing's *It's The Same Old South*, Billie Holiday's *Strange Fruit*, blues bemoaning the status of blacks in this country, even Fats Waller's tremendously moving *What Did I Do To Be So Black and Blue?*, were isolated cries, in the language of their times. The awareness and pride of musicians in the 1950s were different: they changed the music itself.

For all these reasons, the years 1940–1960 can be regarded as a unified period in jazz history, analogous to the Swing era or the New Orleans/early jazz era. From start to finish, the musics are dominated by bop. But that plural word, musics, was intentional. The richness and variety of invention have no parallel in jazz history, and even with the coming of free jazz in the 1960s and the popularity of jazz-rock fusion in the 1970s and 1980s, the music of the 1950s has continued to inform, even to dominate, all jazz heard since.

BIRD LIVES! CHARLIE PARKER (1920–1955)

➤ *Now's the Time*, Charlie Parker. The Charlie Parker Quartet: Charlie
Parker, alto sax; Al Haig, piano; Max Roach, drums; Percy Heath, bass.
Recorded 1953.

This cut is twelve choruses of the 12-bar blues from four pioneers
of bebop. (Heath will go on to be the bassist for the so-called "neoclas-
sical," "cool" Modern Jazz Quartet; see the tune *Django* in the *Bopping
On* section later in this chapter. But remember that cool jazz came
directly out of bop and wasn't completely antithetical to it.) Of the
twelve choruses, the first two are fairly straightforward thematic statements; then we hear five choruses from Parker, three choruses by the
rhythm section, one drum solo (!), and the "out" chorus.

Things to notice: 1) the *light* sound from each of the four players
and from the combo as a whole ("light" in terms of timbre, as with
Lester Young earlier, not in the sense of "easy listening"); 2) the steady
4-to-the-bar in the bass *only*, the piano and drums adding rhythmic
"punctuations" and polyrhythms, and Parker's tremendously varied
rhythms and accents over it all (can you keep the steady 4-to-the-bar
during the drum solo?); 3) the long melodic line, jumping all over the
range (high and low), suddenly juxtaposing long and short notes, playing around with the 4-bar phrase rhythm (analogous to the rhythmic
playing around with the 4-beat meter); 4) the high-energy drive of the
whole, a continuation of earlier Swing music (especially that of the
Kansas City/Basie tradition) but also a function of 1) through 3) above
and of the small-combo format (you can go faster in a Mercedes than
you can in a Mack truck).

➤ *KoKo*, Charlie Parker. Charlie Parker's Re-Boppers: Charlie Parker, alto
sax; Dizzy Gillespie, trumpet and piano; Curley Russell, bass; Max
Roach, drums. Recorded 1945.

This is not a reworking of Ellington's *Ko-Ko*, which was a blues,
but a new tune based on the changes of Ray Noble's *Cherokee*, a Swing-
era big-band staple (the most famous recording of which was probably
that by Charlie Barnet and His Orchestra, included on the Smithsonian
Big Band Jazz anthology). This is like the Swing version of *Cherokee* in

Charlie Parker. Courtesy of the Rutgers Institute of Jazz Studies.

structure and in that the rhythm section seems to work at double-time. The overall layout here is intro (32 bars); two choruses from Bird (64 bars each, aaba); drum break; and coda (32 bars). The intro and coda are unmistakable bop: a fast, difficult melodic "head" played by sax and trumpet *in unison*, then 8 bars each from trumpet and sax solo, then a final 8 from the two in close harmony. Only with the tune itself does the full rhythm section come in. This kind of playing—fast and very difficult—for two players working in tandem—would have been unheard of in earlier generations of jazz musicians; the only thing we've heard that approaches it is Ellington's *Cotton Tail*.

The comments under *Now's The Time* about the light sound, the steady rhythmic foundation in the bass, the melodies and the drive, apply here as well. But listen carefully to Max Roach's drumming, also characteristically bop: for his normal time-keeping work, he uses the ride cymbals, and saves the drums (traps and bass drum) for punctuation (sometimes on strong beats, sometimes for syncopations and off-beat accents) and for his solo. And as with *Now's The Time*, try to keep the basic meter going during Roach's solo. Does he keep it, or does it disappear completely? How long is his break?

➤ *Lady, Be Good*, George Gershwin, Ira Gershwin. Charlie Parker with Jazz at the Philharmonic: Charlie Parker, alto sax; Al Killian, Howard McGhee, trumpet; Willie Smith, alto sax; Lester Young, tenor sax; Arnold Ross, piano; Billy Hadnott, bass; Lee Young, drums. Recorded 1946.

This is three choruses an aaba Swing-era standard which was Ella Fitzgerald's signature tune for many years. This cut begins with an intro and a first chorus from the rhythm section, especially the pianist. Parker's 2-chorus solo is interesting because in the first chorus he seems to be playing from his Kansas City roots and in the second a more contemporary bop improvisation. The moral of that story is that hard-and-fast delineations between contrasting or even just differing styles are not always true to reality. Like any great jazz musician, Parker had many quills to his bow and is too varied to be constrained by any single label.

At any rate, in the first chorus of his solo, Parker stays with the 8-bar phrase units of the original Gershwin tune and, within the phrases, doesn't use the great variety of note values (short and long) or register (juxtaposed high and low) that we hear elsewhere. His timbre is especially reminiscent of the "blues-drenched" Kansas City sound, a little raspy and with an aggressive, swinging edge. Even here, though, he fills the whole 8 bars of each phrase with lots of notes; this continues in the second chorus. That chorus is closer to what we think of as typically bop lines, with the variety of notes and registers, and the unexpected emphasis on notes that seem to come anywhere in the phrase. Parker is here also embellishing the original Gershwin chords with extended harmonies (you won't hear this, necessarily, unless you've had a fair amount of musical training; but you should know that it's happening).

➤ *Klacktoveedsedsteen*, Charlie Parker. Charlie Parker Quintet: Charlie Parker, alto sax; Miles Davis, trumpet; Duke Jordan, piano; Tommy Potter, bass; Max Roach, drums. Recorded 1947.

Who knows what the title means—an anonymous musician is quoted in the *Smithsonian* anthology booklet as saying, "It's a sound, man. A sound." If you say it out loud, it does sound like a bop head, a bop rhythmic figure.

The layout is like that of *KoKo*: 16-bar intro, the first 8 bars from the sax and trumpet in close harmony, the second 8 from the drums;

five choruses of the aaba 32 bars (first, thematic, chorus unison horns
with the bridge from Bird, then solo choruses from Parker and Davis, a
fourth chorus by the rhythm section, the fifth or "out" chorus like the
first), and a coda echoing the intro. By now you should be getting used
to the general bop sound; so listen to this cut several times and concentrate in turn on the melodies (rhythms, range, contour or shape, use
of rests or silences), the bass, and on Roach's drumming. Then put them
all back together and see what you hear. Bop is a multilayered music,
and to really hear it, you need to be able to separate the layers. What is
each musician doing individually? How are they, at the same time,
working together?

> *Embraceable You*, George Gershwin, Ira Gershwin. Charlie Parker Quin-
tet: Charlie Parker, alto sax; Miles Davis, trumpet; Duke Jordan, piano;
Tommy Potter, bass; Max Roach, drums. Recorded 1947.

These are two completely different, but equally wonderful, takes
of the tune, a slow ballad, bop-style, recorded the same day. (We'll hear
another of these, Dizzy Gillespie's *I Can't Get Started*, in the next section.) The versions are different in the lines that Parker improvises for
each and in the overall shape he gives each of his choruses, but they're
alike in that both are harmonic improvisations, new melodies conceived over a given chord progression. Bird sometimes, but much more
rarely, improvised thematically, stuck closer to a song's original
melody. Good examples of that can be found on the album *Bird With
Strings Live*, with such tunes as *Everything Happens To Me*. But such
examples, pretty as they may be, don 't seem to have the inventive
expressiveness or the musical stature of the present selections. Try to
find a copy of the former and compare them for yourself.

In both of Bird's solos here (one chorus each of 32 bars), he sets off
each 8-measure phrase fairly clearly and shows off the various bop
melodic techniques we've mentioned so far: big range, going from one
end to the other in a single gesture; alternating strings of fast notes with
longer, sustained ones; lots of rhythmic play and suppleness in his
melodies; and, *within* the 8-bar phrase, use of rests to set off the smaller
ideas, so that it's not just 4-plus-4 or 2-2-2-2 to equal the 8 measures.

But these same general techniques are just common elements
between two different, individual melodies. In the first version, Bird
uses a lot of repetition. He plays a short figure, as at the beginning,
then repeats it at the same pitch level or maybe higher or lower; he
extends it, and it leads him into a new idea. He seems to have con-

ceived the solo as one single, long, extended line from beginning to end, and even when he rests, there is a concentration in the silences that continues the motion, the unrelenting forward direction. (In this, the cut resembles Bechet's *Blue Horizon* from the first section on early jazz in Chapter One, and Sonny Rollins' *Blue 7*, to come a little later in this chapter.) In the second, slightly faster, version, however, he avoids this sort of repetition and long-range connection. Here we have a succession of ever-new ideas, longer than those of the first version and more varied from one to the next. The sense of overall shape or contour is different as a result: whereas the first solo seemed like one unbroken melody, this is more an alternation of ups and downs, tension and release. A good way to feel the difference between the two solos is to breathe with Parker—hold your breath through a phrase and breathe again during the rests. How does that affect the way you hear the tune?

➤ *Crazeology*, Benny Harris. Charlie Parker Sextet: Charlie Parker, alto sax; Miles Davis, trumpet; J. J. Johnson, trombone; Duke Jordan, piano; Tommy Potter, bass; Max Roach drums. Recorded 1947.

Again, two cuts of the same tune, recorded the same day. The first of these is incomplete, including only the thematic chorus and a solo chorus from Parker. But notice here the quintessential bop nature of the basic tune—rhythms, accents, speed, length of phrases, the whole bag. Also typical of bop is the arrangement, the thematic chorus played by all the horns in unison and then giving way to the solos.

In the second (complete) take, the thematic chorus is identical to what we heard before. Parker's solo is completely different. Notice that little upward rip he begins his chorus with. Even though during his solo, the improvisation seems ever new, one melodic idea pouring out after another, Parker still often refers to or echoes that opening rip. This is more evidence of Parker's melodic genius: even in the midst of improvisations, he's still thinking (at least in part) "motivically," achieving a nice degree of unity within that outpouring of notes by keeping a single little musical germ in a lot of his new ideas.

After Parker's solo, we hear choruses from J. J. Johnson on trombone (muted), Miles Davis on trumpet (emphasizing the low and midranges of his horn), and the rhythm section, with the pianist taking the first two a phrases, the bass on the bridge, and the drummer the final a. In each case, you should listen for the general bop style characteristics, and compare each player individually with Parker, within that general style. Finally, the thematic chorus returns as the "out" chorus, this time with Bird taking a solo on the bridge.

➤   *Parker's Mood*, Charlie Parker. Charlie Parker's All Stars: Charlie Parker, alto sax; John Lewis, piano; Curley Russell, bass; Max Roach, drums. Recorded 1948,

Parker, of course, was a sax player out of Kansas City, and he could play the blues. Here we have four choruses (the third a solo from John Lewis, later of the Modern Jazz Quartet), framed by an intro and coda. Compare this cut to the complete version of *Embraceable You*, above, to Bechet's *Blue Horizon*, and to the other bop in this chapter. You should be able to make connections in all directions—blue notes, bluesy kinds of melody or melodic fragments, blues timbres, but at the same time the cross-phrasing (again, not coinciding exactly with the standard 4-bar phrase pattern of the blues, but working across it, for example beginning the melody in the first measure but carrying through bar 5, 6, or even 7), the big melodic range, and the fast-note figures from bop.

➤   *Ornithology*, Benny Harris, Charlie Parker. Charlie Parker Septet: Charlie Parker, alto sax; Miles Davis, trumpet; Lucky Thompson, tenor sax; Dodo Marmarosa, piano; Arvin Garrison, guitar; Vic McMillan, bass; Roy Porter, drums. Recorded 1946.

This is the tune based on the older standard *How High The Moon* discussed in the essay at the beginning of this chapter, to show the distinctions between Swing tunes and bop tunes in terms of range, phrasing, etc. You'll want to go back and read that again. This cut is classic Bird and a bop standard. The choruses are 32 bars, but the phrase structure is abab. As usual, there are unison horn choruses to begin and end, with solos in between. You'll be able to find your own way through the chart by now; apply the comments for the first four cuts in this section here, too.

➤   *Night in Tunisia*, Dizzy Gillespie, Frank Paparelli. Charlie Parker Septet: same personnel, same date as *Ornithology*, above.

Yet another bop anthem, this one by Dizzy. We have two takes here, the first (again) partial and the second complete. The partial take includes only the end of the first chorus and then Parker's *Famous Alto Break*, an interjection between the statement of the tune's theme and the first solo chorus. For whatever reasons, we don't have the rest of this particular recording. But listen to that alto break: it is as breathtaking as, and in every way on a par with, Louis Armstrong's intro to *West End Blues* some 20 years before.

The tune itself begins with a 12-bar introduction, 8 measures of rhythm section and then 4 more measures with a horn riff added to that. Listen to the rhythmic pattern: $\underline{1}$ 2 3 $\underline{1}$ 2 3 $\underline{1}$ 2, $\underline{1}$ 2 3 $\underline{1}$ 2 3 $\underline{1}$ 2, an asymmetrical subdivision of the eight beats. We haven't heard anything like this yet. The influence is from Afro-Cuban music, which Gillespie had been listening to (has always listened to, throughout his career) and working into his own music. The rhythm and the riff continue into the a phrases of the song proper; in the bridge, the rhythm reverts to the more common regular meter.

The tune is a 32-bar aaba. In the first chorus, Davis plays the a phrase (again the muted trumpet) and Parker takes the bridge. There is then a 16-bar interlude: the first 12 bars are the Afro-Cuban rhythmic/melodic figure, the last 4 are a Parker break (very similar to the intro on the first version, above). In the second chorus, Bird takes the first two a phrases, Miles the ba. For the third chorus, Thompson (tenor sax) is on the aa, then we hear a guitar bridge and a final phrase from the whole ensemble. There is an 8-bar coda. In rhythm, range, contour, and overall sound, this is an exemplary bop melody. And, like most of the earlier cuts in this section, the arrangement is standard, too: written-out unison intros and closings ("out" choruses), and in between a string of solos improvised on the chords of the tune. And, also like most of the sections here, *Night in Tunisia* has become a standard for all types and assortments of jazz musicians and has been recorded by almost everybody.

DIZ (1917–1993) AND MONK (1917–1982)

➤ *I Can't Get Started*, Vernon Duke, Ira Gershwin. Dizzy Gillespie Sextet: Dizzy Gillespie, trumpet; Trummy Young, trombone; Don Byas, tenor sax; Clyde Hart, piano; Oscar Pettiford, bass; Shelly Manne, drums. Recorded 1945.

This song has one aaba chorus, with intro and coda. Listen to the way that Gillespie uses a whole arsenal of bop techniques—enormous range, long phrases, cross-phrasing—but uses them in the service of a

Dizzy Gillespie. Notice his trademarks, the bell of his trumpet bent
upwards, and his little goatee. Courtesy of the Rutgers Institute of Jazz
Studies.

slow, lyrical ballad. This solo is based on a Swing-era standard, like
Parker's *Embraceable You*. But, musically speaking, it's sort of halfway
between that Parker rendition and Billie Holiday's or Bunny Berigan's
versions of *I Can't Get Started*. The latter two stay much closer to the
original melody, and their phrasings and textures are much more
straightforward. Dizzy has the original tune in his head as he's playing, but he's improvising away from it. We do get hints of the original
melody at the beginnings of Gillespie's <u>a</u> phrases, but because of the
cross-phrasing, these hints come at the *ends* of Dizzy's phrases.
Because of these melodic reminiscences, it's as close to earlier styles as
it is to Parker's all-improvised *Embraceable You*. Strictly bop characteristics include the cross-phrasing just mentioned and the layered texture—the rhythm section, the background horns and their phrases,
and Dizzy on top of all that—and Diz's big range. Listen to Gillespie's
tone, too. It's perhaps not as warm as say, Armstrong's, but it does
have more variety and more brassiness than Davis's, and it's a more
characteristically bop timbre than his. With all these ins and outs, the
like-this-but-like-that-too qualities, and because of the emotional
impact of the music, *I Can't Get Started* may remind you of Ella Fitzgerald's *'Round Midnight*.

➤   *Shaw 'Nuff*, Dizzy Gillespie, Charlie Parker. Dizzy Gillespie All Star
     Quintette: Dizzy Gillespie, trumpet; Charlie Parker, alto sax; Al Haig,
     piano; Curley Russell, bass; Sidney Catlett, drums. Recorded 1945.

Shaw 'Nuff (a pun on the expression "sure enough" and the name of a manager, Billy Shaw) is a so-called "*Rhythm* tune," a song based on the chord changes of the Gershwin classic *I Got Rhythm*. The tune, and this recording, will sound very much to you like what we heard from Dizzy in the previous section. The introduction and coda use Afro-Cuban rhythms, as Dizzy especially liked to do, with the horns playing in close harmony. The first and last choruses of the aaba tune are unison between the horns. They are separated by three solo choruses, in order by Parker, Diz, and Al Haig on piano. Everything we've said to date about bebop holds here. But listen to the difference between Dizzy and Miles Davis: Dizzy starts his solo at the top of the trumpet's register, and he stays up there, too. His playing has the same sort of intensity and drive here as Parker's playing does (Davis's intensity is of another kind).

➤ *Salt Peanuts*, Dizzy Gillespie, Kenny Clarke. Dizzy Gillespie, trumpet; Charlie Parker, alto sax; Bud Powell, piano; Charles Mingus, bass; Max Roach, drums. Recorded 1953.

This was some pick-up group: a jazz society in Toronto decided to invite the five "greatest" bop musicians up to do a concert, and they managed to get the Bud Powell Trio, plus Bird and Diz. The gig was billed as "the greatest jazz concert ever," and the recording of the concert goes by the same title. (It's known among fans either by that name or as "the Massey Hall concert," after the site of the gig.) Obviously, though, this wasn't really a pick-up group. These five men had been playing together in various groups and combinations for years by 1953. Of the five, only Powell and Mingus are new to us, and we'll hear from both of them again.

Since this is a live version, it's not limited to the three-minute length that was the norm for studio recordings, and the musicians could stretch out, extend their solos for as long as they had more ideas coming. Does the playing seem freer to you as a result? (You might want to compare this to a studio recording of the same tune. This live version is about twice as long as a typical contemporary studio version.) And, again, everything we've said so far about the bop style—melodies, rhythms, phrasing, texture—goes for this cut as well, and, even though it's much longer than a standard recording, the formal layout is the same. There is an ensemble beginning and end with a string of solos in between, and wonderful Dizzy whooping it up in the background.

There is one important point to make about the rhythm, though, and it's a good example of bop-style "angular" or "asymmetrical" rhythms. Listen carefully to the rhythmic hook of the head, "salt peanuts," and say it to yourself: both times you hear it, it's the same little rhythmic figure, but the accent comes on different notes each time. That is, the rhythm is long-short-short, but the accent the first time comes on the first short syllable ("pea-") and the second time, on the long ("salt"):

		Salt	PEA-	nuts,	SALT	pea-	nuts!
(beat):	1		2		3		4

Clap or tap out the beat, as indicated above, and say the refrain along with it, or just repeat "salt peanuts" to yourself over and over, putting the emphasis on a different syllable each time. What's happening is that the musicians take a simple little rhythm and repeat it, but begin each time in a different part of the measure, so the accent is going to come out on a different note or syllable each time. In a swing riff, by contrast, the figure is repeated literally each time, so the effect is one of balance and regularity, not the asymmetry or angularity here. We'll hear this again, especially in Monk's *Criss-Cross* and *Misterioso*.

➤ *Things to Come*, Dizzy Gillespie, Walter Fuller. Dizzy Gillespie and His Orchestra: Dizzy Gillespie, Dave Burns, Raymond Orr, Talib Saawud, John Lynch, trumpet; Gordon Thomas, Alton Moore, Leon Comegys, trombone; Howard Johnson, John Brown, alto sax; Ray Abrams, Warren Luckey, tenor sax; Pee Wee Moore, baritone sax; John Lewis, piano; Milt Jackson, vibes; Ray Brown, bass; Kenny Clarke, drums. Recorded 1946.

Big-band bebop: five trumpets, three trombones, five saxes, four rhythm. The tune is adapted by Walter Fuller from Dizzy Gillespie's small-combo composition, *Bebop*. This is a terrific example of the big-band *format* and bop *style*. The format is exactly that of the Swing big bands: rhythm, brass, and reed sections, used as such and played off against one another, as in the first chorus, when saxes play the *a* phrases and the brass take the bridge. But everything else about it is bop. The tempo is incredibly fast (even Dizzy seems to have a little trouble keeping up, though Milt Jackson and Ray Brown don't). The original melody is all over the place, with lots of short, fast notes covering a huge range, and the improvised solos are even more so. The beginning cadenza, which Dizzy had played solo in the small-combo version (like Parker on the *Night in Tunisia* cut) is here given to the entire section, and the whole section plays the melodies in unison when we get to the first chorus of the tune proper. (The only time we've heard this before was on Ellington's *Cotton Tail*.) The use of introduction, coda, and interludes between the choruses does turn up occasionally in Swing charts, but, as we've seen, it's also a hallmark of Gillespie compositions. The rhythm section's work is pure bop—regular time is kept only by the drummer's ride cymbals and the bass, and everyone else concentrates on off-beat accents and rhythmic surprises. Finally, the thick, fiery sound of the arrangement, when the whole band is working together, is miles away from that of any Swing group.

So listen to the great arrangement and keep it in mind to compare with the bands we'll hear later, especially those of Woody Herman, Charlie Mingus, and Gil Evans. Solos here are by Dizzy, Milt Jackson, and John Brown on alto. (How many choruses does each play?) And note, in passing, the personnel of the rhythm section: Lewis, Jackson, Brown, and Clarke were the founding members of the Modern Jazz Quartet (Brown and Clarke were later replaced by Percy Heath and Connie Kay), one of the most popular groups during the 1950s and 1960s, and a group not associated with bop.

➤ *Misterioso*, Thelonious Monk. Thelonious Monk Quartet: Thelonious Monk, piano; Milt Jackson, vibes; John Simmons, bass; Shadow Wilson, drums. Recorded 1948.

Monk, whose affectionate nicknames include "The Onliest Monk" and "Melodious Thunk," was the house pianist at Minton's Play House, one of the clubs in Harlem where bop came into being. He's important not just as one of the founders of bop, but as a composer and pianist as well. His compositions usually fall into the normal 12-bar blues or 32-bar aaba patterns, but that's about all that's conventional about them. The melodies are very lean and spare, with a few exceptions such as *'Round Midnight* (which dates from 1939, or just before the crystallization of bop); sometimes they're deceptively simple, more often they're very striking because they're so elliptical and understated, completely unlike tunes such as *Night in Tunisia* or *Ornithology*. Monk's piano playing is equally sparse. He likes well-placed single notes and chords, phrases that seem off balance, surprising accents and chords. Although he might not sound like it on first

Thelonious Monk. Courtesy of
the Rutgers Institute of Jazz
Studies.

hearing, Monk is also a beautifully lyrical and even introspective
musician. Compare him to Ellington (*Clothed Woman*) and Bill Evans in
that regard. And compare him to the other boppers. He may have been
right there at the creation, and a central part of it, but he's a completely
individual voice.

This cut is a straightforward 12-bar blues, although that intro
sounds ambiguous—even directionless—in tempo and tune. Listen
especially to Monk's laconic piano playing, whether under Jackson's
solo or during his own—single-note playing (with a vengeance),
phrases often ending on accented off-beats, cross-phrasing, left-hand
chords used (here) only for occasional punctuation and accenting. You
could describe Jackson's playing the same way, but he uses more notes
than does Monk, and his playing isn't so astringent. One isolated example of the astringency, and of Monk's playing in general, is the way he
hits two notes together with a sharp accent and then releases one of
them. (You can try this for yourself on the piano, playing any two notes
that are right next to each other.) When he does this, he gets the rhythmic punch of the accented attack and the dissonant punch of the notes;
and then, when he releases one of the keys, the other one continues to
sound, but with a sharp ring, almost metallic.

➤   *Evidence*, Thelonious Monk. Same date, same personnel as *Misterioso*.

This side was cut on the same date as *Misterioso* and shares many of its characteristics. After another very ambiguous introduction by Monk, especially in its lack of any clear meter, we hear 3 aaba choruses. The first chorus is taken by Milt Jackson, who begins with clear references to Monk's original melody before moving out into his own improvisation. Monk supports Jackson with propulsive, accented chords that put forth the harmonies fairly clearly in the first two phrases and then move farther out in the last two. Monk's own solo chorus, next, is another single-note one, a kind of direct response to Jackson's, but in Monk's own patented elliptical language. The third chorus amounts to a duet between Monk and Jackson, Monk playing chords and octaves as Jackson uses the vibes' pedal for sustained, ringing sounds in the a phrases, each player moving closer to what the other has played but still maintaining their individuality, especially in timbre.

➤   *Criss-Cross*. Thelonious Monk. Thelonious Monk Quintet: Thelonious Monk, piano, Sahib Shihab, alto sax; Milt Jackson, vibes; Al McKibbon, bass; Art Blakey, drums. Recorded 1951.

A 32-bar aaba, but an angular, asymmetrical composition. Again, phrases end on accented off-beats; given figures are begun in different parts of the measure (as in *Salt Peanuts* and *Straight No Chaser*), which means that the rhythmic accent will come on different melodic notes each time (hence one's calling this angular or asymmetrical). Even the distinction between the a and b phrases is blurred over—the bridge begins with a melodic figure from the end of the a phrase, and comes to a full cadence (returns to the tonic) some two bars in, and then at its end anticipates the a-phrase figures. Perhaps that's the meaning of the title, that the phrases criss-cross. Can you hear a bridge (or contrasting phrase) in the solo choruses? Why, or why not?

A good way to start listening to this cut is to count off the 8-bar phrases (listen to the rhythm section). Then, when you have the phrases isolated, listen to the melodies. How do they play off the foursquare phrase-structure?

➤   *Bag's Groove* (excerpt), Milt Jackson. Thelonious Monk, piano; Percy Heath, bass; Kenny Clarke, drums. Recorded 1954.

"Bags" was a nickname of Milt Jackson, the composer of this tune and the vibes-player we've been listening to on earlier cuts. This excerpt is Monk's solo from a recording by Miles Davis All Stars group. Note that the bass player and the drummer here are two members of the Modern Jazz Quartet.

This excerpt is nine choruses of the blues, cannily built up by Monk in three separate blocks. The first chorus uses a single little motive that may sound to you like a bugle call (though not so intrusive here), or maybe like the first phrase ("Fish gotta swim, birds gotta fly") of the torch song *Can't Help Lovin' dat Man of Mine* from Jerome Kern's landmark 1927 musical *Show Boat*. (I find the latter coincidental. As a music lover of my acquaintance once said, "We've only got 12 notes, everything is going to sound like something else." But one never knows.) The second chorus is still single notes in Monk's right hand, but the melody is a little longer. In the third chorus, there are still more notes in the melody, and Monk adds some chords underneath them. The fourth chorus is primarily chordal, the point of arrival of what's come so far.

In the fifth chorus, Monk plays a little riff as the basis of his line. The sixth chorus is the same riff, but now with added—and accented— notes at the end of each phrase (on the 2nd beat of the bar, i.e. off-beat). The last three choruses do the same thing with a different riff. In the seventh chorus, the little riff is just two notes. In the eighth, Monk does the riff in octaves (opens up the registers, as he had done earlier by adding chords), then pares it down to a fast repeated note which gets us into the last chorus. Surprisingly, once we're into the last chorus, what we hear from the piano is *silence*; and then very spare chords to end the solo.

Could this solo have come from Count Basie? Why, or why not?

➤   *I Should Care*, Paul Weston, Axel Stardahl, Sammy Cahn. Thelonious
     Monk, piano. Recorded 1957.

Working as a soloist, Monk played his own tunes (*Ruby, My Dear*), Ellington compositions (*Solitude*), pop standards such as *April In Paris*, and oddities with titles like *There's Danger in Your Eyes, Cherie*. These solo recordings are often free in tempo and meter (that is, there is no single speed or single metrical pattern that holds throughout) and seem to be free-form as well, changing and flowing with the tides of Monk's meditations. It's here, especially, that Monk shows the lyricism and introspection that I mentioned above, and it's this cut (or other solo recordings) that you should compare to Ellington's *Clothed Woman* and Bill Evans's *My Foolish Heart*. But in doing so, don't just let the quiet beauty of each cut wash over you—think about how these three pianists achieve it.

This cut, as I say, seems to be a quiet meditation or gentle exploration. A lot of standard Monk devices can be heard—the accents, letting single notes or chords ring—but here their context is one of low dynamics and a relaxed, wandering thoughtfulness. Listen to this until you can hear the variety in what Monk does. There's one short phrase, for example, that has a strong, hot meter. Sometimes he plays one or two notes at a time, sometimes bigger chords, sometimes fills out the whole keyboard. The melody may be on top of the chords, but he likes to stick in short 3- or 4-note runs in the middle register. All in all, Monk may have pared the original tune down to a spare scaffolding. But on that scaffolding he builds up his own personal musings, and the music is very, very rich.

➤   *Straight No Chaser*, Thelonious Monk. Thelonious Monk Quintet: Thelonious Monk, piano; Sahib Shihab, alto sax; Milt Jackson, vibes; Al McKibbon, bass; Art Blakey, drums. Recorded 1951.

This is another 12-bar blues and another bop tune featuring the rhythmic variation of a given melodic fragment, as in *Salt Peanuts* and *Criss-Cross*. This cut should present no problems for you. But did you notice that Monk, at the end of his solo, quotes his own *Misterioso*?

VARIETY: SOME SOLOISTS OF THE 1940S

➤   *Lady Bird*, Tadd Dameron. Tadd Dameron's Sextet: Tadd Dameron, piano; Fats Navarro, trumpet; Wardell Gray, Allen Eager, tenor sax; Curley Russell, bass; Kenny Clarke, drums. Recorded 1948.

Dameron had been an arranger/composer during the 1930s for Swing bands; he then wrote charts and did arrangements for Dizzy and other boppers, and he became one of the principal composers and arrangers of bebop. Note that this is a careful arrangement for a small combo, an unusual phenomenon. The earliest work of Fletcher Henderson and Duke Ellington had been for incipient big bands, groups of ten to twelve players. The larger combos of the 1930s, such as Goodman's sextet or the groups which backed up Billie Holiday, didn't play from such carefully worked out and notated arrangements. We will hear such arrangements again, though, form the Miles Davis nonet in the next section, and these small-combo charts did become less rare after the late 1940s, particularly with the "cool school."

Listen to the arrangement, first of all. The close writing for the three horns over the rhythm section makes it sound like an ensemble larger than just a sextet, and the warm colors (a result of the trumpet's playing in the *middle* range and combined with two *tenor* saxes) set up a comfortable context for the solos to come. Those solos are by Navarro, Eager, and Gray, in that order. Navarro's is the one you really want to listen to. He was an enormously important trumpet player in the late 1940s, learning a lot from Dizzy and using what he learned to forge his own style. He ranges all over the horn, for instance, and his use of a lot of fast notes over a more moderately swinging backup, his command of phrasing, may remind you of Gillespie. But his tone is different, and he's not so frenetic. Navarro's career was very short—he was dead in his middle 20s—but he was very influential on the hard-bop school and on trumpeters like Clifford Brown.

The rhythm section here does good, solid bop work, especially Kenny Clarke. Dameron's piano playing helps keep things moving, but it's more the work of an arranger who plays piano than of a pianist who also writes.

The formal layout is also standard bop, the ensemble choruses sandwiching the string of solos. Each chorus is 16 bars, but how long are the phrases—4 bars, 8 bars? How would you label them?

➤　*Night in Tunisia*, Dizzy Gillespie. The Bud Powell Trio: Bud Powell, piano; Curley Russell, bass; Max Roach, drums. Recorded 1951.

We heard Bud Powell in the version of *Salt Peanuts* in the previous section. A completely different pianist from Monk, Powell was more influential than Thelonious as a bop stylist on the piano. You may be reminded of Art Tatum, and you'll hear a lot of Charlie Parker's influence, too. (It's not for nothing that Powell is often called a "horn-like" soloist.) Powell liked long, single-note lines and sometimes his hands work together like a horn soloist over a rhythm section, the driving extended phrases of the melody unfurling over sharp, accented chords. Powell always worked with the best musicians—you'll notice how often Russell and Roach turn up in our examples—

and his recordings, especially those from 1947-1953, are among the greatest of bop.

Compare Powell's solo on this *Night in Tunisia* to Charlie Parker's, above. On all accounts you will hear bop at its most pure, driven, and intense.

➤   *Un Poco Loco*, Bud Powell. The Bud Powell Trio: Bud Powell, piano; Curley Russell, bass; Max Roach, drums. Recorded 1951.

Un Poco Loco (its title is ironic, given the personal problems of Powell and Parker, and the initial reaction to bebop from uncomprehending listeners) is a 32-bar aaba tune with the standard formal layout, thematic choruses to begin and end, with improvised solos in between. Listen to Powell here, and to the way that he and Roach work together. Harmony is maybe the least important, least interesting aspect of this tune, and a lot of the phrases take place over sustained pedals (also called drones), when the chord doesn't change. So what matters is melody and rhythm, and the way those two work together. Powell unleashes those long, driving lines characterized by sharp, off-beat accents. His fierce insistence comes as much from the rhythmic punches as from the great variety in his phrases, sometimes short and repeated, sometimes seemingly unstoppable (even to breathe). Alongside Powell, not really behind him at all, is Roach, who is often called a "melodic" drummer. What that means is that Roach often uses the various timbres he has at his disposal—relative high and low drums, hitting the instruments at different places on their surfaces—to make a kind of melody of colors as well as a polyrhythmic texture. Roach and Powell both begin with the sort of Latin feeling of the rhythms and melody (especially in the first improvised chorus). But the wonder of this tune is the way the two men mix rhythm and melody, each as an individual and the two together. Powell's intensity is unsurpassed, even by Bird.

➤   *Glass Enclosure*, Bud Powell. The Bud Powell Trio: Bud Powell, piano; George Duvivier, bass; Arthur Taylor, drums. Recorded 1953.

This tune is out of the ordinary. *Glass Enclosure* is a composition that falls basically into four sections (that is, not a succession of choruses). The first section is a sort of march, full of big majestic chords, but still driving. (Note that the bass here is bowed, not plucked.) Then there is a section with the standard bop texture, tune, and rhythm work. (How long are the phrases? When does the meter first become clear?) The third section begins slowly and quietly, but it picks up immediately and begins to remind us of the first section. And finally that first section returns to close out the cut.

You'll be able to find your way through the composition without any further guidance. But what does *Glass Enclosure* have to do with bop as a style? What elements do you hear that are characteristic of bop, although used here in an unusual context and in new ways (besides in the second section)? Think about rhythms, phrasing, the asymmetry or angularity we've discussed, the textures of bop piano-playing (Monk?), and the kinds of melody you've heard. The point of such an exercise is not just to listen to the tune more carefully, it's also to suggest something to you about the shortcomings built in when we attach labels to styles, periods, or people. A label is good only as a rank generality, and it works like a kind of shorthand. When I say that x is a typical bop chart, for example, you should immediately have a general idea about what to expect in it—what kind of ensemble, what kind of structure, what kinds of melody, textures, rhythms, and so on. But don't forget that a label always *excludes* a great deal, too, that the short-hand is not the whole message. Not all Swing music, you'll recall, sounds like *Moten Swing* (nor does all big band music), not all bop sounds like *Night in Tunisia*. As will be true with all the rest of the selections in this chapter, the general label is a place to start, a convenient framework for listening. But don't stop with that label: keep *listening*, since it's the music that matters.

➤ *Fantasy on "Frankie and Johnny,"* traditional. Erroll Garner, solo piano. Recorded 1947.

A musical "fantasy" is a more-or-less free improvisation on some preexisting material, whether a song (as here) or some extramusical source (such as the classical composer Tchaikovsky's *Overture-Fantasy* on Shakespeare's *Romeo and Juliet*). *Frankie and Johnny* is a traditional American ballad, or narrative song, using the blues form. Its first line is "Frankie and Johnny were lovers, and oh, Lordy!, how they could love!" The refrain, the b phrase of each chorus, is "He was her man, but he was treatin' her wrong." It was a folk standard in any number of musical styles and contexts, but almost always done, as Garner plays it, in a moderate to quick tempo. It's a story that's usually kind of tossed off, not meant to warn or scare like other narrative ballads such as, for example, *The House of the Rising Sun* or *St. James Infirmary*.

Garner is a very different pianist from Bud Powell, or from anyone else we'll hear in this chapter. He may remind you of James P. Johnson or Fats Waller, with his nonchalant light touch. (Unlike most other pianist of his generation, Garner never learned to read music.) But there are a couple of what sound like post-Tatum touches here, too, in his introduction to the tune and in his use of substitute chords and modulations. The intro begins slowly and then builds up a few sequences, vamps, and so on, before he moves into the tune itself, in a stride texture. Garner plays five choruses of the song, with an interlude between the second and third that recalls the intro. After the first chorus he begins to play with some of his substitute harmonies, and in each of the last two choruses, modulates (changes key) upward for a little added brightness and interest. He's not telling the basic story in his piano playing here, though (in the original, Frankie kills Johnny because he treats her wrong); he's treating the standard only as a tune he enjoys.

➤   *I Got Rhythm*, George Gershwin and Ira Gershwin. Don Byas, tenor sax, and Slam Stewart, bass. Recorded 1945.

As Martin Williams recounts the story in his booklet with the *Smithsonian Collection*, Byas and Stewart played this at a concert in New York when they showed up for the gig at the same time as the audience, but before the other musicians got there. The tune was written in 1930, for the Broadway show *Girl Crazy*; it was introduced by the singer Ethel Merman. *I Got Rhythm* immediately entered the canon of great American songs, and its harmonies have become the framework for any number of other tunes, known as "*Rhythm* songs" or "*Rhythm* changes." You may know the lyrics, too: "I got rhythm, I got music, I got my man [gal], who could ask for anything more?" The ebullience of the words somehow always carries over into every performance of the tune.

Here we hear eleven choruses. In the first, Byas plays the melody straight over Stewart's walking bass. Then there are four more choruses from Byas, whose playing includes elements of both Swing and bop, of other musicians like Coleman Hawkins, Lester Young, and Charlie Christian. He improvises new melodies off the original chord changes, and in every chorus plays the first two phrases as units, then cross-phrases from the bridge into the final a phrase. His playing is always driving and propulsive. In his two solo choruses, Slam Stewart shows off his trademark bow-and-sing sound, and does a kind of condensed version of what Byas has done: he plays close to the tune for the first phrase, less close thereafter, begins his second chorus with a line that sounds like the last movement of Beethoven's 9th, and then does his new melodies over the basic changes. For the last four choruses, they go back to sax improvisation over the walking (plucked) bass, until the last chorus, where Byas plays longer notes, as if torquing back a little. Then a little tag coda, and they're out.

➤ *Body and Soul* (excerpt), Johnny Green, Robert Sauer, Ed Heyman, Frank Eyton. Gene Norman's "Just Jazz," featuring Red Norvo and Stan Getz. Charlie Shavers, trumpet; Willie Smith, alto sax; Stan Getz, tenor sax; Red Norvo, vibes; Nat "King" Cole, piano; Oscar Moore, electric guitar; Johnnie Miller, bass; Louis Bellson, drums. Recorded 1947.

This is the third version of *Body and Soul* we've heard; you might want to go back and listen again to those by Goodman, with Teddy Wilson and Gene Krupa, and Coleman Hawkins. We're closer here to the emotional world of the Goodman version than of the Hawkins.

This excerpt begins with a chorus played by Red Norvo on vibes (aa), Stan Getz (bridge), and Oscar Moore (last a). The first three phrases of the second chorus (aab) are led by Nat "King" Cole, whose first fame came as a bop pianist, then as a singer, especially of ballads, and latterly as father of Natalie. The final a phrase is played by Charlie Shavers on trumpet, supported by the whole group.

➤ *Bikini*, Dexter Gordon. Dexter Gordon Quartet: Dexter Gordon, tenor sax; Jimmy Bunn, piano; Red Callender, bass; Chuck Thompson, drums. Recorded 1947.

As a segue from the variety of this section to the more focused sections to come, we return to classic bebop. Dexter Gordon was a bopper from almost the beginning, and his fascinating career included acting the lead in Bernard Tavernier's film *Round Midnight* (see Chapter Five), playing his own music (that is to say, his own playing in his own style) while acting a character based at least in part on Lester Young and Bud Powell.

The structure of this tune is unusual: aaba, but the a phrases are all 12-bar blues, and the bridge is an 8-bar contrasting phrase. But only that structure should sound new to you. Ensemble, layout, kinds of melody, textures, everything else is classic bop, and should present no problems. The first chorus of the four is still the thematic chorus, Gordon playing his own melody. The second chorus is Gordon again. The third chorus is from Jimmy Bunn on piano, the fourth from Gordon with the bridge by Thompson on drums.

BOPPING ON—SOME SOLOISTS OF THE 1950S; CHARLES MINGUS (1922–1979)

➤ *All of Me*, Seymour Simons, Gerald Marks. Sarah Vaughan and Her Trio: Sarah Vaughan, vocal; Jimmy Jones, piano; Richard Davis, bass; Roy Haynes, drums. Recorded 1954.

This tune will be familiar: earlier, we heard Billie Holiday's 1941 version, and you might want to go back and listen to that again. This *bop* version of the tune is made up of three abac choruses. Vaughan's second, scat, chorus here is one of terrific bebop virtuosity—*huge* range, long phrases, cross-phrasing, and tricky rhythms. Some of the lines may remind you of Dizzy Gillespie, although every time I listen to this, I also hear bits that remind me of Billie, Ella Fitzgerald, Carmen McRae, and even Louis Armstrong. "Sassy" (one of Vaughan's nicknames, another being "The Divine One") listened to a lot of people, and a lot of people listened to her. (She was also not a bad pianist.)

Pay some attention to the first and third choruses, as well as to the middle one. Vaughan always improvised further away from the original tune than did Billie Holiday; she varied her timbre and her vibrato to color the lines and the words (also depending on which of her many registers she was using); and her phrasings and rhythms are good bop, as opposed to pure Swing.

➤ *All Alone*, Irving Berlin. Sarah Vaughan, vocal; Clark Terry, Charlie Shavers, Joe Newman, Freddie Hubbard, trumpet; J. J. Johnson, Kai Winding, trombone; Phil Woods, Benny Golson, reeds; Bob James, piano. Recorded 1967.

Here we have another idiomatic approach to a bop ballad. Vaughan swings the tune at a moderate tempo, improvising new melodies with every phrase, changing the import of the lyrics from a complaint to a kind of teasing, "So what are you going to do about it?" What does she do here in terms of phrasing, tone color, improvising, and so on? Is it really right to label this "bop"?

➤   *I Ain't Got Nothin' But the Blues*, Duke Ellington, Folin, George. Sarah Vaughan, vocal; Mike Wofford, piano; Joe Pass, guitar; Andy Simpkins, bass; Grady Tate, drums. Recorded 1979.

Although Sarah Vaughan often moved over to pop tunes and concert venues, especially in the latter half of her career, she never moved completely away from jazz. This tune from her 2-CD set, *The Duke Ellington Songbook*, is a prime example, and this is about as blue as you can get. The tune is a 32-bar aaba. She sings the first phrase completely unaccompanied, and the rhythm section comes in with the second a phrase. She begins the 2nd chorus over a stop-time accompaniment for the first two a phrases; Joe Pass solos in the bridge, with Vaughan singing some wordless responses behind him. She returns in the last phrase, and then sings a coda or "out" chorus, again completely *a cappella* before the rhythm comes in for the final cadence.

Again Vaughan uses her formidable vocal range and variety of timbres, especially bluesy and gut-bucket in her lower registers. She means business here.

➤   *By the Bend of the River*, B. Haig, Clara Edwards. Betty Carter and the Norman Simmons Trio: Betty Carter, vocal; Norman Simmons, piano; Lysle Atkinson, bass; Al Harewood, drums. Recorded early 1970s.

As a 16-year-old high-school student in Detroit, one of the hotbeds of hard bop, "Betty Bebop" (1930–1998) sat in with Bird, Miles, and others. She worked constantly ever after, and her repertory might well have been larger than that of any other singer around. She did tunes like this one, romantic ballads like *This Is Always* (below), newly composed tunes and original compositions, and standards like *All the Things You Are* and *When It's Sleepy Time Down South*, even show tunes like *Surrey with the Fringe on Top* from Rodgers and Hammerstein's *Oklahoma!* and *My Favorite Things* from *The Sound of Music*. In the early

Betty Carter. Courtesy of the
Rutgers Institute of Jazz Studies.

1960s, she toured with Ray Charles and did a famous version of *Baby, It's Cold Outside* with him. At her best, Betty Carter was a nonpareil singer: she didn't just improvise, she worked without a net, and her live performances were electrifying. She was another example (like Billie Holiday, Miles Davis, or John Coltrane) of a musician who has transcended a label to develop a compelling personal language.

This recording is two choruses of a 32-bar aaba plus coda. Characteristics to listen for include the melodic improvisations all over the ballpark, using an enormous range (both in the song overall and in some individual phrases); the rhythmic work and the drive; her pitch-slides and bends (which also affect the rhythms of her delivery) and her exploitation of vocal timbre; and the interplay with her rhythm section.

➤   *Frenesi*, Alberto Dominguez, Ray Charles, Bob Russell. Betty Carter, vocal; Bernie Glow, Nick Travis, Conte Candoli, Joe Ferrante, trumpets; Urbie Green, Jimmy Cleveland, trombones; Sam Marowitz, Seldon Powell, Al Cohn, Danny Bank, saxes; Hank Jones, piano; Milt Hinton, bass; Osie Johnson, drums; arranged and directed by Gigi Gryce. Recorded 1956.

Frenesi was a big hit for the bandleader Artie Shaw in the late Swing era, and stayed popular, especially with pop musicians, through the 1950s, when there was quite a rage for Latin and Latin-sounding music. The tune is another 32-bar aaba chart. The joy here lies in Carter's two scat choruses, after the flirtatious and fun-seeking thematic chorus. The exuberance of Carter's rhythms is a marvel, and although she cuts the tempo of the tune slightly from the first chorus, it sounds as if she's singing faster. She's certainly picked up the energy. In the first scat chorus, she sings the a phrases over just the rhythm section. (Hank Jones and Milt Hinton have been major players since they came on the scene. Jones and Carter were both from Detroit; Hinton is also well known as a remarkable photographer, especially of his jazz colleagues and their world.) The brass and most of the band come in to accentuate the bridge. In the second chorus Carter and the band trade 4s for the first two a phrases, and then jack the energy even higher by trading 1s in the bridge. For the final a phrase, she returns to the lyrics, only to break into scat yet again for her final frenzy.

➤ *This Is Always*, Harry Warren, Mack Gordon. Betty Carter, vocal; Harold Mabern, piano; Bob Cranshaw, bass; Roy McCurdy, drums. Recorded 1964.

This ballad, like *By the Bend of the River*, above, is more typical of Betty Carter's club and concert appearances, with just a trio behind her. Again, it shows what she was capable of with rhythm and handling time: although the tempo isn't as glacial as she sometimes used, most of the tune sounds almost out of time, appropriate to the lyrics' theme of endless love and the title, "This is always." When it sounds as if the trio picks up the tempo for that one phrase where she drops out, they actually stay with the same beat; it's just that the activity heightens and nicely sets up the return to the vocal and her theme, "This is always," with a return to the original slow feel.

➤ *Blue 7*, Sonny Rollins. The Sonny Rollins Quartet: Sonny Rollins, tenor sax; Tommy Flanagan, piano; Doug Watkins, bass; Max Roach, drums. Recorded 1956.

An amazing, extended (eleven minutes) 12-bar blues. Rollins was one of the greatest hard-bop musicians (he also adopted the "New Thing" for a time in the early 1960s), and this is one of his greatest compositions and improvisations. Those two terms aren't really a contradiction with Rollins: one of the traits most widely noted in his play-

Sonny Rollins. Music Division, The
New York Public Library of the Per-
forming Arts, Astor, Lenox and
Tilden Foundations.

ing is the way he builds his solos carefully and with such precision that
they seem to combine the fervor of spontaneous improvisation with the
monumental "rightness" of a fully worked-out composition. *Blue 7* is
extraordinarily rich, and it requires careful and repeated listening.
After the ambiguous walking-bass intro (see Monk's *Misterioso,* above),
Rollins enters with the theme on which the rest of the improvisation is
based. Listen repeatedly to the first couple of choruses, until you have
them firmly in your ears. The figures are short (remnants of the 2-plus-
2 phrase structure of the blues), but they combine into longer lines. As
with Bird on *Embraceable You,* Rollins's intensity continues even across
his silences. Listen to how he gives shape to his solo with register,
rhythmic activity, accumulation of notes, and length of phrase, so that
ultimately the whole improvisation sounds like one continuous line,
broken only by the solos of the other instruments.

Pay special attention to Roach's long drum solo; it's as subtle,
complex, and well constructed (choose your adjective) as Rollins's.
Roach uses two principal rhythmic figures, a triplet motive (the <u>ba</u>-be-
<u>bah</u> on the ride cymbal) and the drum roll. And here, as in *Un Poco Loco*
with Bud Powell (above), he also exploits not only the various timbres
he has available, but also register (cymbals, high drums, low drums) to
give variety and shape to his solo, to keep his polyrhythms clear to the
listener, and to create the percussive "melody" for which he's always
been famous. Even more, listen to the beginning of his solo: he's playing blues choruses on the drums, clearly laying out the <u>aab</u> phrase
structure with his motives and colors. All this builds and combines, and

the final choruses are a masterful, triumphant combination of everything we've heard since the beginning of the cut.

➤ *Pent-Up House*, Sonny Rollins (abridged). Sonny Rollins Plus Four:
Sonny Rollins, tenor sax; Clifford Brown, trumpet; Richie Powell,
piano; George Morrow, bass; Max Roach, drums. Recorded 1956.

Like the *I'll Remember April* below, played by the same musicians,
this is a cheerful bop number that shows off the difference between two
great horn men, the trumpeter Clifford Brown and the tenor sax player
Sonny Rollins. "Brownie" always seemed to be smiling when he
played, and he was never as frenetic as, say, Dizzy Gillespie. You
should compare him to Diz, and to Fats Navarro, whom we heard
above with Tadd Dameron. Brown's phrases are incredibly long and
smooth, and his tone is brassy but not aggressive. Rollins, by contrast,
has a raspier timbre, and often likes to build up his lines gradually from
small figures into longer phrases, as we heard on the last cut. This tune
is a 32-bar aa (the same 16 measures repeated). After the thematic chorus, we get three choruses from Brown, three from Rollins, one from
Richie Powell, the pianist (Bud Powell's brother), trading 2s by the
horn soloists and Max Roach, a solo from Roach, and then the out chorus. The version of this tune on the *Smithsonian Collection* is abridged;
the compiler shortened Powell's piano solo.

➤ *I'll Remember April*, Don Raye, Gene De Paul, Pat Johnston. The Clifford
Brown/Max Roach Quintet: Clifford Brown, trumpet; Sonny Rollins,
tenor sax; Richie Powell, piano; George Morrow, bass; Max Roach,
drums. Recorded 1956.

Clifford Brown (1930–1956: he and his pianist, Richie Powell, were
killed in a car accident) was, with Dizzy and Miles, the preeminent
trumpet player of the 50s, and in some ways he was more representative of the 50s bop school than either of them. He learned from Dizzy
(as did everyone) and Fats Navarro, but developed those lessons into
his own style. (Davis, as we'll see below, also came out of bop, but he
moved radically away from it during the 50s and 60s.) Brown shared
the boppers' technical mastery and their ability to improvise new, long
melodies over the fastest and most difficult chord changes. He could
play with ease in all registers of the horn, and his long phrases can go

from one end of the range to the other without break. Brown's tone is different from Gillespie's or Davis's, lighter and less astringent. His phrases are warm and elastic—in this cut, like *Pent-Up House*, they're joyful—but one thing you want to listen to especially is their sheer length. Brown had amazing lungs and lips, and you'd think he could play forever without having to breathe. (I made a similar point earlier about Bud Powell's lines, but the effect with Brown is one of exuberance rather than of Powell's driven fierceness.) You'll hear this immediately when Sonny Rollins begins his solo, just after Brown's, with his rougher tone and shorter, pushier phrases.

I'll Remember April is a <u>48</u>-bar tune, aba, each phrase being 16 measures long, those 16-bar phrases 4 plus 4 plus 8. The quintet's version begins with a long vamp, building up riffs from the drums, then bass, then piano, and then the two horns together, again with the Latin feeling that we've often in bop (see *Night in Tunisia* and *Un Poco Loco*). From there on the formal layout is standard bop: a thematic chorus from Brown on the <u>a</u> phrases and Rollins on the <u>b</u>; two solo choruses each from Brown, Rollins, and Richie Powell; the drum solo from Roach; two more improvised choruses from the horns, in the first of which they trade 8s and in the second, trade 4s (this increase in activity builds up the excitement and makes a drive to the climax); the final, out chorus, like the first one; and a concluding return to the opening vamp, rounding off the tune and fading out.

The overall sound, the way the solos work over the rhythm section, is also normal bop. So listen in this cut to the differences among the soloists, each of whom has a personal, individual voice within the general bop style. Brown's solo, as I said, shows off his speed and dexterity over the basic tempo (already as fast as it can be). His phrases are so long that the term cross-phrasing is almost meaningless. The light tone, the endless stream of fast notes and the bounce in his rhythms are a real contrast to Rollins's earthier tone and punchier rhythms. Rollins rides the tempo with longer notes in his first chorus and then meshes into it when he picks up the action in his second. Powell's melodies are more like Rollins's than like Brown's, but his playing, especially the second of his two choruses, is a lot more bluesy than either. The rhythm section, in general, really drives here, especially because of Morrow on bass, giving his rock-solid support to Powell's inventions. All around, you can't do much better than the playing you hear here.

➤ *Moon Rays*, Horace Silver. The Horace Silver Quintet: Horace Silver, piano; Art Farmer, trumpet; Clifford Jordan, tenor sax; Teddy Kotick, bass; Louis Hayes, drums. Recorded 1958.

This is a rather unusual tune from another classic hard-bop group (you may have noticed how popular quintets are in this era). *Moon Rays* is a 64-bar aaba, each phrase 16 measures long, and the bridge being the same tune as the a phrase, but in a higher key. The tune is a relaxed sort of ballad, at a moderate tempo, that picks up some rhythmic activity (though still at its moderate tempo) when the solos begin. The solos are by Jordan on tenor, Farmer on trumpet, and Silver on piano. Notice toward the end of Silver's solo that he begins to get a little "funky," a little more soulful (in the 60s sense) than other jazz pianists do very often. This was Silver's stock in trade, and set him apart from most other jazz pianists of his generation.

➤   *A Foggy Day*, George Gershwin, Ira Gershwin. The Charles Mingus Quintet: Charles Mingus, bass; Mal Waldron, piano; Eddie Bert, trombone; George Barrow, tenor sax; Willie Jones, drums. Recorded 1955.

We end this section with four selections from Charlie Mingus, a bass player out of the bop tradition (we heard him with the Bud Powell Trio, Diz, and Bird on *Salt Peanuts*). As a bassist, composer, and leader, Mingus moved beyond. He was an extraordinary source of black pride all his life, and was especially important in the late 1950s when the drive for civil rights began to take on more urgency and more strength in the United States. Mingus stood up to be counted—demanded, in fact, to be counted—when many others did not. He was also a great source of professional pride to the jazz musician. Mingus had an enormous knowledge and love of the traditions and roots of jazz, and paid tribute to his jazz heritage in his music. We'll hear that particularly in the selections after this one.

A Foggy Day is a 32-bar abab', in a typical bop layout (i.e., in overall structure, kinds of solo lines, drumming and rhythms, and so on). The ensemble, however, is unusual in that the two horns are both low instruments. This gives the cut a darker, heavier timbre than we've heard before. (Compare the tenor and trombone here with, say, the alto and trumpet of Bird and Dizzy. Or compare the timbres of these particular players with those on Woody Herman's *Four Brothers*, in the next section, where the tone is much lighter, not so dark or heavy.) *Foggy Day* is also unusual in its free-form intro, coda, and interlude just before the final chorus, where the sound anticipates the "New Thing" (free jazz) of the early 1960s, and in the naturalistic device of using the bass and trombone to imitate a foghorn. (This last bit also shows up occa-

Kenny Clarke and Charles Mingus. Music Division, The New York Public Library for the Performing Arts, Astor, Lenox and Tilden Foundations.

sionally in the solo choruses, always dissonant, clashing or intrusive, with the solo line.)

➤ *Haitian Fight Song*, Charles Mingus. The Charles Mingus Quintet: Charles Mingus, bass; Jimmy Knepper, trombone; Curtis Porter (Shafi Hadi), alto sax; Wade Legge, piano; Danny Richmond, drums. Recorded 1957.

From the very opening of this cut you will hear Mingus's unmatched virtuosity on the double bass—in range, rhythm, tonal control, everything. It's as if the bass *sings* here—and weren't a manufactured instrument. Mingus's virtuosity is also a sign of his extraordinary and unyielding energy, energy he devoted to composition and leading, to speaking out for basic civil rights for blacks, to proselytizing for black music and jazz. In this cut and the last of this group, especially, we hear his use of traditional black and/or jazz elements for new and fresh compositions.

After the solo bass intro, Mingus sets up a 4-bar riff that is as funky as you can get. This riff continues and serves as the underpinning for all the rest of the group, entering one by one. Next in is the percussion, then the trombone, then everyone, a great buildup of energy and excitement that makes the quintet sound like a much bigger band. These riffs yield to blues choruses, beginning where the trombone starts to play solo. The trombone plays five choruses of the blues. Notice the third chorus, where Mingus and the rest of the group seem to move into double time. The fourth chorus is stop-time, and the fifth goes back to the normal hard bop texture. This will happen in the later solos, too; Mingus's unflagging energy never meant loss of complete control, and here he does the same (or similar) things at the same (or almost the same) place in successive solos. After the trombone solo, the piano also plays five choruses; the third chorus is a stop-time one. Next comes a solo by the alto, in which the third is again double-time and the fourth stop-time. Then Mingus plays his solo, a bass solo such as we have not heard yet in this history. Again, he's all over the range, and shows an amazing variety in timbres, rhythms, and phrasing. The rest of the rhythm section drop out, and he plays completely solo until he moves back into the 4-bar riff from the top of the chart and the quintet repeats the same buildup. Finally the group slows down and fades out.

This cut is classic Mingus for a lot of reasons: its energy, its dark colors, the riffs and the funk, the virtuosity, the clear structure. For other musicians, Mingus's music was as difficult as Monk's. But he was as popular as any of his bop contemporaries, and his music continues to live.

➤   *Goodbye Pork Pie Hat*, Charles Mingus. Charles Mingus, bass; John Handy, Booker Ervin, tenor sax; Horace Parlan, piano; Danny Richmond, drums. Recorded 1959.

Mingus's own composition, and an elegiac tribute to Lester Young, who died in 1959. (Prez used to wear a pork pie hat.) Like the Modern Jazz Quartet's *Django* in the next section, this is a loving memorial from the musicians to one of their own. It is also a kind of Ellingtonian portrait (Mingus held Ellington in awe). In her 1979 album

Mingus, done in collaboration with him but completed after he died, Joni Mitchell did *Goodbye Pork Pie Hat* as a tribute both to Lester Young and to Mingus himself, and by extension to a whole generation of jazz history.

The tune is a slow 12-bar blues. The first chorus is played by the tenors in unison—note, again, the dark and low sound of the ensemble. The two-chorus solo is by Handy, and there's a wonderful moment at the beginning of the second chorus, when Handy goes into a sort of flutter-tongue sound supported by the same shake, the same trembling, from Mingus on bass. After the solo, they expand the range to play the same melody in different registers (in octaves). The result is one of expansion, of opening out the dark and constrained emotions that had preceded. Notice, as with *Django*, the solidity of the music. No cheap show here: a great musician may have passed, but his colleagues' memory of him, the music with which they express that memory, and the tradition which he carried on himself and transmitted, all that shall live.

➤   *Hora Decubitus*, Charles Mingus. Charles Mingus and His Orchestra: Charles Mingus, bass; Eddie Preston, Richard Williams, trumpet; Britt Woodman, trombone; Don Butterfield, tuba; Eric Dolphy, alto sax; Dick Haffer, tenor sax and clarinet; Booker Ervin, tenor sax; Jerome Richardson, soprano sax and baritone sax; Jaki Byard, piano; Walter Perkins, drums. Recorded 1963.

The title means, we're told, "At Bedtime"; who knows what that has to do with the music itself. But rejoice, folks, this is a riffed 12-bar blues (remember them?), the sort of thing we heard from Moten, Lunceford, and Basie. Soloists are Ervin (tenor), Dolphy (alto), and Williams (trumpet). The cut swings like all hell and more. There's lots to dig: the old riff layout and the accumulation of riffs, more in each succeeding chorus, that we heard back with the Kansas City/Southwest bands in the 1930s, piling up section onto section; the sectional treatment of the band, brass against reeds; the hot 4-to-the-bar bass; and, by contrast, the post-bop solos (can you imagine those coming from even such a progressive player as Lester Young?), especially the solo from Dolphy; and the bop rhythm-section work under the solos, contrasting with the hot, *swing*, ensemble choruses (especially the last one). The energy comes from both bop and Swing. As with the previous Mingus cuts, listen to how all this works *together*. If you heard this on the radio, unannounced, what would you think it was?

INTO THE COOL

➤   *Four Brothers*, Jimmy Giuffre. Woody Herman and His Orchestra: Stan
    Fishelson, Bernie Glow, Marky Markowitz, Shorty Rogers, Ernie Royal,
    trumpet; Bob Swift, Earl Swope, Ollie Wilson, trombone; Woody Her-
    man, clarinet, alto sax; Sam Marowitz, alto sax; Herbie Steward, alto
    and tenor sax; Stan Getz, Zoot Sims, tenor sax; Serge Chaloff, baritone
    sax; Fred Otis, piano; Walt Yoder, bass; Don Lamond, drums. Recorded
    1947.

We include this cut because of the sound of the saxes, the "Four
Brothers" of the title, and the melodies in the main tune and the solos.
The "Four Brothers" were three tenor saxes—Stan Getz, Zoot Sims, and
Herbie Steward—and a bari (or baritone) sax, Serge Chaloff. Given the
size and the low register of their instruments, all four play with a surprising and ingratiating lightness of timbre and a real lilt to their swing.
Their solos are smooth in contour and rhythm, not so aggressive or hot
as the contemporary boppers. But the rest of the group and the tune are
more in line with the usual band sound of the late 1940s and early
1950s. The drummer is much more active than a cool drummer will be
(for example on the next cut, or the tunes from Miles Davis's *Birth of the
Cool*). Once the whole band begins to work, after the two solo choruses,
the chart is not in a cool style, but that of a Swing/bop big band. The
trumpets are brassy and hot, and the rhythm section is working hard.
    The tune is a 32-bar aaba. The thematic chorus at the beginning is
played by the Four Brothers, who then take 16-bar solos in turn: Sims,
Chaloff on bari, Steward, and Getz. In the next ensemble chorus, the
clarinet solo in the bridge is Woody Herman, the band's leader. At the
end, we hear 2-bar licks from Getz, Sims, Steward, and Chaloff. The
main tune of the chart comes only at the beginning; there's no thematic
"out" chorus at the end. So the overall shape of the arrangement is one
big crescendo, from the laid-back, "cool" sounding main tune and sax
solos through the ensemble buildup to the climax at the end.

➤   *Subconscious Lee*, Lee Konitz. The Lennie Tristano Quintet: Lee Konitz,
    alto sax; Lennie Tristano, piano; Billy Bauer, guitar; Arnold Fishkin,
    bass; Shelly Manne, drums. Recorded 1949.

Tristano and Konitz were musicians instrumental in the evolution
of bop to what has since become known as the "Cool School." Like bop
some ten years before, cool jazz was the development of a small num-

Lee Konitz. Music Division, The
New York Public Library for the
Performing Arts, Astor, Lenox
and Tilden Foundations.

ber of musicians working very closely together and trying consciously
to create a new sound. The dividing line between bop and cool isn't
always so clear as that between bop and Swing, especially at the beginning; but work on it throughout this section, and contrast it especially
with the bop soloists we've just listened to. A good contrast of the two
styles is *I'll Remember April* by Clifford Brown et al. and the Lee
Konitz/Gerry Mulligan recording of *All The Things You Are*, below.

Although the harmonies in cool jazz could be just as complex and
rapidly changing as those of bop, the emphasis in cool is on melody—
long, flowing lines that work across the standard 8-bar units (as in
bop), but which are more restrained, less earthy or "funky" than those
we've heard from Bud Powell, Sarah Vaughan or Betty Carter, Sonny
Rollins and the rest. Sometimes these flowing melodies are combined
into an easygoing polyphony that brings them into even greater relief
at the expense of the harmonic background. Dynamics (relative loudness or softness) rend to be lower, softer in cool jazz than in bop. The
horns' timbre is very light, even a little dry, and with very little vibrato.
The rhythm section, especially the bass and drums, is relegated almost
completely to a secondary, time-keeping role. All these characteristics—emphasis on smooth lines rather than on harmonies or harmonic
complexity, or on rhythm as such; softer dynamics; lighter, sparer

sound—give this music an emotional pitch lower than that of bop, one that's easily summed up in the term "cool."

Note: "cool" jazz is also sometimes referred to as "West Coast jazz," to distinguish it from "East Coast jazz," or hard bop. The terms are a little misleading, however. Cool jazz may have been more prevalent in California than in the East, but the style was evolved in New York as much as anywhere else. Similarly, hard bop may have been king in New York, but it was heard all over the country and in Europe, too, in the 1950s. In addition, a lot of the boppers of the 50s came from places like Detroit or other large Northern cities. So "West Coast" and "East Coast" may be convenient labels at times, but they don't reflect the real story any more than do stylistic distinctions along racial lines, or the old New Orleans/Chicago/New York line.

Back to *Subconscious Lee.* The music is based on Cole Porter's song *What Is This Thing Called Love?*, a 32-bar aaba. If you can focus on the chords of *Subconscious Lee,* you'll hear that same structure; but if you focus on the tune of the thematic chorus, played by Konitz and Bauer, you won't. What you'll hear is a succession of four 8-bar phrases, all with a sort of family resemblance, but not in an aaba phrase structure. As the boppers had done, and Lester Young and Coleman Hawkins before them, Konitz has put a new and contemporary melody over a preexisting framework. After the thematic chorus, we hear solo choruses from Tristano, Bauer, and Konitz, and then a final chorus with solo phrases from Tristano, Bauer, Konitz, and Tristano again, and finally the last a phrase of the beginning thematic chorus, as the send-off. Notice how similar all the soloists sound, especially Tristano and Bauer (or Konitz and Bauer in the first chorus), in their touch, the rhythms, the cross-phrasing, the legato smoothness of their lines, the light timbres, and so on. One of Konitz's desires was to set himself up as a kind of contrast to Charlie Parker; there were so many sax players in the late 40s who sounded like Bird (or tried to), that Konitz wanted to sound different. How would you compare and contrast him to Parker?

➤   *Jeru,* Gerry Mulligan. Miles Davis and His Orchestra: Miles Davis, trumpet; Kai Winding, trombone; Junior Collins, French horn; John Barber, tuba; Lee Konitz, alto sax; Gerry Mulligan, baritone sax; Al Haig, piano; Joe Shulman, bass; Max Roach, drums. Recorded 1949.

Like the next two cuts, *Jeru* is from the record called *Birth of the Cool,* one of Davis's most famous and influential sessions, and one of the most famous in jazz history. (Davis went from strength to strength in the 1950s; see the section on him, below.) The first thing to notice here is the ensemble—nine instruments, with no doublings (i.e., there's only one of each kind), and including tuba and French horn. We haven't heard a tuba in years, and jazz French horn was (and is) so rare as to be virtually nonexistent. The initial conception for this group came from the composer/arranger. The group didn't just find themselves together one day and say, "Well, what can we play?" Instead, Davis, the arranger Gil Evans, Gerry Mulligan, and others brought these musicians together and did the charts with these particular sounds in mind. The band did a few brief public appearances (their first was in New York in 1948), cut these compositions in 1949–1950, and then disbanded.

Pay attention to several things: the arrangement itself, with its cross-voicing (as we heard from Duke Ellington), carefully planned out in terms of texture and timbre; the sound of the soloists, again the light, dry timbres, and especially Davis's breathy, almost detached-sounding tone, staying pretty much entirely in the trumpet's middle register (Davis sounds very different here from the way he had played earlier with Parker, and this is the sound he's been identified with ever since); Roach's drum work, underlying the cool, "laid-back" melodies and tone with a hotter, more forward-driving rhythmic play; the kind of melody that Mulligan wrote (a bop tune? cool?); and the phrase structure. Can you hear the cross-phrasing in the horns? Is there any larger structure to the phrases—aaba choruses, for example?

➤ *Boplicity*, "Cleo Henry," i.e. Davis. Miles Davis and His Orchestra: Miles Davis, trumpet; J. J. Johnson, trombone; Sandy Siegelstein, French horn; John Barber, tuba; Lee Konitz, alto sax; Gerry Mulligan, baritone sax; John Lewis, piano; Nelson Boyd, bass; Kenny Clarke, drums. recorded 1949.

There are some changes in personnel here, but the same instruments as on *Jeru*. *Boplicity* was arranged by Gil Evans, who ten years later again collaborated with Davis on the famous and wonderful albums, *Miles Ahead*, *Porgy and Bess*, and *Sketches of Spain*. *Boplicity* is basically a 32-bar aaba; how many choruses are there? You should be able to hear the 4- and 8-bar units fairly readily. Listen again to the arrangement itself, and especially to the solos from Mulligan and Davis. Mulligan was very important as a player/arranger/composer for cool jazz, especially after 1952, when he formed his famous pianoless quartet in California. (We'll hear that quartet, with Lee Konitz, below.) He also rerecorded these same charts, with different players, in the early 1990s; you might try to get your hands on that to compare. How would you describe Mulligan's sound on baritone sax? Is he working in the same style as Davis, or that of Konitz on the other cuts in this section?

➤ *Israel*, Johnny Carisi. Miles Davis and His Orchestra: same personnel, same date as *Boplicity*.

This is a 12-bar blues, with two thematic choruses after the intro, and then the solos. Concentrate here on the original theme and on the improvised solos—can you hear resemblances to bop melodies? to cool textures, doublings, melodic flow? Is there a "blues feeling" here?

➤ *All the Things You Are*, Jerome Kern, Oscar Hammerstein II. Lee Konitz with the Gerry Mulligan Quartet: Lee Konitz, alto sax; Gerry Mulligan, baritone sax; Chet Baker, trumpet; Carson Smith, bass; Larry Bunker, drums. Recorded 1953.

Here we have Konitz soloing over Mulligan's famous and innovative "pianoless quartet"—that is, two melody instruments (trumpet and baritone sax, high and low) over bass and drums, with no chordal instrument such as piano or guitar. Remember the comments above about cool jazz's emphasis on melody above all, at the expense of harmonic hegemony. This is not at all to say that harmonic considerations have gone by the board, but without a piano insisting on specific chord changes, the harmonies of a tune are implied (in the bass and in the tune) rather than overtly stated, and this gives the melodists a little more elbow room, a little more space to stretch out in. *All the Things You Are* has always been a bop favorite, precisely because of the strength of its chord changes. In this version, the changes still give the cut a solid foundation, but because we never hear the chords as such, we can focus our ears on Konitz's expansive melodies. This focus on Konitz's lines is also possible because of the ensemble itself. With no chordal instrument, no piano or guitar, to fill up the musical "space," to connect the low bass with the higher sax, we're given a beautifully lean and clear texture. This is the first thing to notice in the opening, Konitz's thematic chorus over just bass and drums; and the typically cool emphasis on melody *per se* is heightened even more when Mulligan and Baker enter with their quiet, sustained support.

All the Things You Are is a 36-bar aaba, four 8-bar phrases plus 4 extra measures at the end. Listen first—and repeatedly—to Konitz's opening chorus. You can get the song's phrasing from the bass, playing at a steady (if quick) 4 to the bar. But where's Konitz? From the very outset, his phrasing has great freedom and a very assured plasticity. The silences, which one also must listen to, seem very casual over that forward-moving bass. But not to worry: "cool" doesn't mean "nonchalant," and what we hear in this first chorus is really a signal of all the variety that's to come.

That variety starts with the phrasing, the way Konitz works over the 4-to-the-bar and 8-bars-to-the-phrase of the rhythm section (actually of the bass, since the discreet, well-placed drumming is the kind of thing you'd really notice only if it were missing). On their chosen turf, the cool jazz musicians had as many resources and as many turns as the boppers did on theirs. Listen to the changes in dynamics, in timbre, in attack (the way he hits a note) that Konitz uses. This is as much an individual "voice" working as the music we've heard from Bird or Rollins or Miles Davis, and the various inflections of that voice spin out long melodies in always fresh and exhilarating solos.

Pay attention, too, to Mulligan and Baker when they come in. At first they're at the level of the drummer, playing at the back reaches of your awareness. But—again within their chosen limits—they build as the solo goes on, becoming more active in their support. By the last chorus, Konitz has returned to the original melody, now stabbing out its most essential notes (compare it to his first chorus), and Mulligan is playing up-tempo, riff-like figures underneath. Mulligan and Baker are still accompanying Konitz, but their backup helps drive the cut to its conclusion.

➤   *Django,* John Lewis. The Modern Jazz Quartet: John Lewis, piano; Milt Jackson, vibes; Percy Heath, bass; Connie Kay, drums. Recorded 1960.

In contrast to Mulligan's pianoless quartet, this is a quartet that's all rhythm section. I've mentioned the MJQ several times in this chapter. They came originally, as individuals, from the rhythm section of Dizzy Gillespie's big band. But throughout their career as a quartet, they were associated with the cool, "neoclassic" side of the street. "Neoclassic" is a term that was used to describe certain symphonic and chamber music after 1920—for example, that of the composer Igor

The Modern Jazz Quartet: bassist Percy Heath, drummer Connie Kay, pianist John Lewis, vibes player Milt Jackson. Music Division, The New York Public Library for the Performing Arts, Astor, Lenox and Tilden Foundations.

Stravinsky. Such music supposedly took as its model the "classical" compositions of the late eighteenth century by such composers as Mozart or Beethoven. In our context, the term "neoclassic" refers to the MJQ's performances of, and improvisations on, works of J. S. Bach, or John Lewis's original compositions, whose formal layout came from classical, not jazz, patterns. (Also related is the "Third Stream" music that was developed in the 1950s. Since "Third Stream" music hasn't turned out to be a jazz genre of major historical importance, we aren't treating it in this book, but see the Glossary for a very short discussion of it.)

   Django is an elegy in memory of Django Reinhardt, and, as such, it's of a piece with Benny Golson's *I Remember Clifford* (Clifford Brown) and Charles Mingus's *Goodbye Pork Pie Hat*, in memory of Lester Young. Tunes like this mark a new stage in the tradition of jazz lore. From the beginning—or maybe from the stage just after the beginning—jazz has celebrated its history and its heritage with songs like

Basin Street Blues (Basin Street is in New Orleans), *Beale Street Blues* (Memphis), or *Do You Know What It Means to Miss New Orleans*. With the 1950s we get to an era in which the music didn't just evoke the aura of a time and place now lost to the past, didn't just sing about going back to Kansas City, but instead paid tribute to particular individual musicians, to people who were important and who were loved. Jazz has become by this point an outspokenly proud and assertive music, aware of its own traditions and history.

Just as one learns about oneself by thinking about one's parents and family, jazz musicians extended themselves in celebrating their musical parentage. There are individual tributes like *Django* or *Goodbye Pork Pie Hat*, more general internalizations in the music of Ellington or Parker, and finally a very broad attention given to all of jazz history as well as to prejazz musics and prejazz instruments (see the section on free jazz in Chapter Four, and most of Chapter Five). All of this accompanies the more systematic and perhaps musically more wide-ranging explorations that went into the makeup of jazz after the late 1940s. It constituted a real watershed in the history of jazz, especially in the history of jazz musicians. It affects not only the ways in which they see themselves, but also provides a new richness and variety in the music, comparable only to the coalescence we saw in the 20s and 30s, when local styles and preferences merged into a national, and then international, language.

But to get back to *Django*: the tune is a 20-bar chorus, 12 measures plus 8. Both phrases are based on a device called the *sequence*, the repetition of a melodic figure at a higher or lower pitch level. In the first, 12-bar phrase it's a 6-note figure, 2 bars long, that goes up, then is repeated at successively lower levels, then goes up again; the second, 8-bar phrase is built on a 2-note figure that is played at successively lower levels with each measure. (The sequence is different from the riff. The latter is simply a repeated figure that works rhythmically as well as melodically, and usually at the same pitch level. Riffs tend to build up tension and drive; sequences are used to spin out long *melodies* based on a single little fragment.) The use of the sequence here gives *Django* its meditative, elegiac flavor, and its bluesy quality.

The solos are equally thoughtful. Listen especially to Milt Jackson's playing, and compare it to what we've heard from him before, with Gillespie and Monk. We've also heard John Lewis, with Bird (*Parker's Mood*), Dizzy (*Things to Come*), and Miles Davis (*Boplicity* and *Israel*). What are the contributions of the drummer and bassist, Kay and Heath? What's "cool" about this cut? How did these folks get here from bop, from Dizzy in the late 1940s?

➤   *West Coast Blues*, Wes Montgomery. The Wes Montgomery Quartet:
    Wes Montgomery, guitar; Tommy Flanagan, piano; Percy Heath, bass;
    Albert Heath, drums. Recorded 1960.

A little gimmick here is the meter. Instead of being 4 beats to the
bar, as every other blues we've heard, this tune is in what's called com-
pound duple meter—2 beats to the bar, each beat divided into threes,
or triplets. You can hear this set out clearly in the first two choruses. In
the first chorus, the bass plays on each beat, and then in the second chorus, fills in the off-beats as well, so that first you'll hear a moderate but
swinging 1-2-1-2, then 1-and-uh-2-and-uh. Once you've got that down,
you'll hear the standard blues chord progression and be able to count
off the 12 bars of each chorus.

Montgomery's solo starts with the bluesy licks of the thematic
chorus, expands into longer single-note melodies, then into melodies
played in octaves (a device for which he was famous), and finally into
full chords. The last chorus is another thematic one, like the first chorus. This gives a certain propulsion to the chart as a whole, but Montgomery always maintains a kind of easy, loping swing that was also
one of his trademarks. The rest of the quartet here, in its way like the
Mulligan quartet backing up Lee Konitz, serves as backdrop and support. The piano is almost inaudible, again the kind of thing you don't
really hear, but would miss if it weren't there. The bass swings along on
its 6-to-the-bar and helps Montgomery define the chord structure of the
blues. The drummer is the most noticeable, giving the cut a lot of its
infectious rhythmic bounce, and playing off Montgomery to keep the
music moving.

MILES DAVIS, GIL EVANS, AND BILL EVANS

➤   *Oleo*, Sonny Rollins. The Miles Davis Quintet: Miles Davis, trumpet;
    John Coltrane, tenor sax; Red Garland, piano; Paul Chambers, bass;
    Philly Joe Jones, drums. Recorded 1956.

We heard Davis (1926–1991) about ten years ago with Bird (*Klacktoveedsedsteen*, *Ornithology* and *Night in Tunisia*, 1946–1947), and you
may want to refer to those cuts again. In the preceding section, we also
heard his work from the late 1940s, three cuts from *The Birth of the Cool*.
Oleo is a continuation of Davis's bop playing, and we hear him here

paired with John Coltrane who, just as Miles began with Bird and moved on, began with Miles and moved on as well. More of Trane in the final section of this chapter.

This is a 32-bar aaba. In the first chorus, Davis plays the first phrase alone; in the second phrase, the trumpet is doubled by piano, and the bass is added; then comes a bridge, in the rhythm section; and the last phrase has Coltrane lead with Davis doubling (almost inaudibly). This is a typical bop tune in many ways—the asymmetrical rhythms and phrases; the way the whole tune comes out of the first three notes (how often do you hear that figure during the a phrase? compare this to Monk's *Straight No Chaser* and another Rollins composition, *Blue 7*); the standard form, standard ensemble, and polytextures during the solos. But many elements of the cut are less typical of bop as a genre and more so of Miles as an individual player and leader.

Listen first to Davis's tone—muted, breathy, with a much different kind of attack from any trumpeter we've heard so far. You often hear not just the beginning of the note, but the sound of his tongue and his breath as well. Davis stays primarily in the middle register of the horn, unlike Dizzy or anyone else; most trumpet players exploit the whole range, and a majority of them like to concentrate on the upper reaches. Davis's phrasing is also peculiar to him. He doesn't just start and blow for 8, 16, or 32 bars at a stretch. Rather, he often uses short licks, carefully placed within or across the 8-bar phrases, and these brief melodic ideas somehow add up, across the silences, to longer melodic phrases. Listen to the variety of textures, too. When is it just trumpet and bass, when does the rest of the rhythm section come in? How many choruses does Miles play before Coltrane takes over?

Coltrane's lines are a little different from Miles's—put simply, he plays more notes. (We'll wait to concentrate on Coltrane till the next section.) Garland's solo here should remind you of Bud Powell. How about the rest of the rhythm section? How does the whole ensemble work together?

It may take practice to hear the aaba structure and to keep the meter in this cut. But it's important to do so; keep at it. Listen also for the little piano figure (syncopated right-hand octaves) that Garland often plays in the third bar of the last a phrase—a little signpost to remind you where you are, and an element of overall unity in the cut.

➤   *My Ship*, Kurt Weill. Miles Davis and the Gil Evans Orchestra: Miles Davis, fluegelhorn; Bernie Glow, Ernie Royal, Louis Mucci, Taft Jordan, John Carisi, trumpet; Frank Rehak, Jimmy Cleveland, Joe Bennet, trombone; Tom Mitchell, bass trombone; Willie Ruff, Tony Miranda, French horn; Bill Barber, tuba; Lee Konitz, alto sax; Danny Bank, bass clarinet; Paul Chambers, bass; Art Taylor, drums. Recorded 1957.

This cut is from an album called *Miles Ahead*, the first collaboration between Davis and arranger/composer Gil Evans (1912–1988) since the landmark *Birth of the Cool* (see the section *Into the Cool*, above), and the first of three Davis/Evans albums in the late 1950s (see the two following cuts). Notice that Miles is not playing trumpet on this date, but fluegelhorn. This instrument is an oversized cornet, like a trumpet but with a warmer, mellower tone than the brassy trumpet. Clark Terry, with the Ellington band in the 1950s and now a soloist and leader in his own right, specializes on fluegelhorn; it's also the instrument of Chuck Mangione.

My Ship is a 32-bar aaba tune, with an orchestral intro (the song's principal melody) and coda. You should be able to get the form on first hearing, so after that listen to the beautiful arrangement. Compare the arrangement to *Birth of the Cool*, to the standard big band, to Ellington and Tadd Dameron, to Woody Herman. How does Evans use the resources at hand? For one thing, he mixes timbres, uses the cross-voicing we heard first from Ellington but have also heard elsewhere. The overall sound here is warm and rather light, matching orchestrally what Davis does as a solo. And look at the composition of the band itself—only two reeds, and no piano.

The band is like Herman's in the group phrasing of the intro, especially for the a phrase at the end of the introduction. And listen to the colors of individual lines against those of the group in the intro. All in all, a quiet, cushioning background for Davis's gorgeous solo. Davis's tone here is like that in *Oleo*, breathy and almost without vibrato. (The story is that Davis's teacher in St. Louis told him to play without vibrato, since he was going to "get old and start shaking anyway." Didn't happen—Davis got older, but his tone never shook.) His phrases, though, are much longer here, as suits a lyrical ballad. If you heard this unannounced on the radio, would you think it was jazz? Why?

➤   *Summertime*, George Gershwin. Miles Davis with the Gil Evans Orchestra: Miles Davis, trumpet; Louis Rucci, Ernie Royal, John Coles, Bernie Glow, trumpet; Jimmy Cleveland, Joseph Bennet, Dick Hixon, Frank Rehak, trombone; Willie Ruff, Julius B. Watkins, Gunther Schuller, French horn; Bill Barber, tuba; Julian ("Cannonball") Adderley, Danny Bank, sax; Phil Bodner, Romeo Penque, flute; Paul Chambers, bass; Philly Joe Jones, drums. Recorded 1958.

Summertime is from the second of this series of Evans/Davis collaborations, the orchestral-jazz reading of Gershwin's opera *Porgy and Bess*. Each chorus of this famous song is 16 bars (two 8-bar phrases, aa'). As with *My Ship*, listen to the colors and motives of the arrangement, and notice again that since Evans is not using piano in the rhythm section, there is no single instrument laying down the harmonies—so one is as aware of colors and mixes as one is of chords. Davis plays with his unique tone, breathy and distant and detached-sounding, but at the same time lyrical and inviting, a real combination of warm and cool (that last word not necessarily in the sense of the jazz label). Notice the rather jaunty tempo for this lullaby, the sequence motive in the accompaniment, and Davis's inexhaustible variations on the original melody that still never stray too far from it or get in its way.

➤   *Concierto de Aranjuez*, Joaquin Rodrigo, arranged by Gil Evans. Miles Davis, trumpet, with the Gil Evans Orchestra. Recorded 1959.

This cut is based on the slow movement of a concerto for guitar and orchestra by the 20th-century Spanish composer Joaquin Rodrigo. Its translation into a jazz idiom is an amazing and beautiful feat accomplished by Evans and Davis. The orchestra here consists of winds (both brass and woodwinds), percussion, bass, and harp. The color mix of the band resembles what Evans has done before, since his work on *The Birth of the Cool*, but carried much further. Davis is, according to the liner notes, playing around a sketch given him by Evans, but (still according to the notes) not improvising very far away from the melody. Indeed, in those sections that are directly based on the original Rodrigo, you can follow Davis along with the score. His ornamentation and some of his phrasings are different, but he's playing a melodic meditation on Rodrigo's themes. What is different here—besides Evans's original orchestration—is the percussion which gives the tune so much of its color and its atmosphere; the less metrical feeling that comes from the use of the rhythm section and the low brass (the Rodrigo is much more like a stately procession); and a couple of original sections inserted into the Rodrigo, one that begins toward the middle of the cut, with repeated notes over a walking bass and the drummer's using brushes, so that it suddenly sounds more typical of a jazz band, and the other a little later, after some quick, glittery triplets.

But what do you think—is this jazz? Does it have any of the characteristics we've stressed throughout this book as central to jazz? Does the question even matter? There certainly are some of the usual jazz traits—the instrumentation, the harmonies, the occasional surfacing of a metrical swing. A cheap answer is that Davis and Evans are jazz artists, and whatever they do is by definition jazz. But that answer is obviously completely unsatisfactory, since it just begs the question. A better answer is to consider the enormous range of musics included in the jazz tent since the beginning, and to remember that jazz is not just an expanding repertory or a growing genre, but that it has *always* been a hugely varied field. This is a point we'll take up again in the next two chapters.

➤   *So What*, Miles Davis. The Miles Davis Sextet: Miles Davis, trumpet; Cannonball Adderley, alto sax; John Coltrane, tenor sax; Bill Evans, piano; Paul Chambers, bass; James Cobb, drums. Recorded 1958.

This cut and the next are from Davis's album *Kind of Blue*, recorded between *Porgy and Bess* and *Sketches of Spain*. For many people, *Kind of Blue* has become one of the essential jazz recordings, and *So What* has become a standard, performed and recorded by legions of jazz artists since 1958.

The form of *So What* is a 32-bar aaba, after a slow intro by Evans and Chambers. But the music is built here in a way different from anything we've heard to date. It's based not on a series of chord changes, of different chords that follow one another in a set pattern, but on a *mode*, a scale or arrangement of individual pitches. The different combinations you hear during any given phrase are all drawn from that single arrangement of seven pitches, and the solos are based on it, too. Modal jazz is characterized by a very restricted use of chords. Whereas earlier tunes we've heard use many chords in the course of a phrase, *So What* uses only one. The bridge uses the same mode as the a phrases, but at a slightly higher pitch level (as if it were a long, 8-measure sequence). The result of all this is a real harmonic stasis, not the drive of the basic Swing or bop chart. And this harmonic stasis suits the tempo, the "kind of blue" solo melodies and their colors, the overall mood of the music.

How would you describe the soloists' melodies here? Are they like those of Parker, Tristano, Konitz, earlier Miles, or anyone else we've heard? What's the relationship of this music to bop, cool, and/or hard bop? (Think about kinds of melody, rhythms, textures, and use of the instruments.)

> *Blue in Green*, Bill Evans, although sometimes wrongly attributed to Davis. The Miles Davis Quintet: as above, minus Adderley.

> *Blue in Green*, Bill Evans. The Bill Evans Trio: Bill Evans, piano; Scott LaFaro, bass; Paul Motian, drums. Recorded 1959.

A 10-bar (!) form, of the variety called "circular" because the last measure of the ten feeds seamlessly into the first, without the feeling of closure or strong return that you usually hear at the end of a chorus of blues, aaba, or other strophic form. To follow the form, count in a slow 4; you can get the tempo from the bass and the piano's left hand in the 4-measure intro before Miles comes in, in his quintet's version of the tune. Count off ten bars at a time. Those of you with some experience in hearing chord changes will hear that the eleventh bar is the same as the first: a new chorus. But the solos don't stop; the melody continues. The point here is not the agglomeration of choruses into the solo, it's the way the players work *without* stopping, in an endless flow. That continuity—not broken up into choruses—the quiet dynamic level, the descending melodic lines, Davis's far-off muted tone, the lyricism in everyone's playing (bass and drums as well as piano and the horns), all these qualities add up to the blue mood of the title of Davis's recording and the title of this tune.

A second version is by the composer, Bill Evans (1929–1980) and his trio. Evans as a pianist matched the emotion of this particular composition—lyrical, sometimes introspective, harmonically intriguing, a beautiful melodic sense, and the ability to swing. In Evans's recording, the mood at the beginning is the same as in that of the Davis quintet; but then the tempo picks up a little, the drumming becomes more regular, and while still lyrical, the music moves away from the almost static, out-of-time world of the Miles Davis recording.

> *My Foolish Heart*, Ned Washington, Victor Young. The Bill Evans Trio: Bill Evans, piano; Scott LaFaro, bass; Paul Motian, drums. Recorded 1961.

Do not confuse Bill Evans with Gil Evans. The latter is the arranger who worked with Miles on *The Birth of the Cool* and then the three recordings from the late 1950s. Bill Evans was a pianist (and sometime composer) whom we've just heard with Miles's small groups in the late 1950s and who then moved out on his own. Almost everything about Bill Evans's playing set him apart from his contemporaries—his touch and tone; his harmonic imagination, very individual in choice of chord and spacing; using his left hand to sustain chords to let them sound more often than to kick off or punctuate the right-hand lines; rhythms that sound less subtle than they are because of the flowing continuity of the music; great concision and avoidance of the unessential or the banal; and, always and ever (even in up-tempo numbers), an unassertive lyricism that worked a great influence on later pianists such as Herbie Hancock, Chick Corea, and Keith Jarrett (all of whom we'll hear in the next chapter). This particular trio is the most famous of Evans's groups—it was also the first—principally because of LaFaro, the bassist.

There are two choruses of 32-bar abab'. There's a lot to listen for— the melodies and phrasings of the right hand (could you compare this with Davis's playing on *My Ship*?), the chords and rhythms of the left, the individual playing of LaFaro and Motian (sometimes supporting Evans, often adding their own ideas), the interplay of all three. The tune and the performance are lyrical and tinged with sadness; but don't let the quiet mood mislead you into thinking that this is superficial, easy-listening music.

JOHN COLTRANE (1926–1967)

➤   *Good Bait*, Tadd Dameron, Count Basie. The John Coltrane Quartet: John Coltrane, tenor sax; Red Garland, piano; Paul Chambers, bass; Art Taylor, drums. Recorded 1958.

The tune is a 32-bar aaba. Compare Coltrane's playing to his work with Miles Davis we heard earlier (*Oleo*, from 1956, and the two cuts from *Kind of Blue*, 1958), and compare him to his contemporary Sonny Rollins (*I'll Remember April*, *Pent-Up House*, and *Blue 7*, 1956).

Among the standard hard-bop characteristics are: ensemble, texture, timbre; overall layout (thematic choruses to begin and end, the string of solos in the middle); concentration on chord changes and harmonic improvisation; length, on every level—long phrases, long solos from every player (except, in this case, the drummer, who only gets a chance to trade 4s with Coltrane for a number of choruses toward the end), and overall length, here about twelve minutes. Further traits of

Coltrane which you should listen to include his tone and timbre, strong in all registers; his big range; and his preference for long, legato lines, with lots of fast notes (this eventually becomes one of Trane's trademarks, what the jazz writer Ira Gitler called "sheets of sound").

Listen to the rest of the quartet as well as to Coltrane. During his solos their playing is good hard-bop rhythm work, laying down a solid foundation for him to work from and work across. But what about their solos? Are the phrasings and the melodies like Coltrane's? Are they similar to the playing we've heard in other bop groups in this chapter?

➤ *Giant Steps*, John Coltrane. The John Coltrane Quartet: John Coltrane, tenor sax; Tommy Flanagan, piano; Paul Chambers, bass; Art Taylor, drums. Recorded 1959.

This is a 16-bar tune, aa'b (4 plus 4 plus 8, the 8-bar b phrase being a rising sequence of a motive from the a phrase). The cut begins with

John Coltrane. Courtesy of the Rutgers Institute of Jazz Studies.

two identical 16-bar choruses. As with compositions since James P.
Johnson's *Carolina Shout* (see Chapter One) and beyond, this became
not just a jazz standard but a "test piece" as well. Because of the chord
changes (unusual for jazz charts of the time and *very* difficult for
soloists, not to mention the luckless piano player) and the tempo (basically faster than is humanly possible), musicians really have to have it
together to get through the tune. And they also have Coltrane's solo to
match themselves against. Read again the general comments under
Good Bait; they apply here, too.

➤   *Naima*, John Coltrane. The John Coltrane Quartet: John Coltrane, tenor
     sax; Wynton Kelly, piano; Paul Chambers, bass; Jimmy Cobb, drums.
     Recorded 1959.

   This slow ballad has two connections with the kind of music we
first heard on Miles Davis's *Kind of Blue*. First, it's related to *modal* jazz,
as was *So What*, built on the notes of a particular scale as opposed to a
succession of chords. Listen to the bass line—for the first 8 bars, Chambers plays only one pitch (this is called either a drone bass or a pedal);
in the next 8 bars, he switches to another note; and in the last 8, he
returns to the first pitch. This pedal and the small number of chords
used combine to create the sense of harmonic stasis that I mentioned
earlier, the lack of forward direction or insistent forward drive such as
we just heard in *Giant Steps*. The sense of stasis suits the slow, floating
tempo and the quiet, thoughtful mood of the piece; it also fits with the
second connection to *Kind of Blue*, the circular form which we heard in
Blue in Green. *Naima*, as it's notated, is a 20-bar piece (aba', 8 plus 8 plus
4); the 8-bar a phrases consist of two identical 4-bar units, and that 4-
bar unit is the final 4-bar a'. So, again, the end of each "chorus" feeds
seamlessly into, and is in fact indistinguishable from, the beginning of
the next. The music moves around the circle without the kind of built-
in, necessary stopping place that one has with the blues, the 32-bar
aaba, or any other standard closed form. The layout of this version is a
20-bar chorus from Coltrane; a chorus from Kelly; Coltrane reentering,
but with the b phrase (8 bars), then a (8 bars, plus an extension, or repetition of the 4-bar unit), and then a 4-bar coda.

➤   *My Favorite Things*, Richard Rodgers, Oscar Hammerstein II. The John
     Coltrane Quartet: John Coltrane, soprano sax; McCoy Tyner, piano;
     Steve Davis, bass; Elvin Jones, drums. Recorded 1960.

The original tune, from the Broadway show *The Sound of Music*, is a 32-bar aabc. In this version, notice the drone bass and the static, circular harmonies. The original melody is also static to some degree, with its insistence on two primary pitches all the way through (the first two notes of the tune); both Coltrane and Tyner emphasize these melodic pitches in their solos.

Tyner's playing is different from other hard-bop pianists we've heard (Bud Powell, Al Haig, Tommy Flanagan, Red Garland). His work is more chordal, away from the single-note "horn-lines" of the others, closer (in some ways) to Bill Evans and Wynton Kelly. The static circularity of this reading also permits the group a kind of additive structure (at both the phrase and the overall levels) that may also reflect Coltrane's interest in African music. And this sort of cumulative, incantatory music was Coltrane's stock in trade with his turn to intense religious mysticism and search for transcendance in the 1960s.

➤ *Bessie's Blues*, John Coltrane. The John Coltrane Quartet: John Coltrane, tenor sax; McCoy Tyner, piano; Jimmy Garrison, bass; Elvin Jones, drums. Recorded 1964.

This is a 12-bar blues by the "classic" Coltrane group. The general scheme is straight-ahead hard bop, but the lines are pure Trane. Listen especially to Jones's drumming in the choruses where Tyner lays out.

➤ *Alabama*, John Coltrane. The John Coltrane Quartet: same personnel as *Bessie's Blues*. Recorded 1963.

In his notes with the Smithsonian anthology, Martin Williams refers to this piece as "holy," and, given its composer and performers, that is certainly not far off the mark. These were bad times in this country: there was the March On Washington, during which Dr. Martin Luther King delivered his famous and eloquent "I Have A Dream" speech (the curious can read the Lorraine Hansberry play, *Raisin in the Sun*, and the Langston Hughes poem where Hansberry found her title, "What happens to a dream deferred? It withers, like a raisin in the sun. . . ."). That was also the occasion for Mahalia Jackson's singing *I Been 'Buked and I Been Scorned*; and it was the year that *We Shall Overcome* seemed for many Americans about ready to supplant *The Star-Spangled Banner* as the national anthem. In the year 1963 four young black girls were killed by a bomb in a Birmingham church one Sunday morning. It was the year that President Kennedy was shot (four days after this cut was recorded). It was a year, the first year, of explosions from blacks in United States cities, who did not yet have basic civil rights; it was the year that a major statement appeared in LeRoi Jones's (now Amiri Baraka) *Blues People*, a book as valuable for its recounting of the position of blacks in this country and for its historical status as the angry and articulate statement of a major black poet, playwright, and leader as it is for its insights into jazz. It is indispensable both as a primary and as a secondary source.

It was a bad time, then, 1963—and good riddance to it. But because of the time, because of the musicians, Williams refers to this cut with the terms "prayer" and "meditation." Listen to the textures (the overall structure is ABA), to Coltrane's modal melodies, to the static drone background, and simply to the sounds of the group and especially of the percussion. "Holy" as a description seems not too far off the mark.

➤ Chapter 4

Free Jazz and Fusion
(Directions)

The two sections of this chapter are not surveys of, but introductions to, jazz's most striking developments in the 1960s and 1970s. A full survey of free jazz would require much more space and time than the scope of this book permits. Electronic jazz and fusion might be dealt with more succinctly; this music was widely heard and popular for some 15 years, but most recently has seemed to retreat before a resurgence of mainstream bop and post-bop and the developments we'll discuss in Chapter Five. So treat the section on free jazz as an introduction to the style, to its sounds and musical concerns, and to its enormous variety; and read the section on electric jazz and fusion less as a survey of the music and its most important groups than as an introduction to its historical and musical context and some of the principal people involved.

Free jazz—also known at its inception (ca. 1960) as "The New Thing"—was the creation of many individuals like Eric Dolphy, a reed player, the alto sax player Ornette Coleman, the pianist Cecil Taylor, Sun Ra, and others. The label "free jazz" is helpful, although it will mislead you if you take it too literally. Free jazz is based on melody and on mood, if we may use a word that can be general to the point of meaninglessness. This kind of music is "free" of most of the building blocks of earlier jazz: free of strict meter and tempo, of preset chord progressions, of standard forms such as the blues or the 32-bar aaba, of the convention that all phrases and choruses be of the same fixed length, even free from any standard performing ensemble. But be warned: this freedom does not add up to chaos. Once your ears are used to what's not in the music, pay attention to what *is* there; it's a music of great power and expressiveness.

Free jazz is also difficult to summarize because of its variety: the musicians discussed here will not sound like each other to you, and even the selections by Ornette Coleman will probably seem radically different from one another. But there are generalizations that can be made. The first of these is the addition to the previously conventional jazz instruments of a great many new ones. Foremost among these is the expansion of the drummer's equipment to include a vast battery of new instruments, gongs, bells, rattles, many instruments taken from African musics. (This has in part to do with the new pride in black heritage that I mentioned in the previous chapter, as well as with jazz musicians' unending inventiveness and desire to expand their music.) Free jazz ensembles have no rhythm section, as such; the rhythm section has expanded to a *percussion* section.

As the instrumental resources expand, the musicians themselves become, to a much greater degree than before, performers on more than one instrument. Ray Nance, a trumpet player with Ellington, also played violin, and most Swing-era reed players were professionally competent on more than one instrument. But free jazz musicians often seem to play everything, and to play all their instruments in a single set. An extreme example is Rahsaan Roland Kirk, who could play three saxes *at the same time.* Eric Dolphy played all the saxes, clarinet and bass clarinet, flutes, in short all the reeds. Sam Rivers plays all the reeds and the keyboards, including a great gospel piano. The best example from the selections to come is the individuals of the Art Ensemble of Chicago.

Free jazz groups also make their music from a wide range of sources. I've mentioned the interest in African musics, which is reflected principally in the textures of free jazz, as well as in its rhythms and forms. In the previous chapter, we heard Mingus's *Hora Decubitus,* with its free jazz solos (especially Dolphy's) over a Kansas City-style riffed blues. In the Art Ensemble's *Thème de Yoyo,* a very funky riff is combined with free polyphonic interludes and the vocal work of a classic R & B singer. Ornette Coleman's *Skies of America* is an enormous composition for a large symphony orchestra. And on the same recording as *Thème de Yoyo,* the Art Ensemble plays variations on a theme by Claudio Monteverdi, an Italian composer of the late sixteenth and early seventeenth centuries. These various sources are sometimes used literally, sometimes juxtaposed, and sometimes forged with new textures and melodies to create original and arresting music.

The best way to begin listening to free jazz is probably to listen to its textures, melodies, and successions of sections, its forms. The basis of free jazz improvisation, as I've said, is melodic, textural, and based on mood. The textures are often polyphonic, sometimes based solely on simultaneous melodies (as in Coleman's *Free Jazz*), sometimes using static, dronelike backgrounds from the bells, gongs, and piano. Forms tend to be additive, whether at the phrase level or for the whole composition. Many free jazz compositions are entire albums or entire sets—anywhere from 35 to 90 minutes of uninterrupted music. To stay with the music, listen to the ways the players use their instruments, to the way they make melodies and phrases, to their treatments of rhythm, meter and tempo, to textures, to their collective improvisation, and on the large scale, to the way they alternate or juxtapose contrasting sections and create the feeling of general tension and release (instability and stability, variety and unity). Finally ask yourself—here, as with fusion—whether this is really jazz. Given what you know of jazz history, what connections can you hear to earlier music?

Fusion is distinctive in its instruments—notably the use of electronic keyboards and the electric bass—its textures, and its adoption of devices, principally rhythmic patterns and bass lines, from the rock music of the late 1960s. The term "fusion" refers to this combination of elements from jazz and rock, a combination which makes perfect historical sense, since many of the fusion musicians grew up playing both rock and jazz (or first rock, and then jazz). It was only natural for the musicians to bring the two together, and the result was not just fusion, but the "jazz-oriented rock" by groups like Chicago or Blood, Sweat, and Tears, that was very popular in the 1970s. The adoption of rock devices is also the source of many people's objections to fusion. For many jazz musicians and jazz fans, fusion is not jazz, but commercial popular music, appealing to the lowest common denominator rather than to the musically literate. It's possible to dispute that position, and it's also possible to accept it and then ask, "So what's wrong with that?" There's no point in arguing the case here. The important thing is to listen to the music.

The addition of electric instruments and the use of rock's repetitive and fairly simple bass lines will be obvious when you hear the music, so we don't need to spend time on that. What is most immediately striking about fusion, and what is also most different from earlier styles and from free jazz, is its textures, its overall sound. The electric keyboards (piano, organ, synthesizer) are used to fill up the entire musical "space." With thick chords, frequent quick scales and arpeggios up and down the keyboard, lots of "filigree" fast notes and noodles, fusion's basic texture is a sort of wallpaperlike background on top of which the soloists lay their individual lines. But because of the repetitiveness of the bass lines and the slow chord changes (that is, the chords are sustained much longer and change much less often than in 1950s jazz), this background is often quite static. The music floats in a way new to jazz, and whatever rhythmic play there is exists in the solos.

Fusion music also borrowed elements from musics neither native to the United States nor in the Afro-American tradition. The most important of these was the Brazilian, with its attractive, lilting melodies and invitingly supple rhythms. (Two important fusion musicians were the percussionist Airto Moreira and the singer Flora Purim, both natives of Brazil.) Fusion has also been readily adopted by European musicians who are equally familiar with European jazz and with the derivative of American rock commonly called Europop. One thinks here of the Czech bassist Miroslav Vitous and the Austrian pianist Josef Zawinul. These two, however, are better considered as American musicians: their best-known work has been done in this country, with United States players. Both worked with Miles Davis in the 1960s, and, with other Davis veterans, formed the group Weather Report in 1971. Before then, in the late 1950s, Zawinul had worked with the alto-sax man Cannonball Adderley as pianist and composer, and had written one of Adderley's biggest hits, the funky *Mercy, Mercy, Mercy*. Another example of fusion's international side was the group headed by Polish violinist Michal Urbaniak, often including the singer Urszula Dudziak.

All this is to show fusion's variety and its wide appeal, qualities which can support either side of the dispute mentioned earlier. For fusion's fans, these qualities are a sign of the music's validity. For others, the distance of fusion from jazz's Afro-American tradition is proof that the music is not jazz, but pop. Again, the argument isn't worth pursuing here. But perhaps we can fuel the fires further by noting fusion's development, largely from the music of Miles Davis—indisputably a jazz musician, and one who was at the forefront of every style except free jazz from his playing with Charlie Parker in the mid-1940s—and from Davis's sidemen, continuing that music in their own groups. The beginning of this history lies in two Davis albums from 1969, *In a Silent Way* and *Bitches Brew*.

The personnel of these two albums is a roster of fusion's most important musicians. *In a Silent Way* was recorded by Davis, trumpet; Herbie Hancock, electric piano; Chick Corea, electric piano; Wayne Shorter, tenor sax; Dave Holland, bass; Joe Zawinul, electric piano and organ; John McLaughlin, guitar; and Tony Williams, drums. On *Bitches Brew*, Davis used Shorter again, this time on soprano sax; Lenny White, drums; Bennie Maupin, bass clarinet; Chick Corea, electric piano; Jim

Riley, percussion; Jack DeJohnette, drums; Harvey Brooks, Fender bass; Charles Alias, drums; Dave Holland, again on bass; John McLaughlin, again electric guitar; Joe Zawinul, again electric piano; and Larry Young, electric piano. The instrumentation of the groups—with the emphasis on electric sounds and percussion rather than drums—is a demonstration of the characteristics of fusion already mentioned and which will be brought out again in the discussions of particular selections. The personnel of the groups includes almost all those musicians most central in the formation of the fusion style.

Our discussion of fusion will treat that background and formation, beginning with three pianists also noted for their work with Davis—Keith Jarrett, Herbie Hancock, and Chick Corea. Our first example of real fusion—or, perhaps, of the connecting link between earlier jazz and fusion—is *Miles Runs the Voodoo Down* from *Bitches Brew*. We then turn to the first major fusion group, the ensemble that pointed the way for the 1970s, Weather Report. Finally, we close with two examples from fusion musicians who are still current, the guitarists Pat Metheny and Sonny Sharrock (Sharrock would probably be more accurately described as a "post-fusion" musician).

FREE JAZZ—"THE NEW THING"

➤ *When Malindy Sings*, Oscar Brown, Paul Laurence Dunbar. Abbey Lincoln, vocal; Max Roach, drums; Booker Little, trumpet; Julian Priester, trombone; Coleman Hawkins, Walter Benton, tenor sax; Eric Dolphy, reeds; Mal Waldron, piano; Art Davis, bass. Recorded early 1960s.

Technically, this is probably not a "free jazz" recording, except for its free-form intro and coda. But it was done by a number of musicians at the forefront of what was then called the black pride movement, which continues today as Afrocentrism and which is one of the principal threads running through a great deal of free jazz. This emphasizes traditional expressive means that have been heard in black music since the nineteenth century, and that we discussed in the very first sections of the first chapter of this book, among them immediacy, spontaneity, individual use (often improvised) of a communal tradition. One message is clearly stated in the lyrics, taken from a poem by the great black poet Paul Laurence Dunbar: music is not what the white folks (Miss Lucy) make when they sing from printed sheets and books, but what the servant (or slave) girl Malindy sings when she's outside, in her own natural setting, away from her white masters and as free as she can ever be. But note that there's no rage in this tune, as you can hear in some other black music of the era (or in earlier songs). This is celebration.

Musically the tune is very straightforward: between the intro and coda, when "Malindy" is singing over the ametrical and sustained chords in the band, we get a strophic, 16-bar aa'ba (the first two a phrases will sound to you like the first two phrases of a blues). Lincoln, who in the early 1990s has gotten a great deal of excited critical and popular reactions for her new recordings and concerts, sings three choruses and then yields to a trumpet solo by Booker Little, his melodies in the same vein as hers. She then closes with another chorus in praise of "When Malindy sings." The formal layout is thus just like that of mainstream bop charts (or earlier Swing charts); the texture underneath Lincoln's singing is also bop, with so much of the drive coming from the drums and the bass.

➤   *Out to Lunch*, Eric Dolphy. Eric Dolphy, alto sax; Freddie Hubbard, trumpet; Bobby Hutcherson, vibes; Richard Davis, bass; Anthony Williams, drums. Recorded 1964.

We've already heard Dolphy's work with Mingus, on *Hora Decubitus* (1963, Chapter Three). In his liner notes to the album *Out to Lunch*, Dolphy said:

> This is a recurring figure around an improvised chorus. This figure, in 5/4, sets the rhythm section up with a definite solo feeling. In the improvised sections, the rhythms overlap. The bass follows no bar line at all. Notice Tony [Williams]. He doesn't play time, he plays. Even though the rhythm section breaks the time up, there's a basic pulse coming from inside the tune. That's the pulse the musicians have to play.

Listen to the cut carefully several times, and then go back and reread Dolphy's comments.

Some aspects of this music are familiar to us, others are less so. The overall structure is standard—thematic choruses, the horns in unison to begin and end, with a string of solos in between. But the solos are longer than we're used to, they don't fall into regular choruses, and the kind of playing is new to us. Pay attention to the tremendous variety in the solos. Both Dolphy and Hubbard play free-sounding, angular lines, but both also play phrases or short sections in older styles: Dolphy a regular, bluesy sort of melody during his solo, Hubbard a

"Spanish" kind of line. The bass also uses devices that we haven't heard much before: double-stops, or playing more than one note at a time; glissando, sliding from one pitch to another; and the kind of pitch-bending or circumlocution that we haven't heard from earlier bass players.

Listen, too, to the changes in texture and the relationship or interplay among the musicians; this is what gives the music its overall variety, overall sense of "up" and "down," of tension and release, in short, its shape. After the first, thematic chorus, in which we hear ostinatos in the vibes and then later in the bass, there are the long solos without any chordal accompaniment. (The vibes, a chordal instrument like the piano, is used for melody and percussion here.) You can hear changing metrical patterns in the bass and different simultaneous meters and rhythms in bass, drums, and vibes. Occasionally, most notably during Hubbard's trumpet solo, there is a regular, repeated pulse in the lower instruments. After Hubbard's solo, you hear a terrific duet between drums and bass, with real call-and-response, give and take. Then all drop out except the bass. The ensemble erupts, as if Dolphy and Hubbard were trading 4s over the group background (remember that from Swing), then comes a final drum solo and the concluding thematic chorus.

Not only do the shape and sense of flow of this music come from the interplay of the five musicians. Each of these players himself shows a great variety of rhythms and phrase lengths. Listen once to this and concentrate on the drummer—what does he do with the ride cymbal? What does he do with the rest of his equipment? How is he interacting with the various soloists?

The heart of this music is in its collective improvisation. And, maybe paradoxically, this is easier to hear here than it was back in the New Orleans style; in that music, the front line (clarinet, trumpet, trombone) worked so closely together, and the texture was so much thicker, that they can sound like a single instrument. Here, the instruments are so different in timbre and in activity that you can separate them quite easily and listen to what each is doing individually, as well as combine them in their spare texture to hear the collective ensemble. It's the style of the music, not the format, which may be new to you. That style and its texture, however, are straightforward and easy to *hear*; so one simply needs to learn how to *listen* to it.

➤ *Lonely Woman*, Ornette Coleman. Ornette Coleman, alto sax; Don Cherry, trumpet; Charlie Haden, bass; Billy Higgins, drums. Recorded 1959.

➤ *Congeniality*, Ornette Coleman. Same personnel, same date as *Lonely Woman*.

These two tunes from the same recording session give us two different sides of Ornette Coleman's personality, but at the same time they also give us the stylistic similarity that underlies his different compositions. Coleman has gone on, since his early days, to learn violin and trumpet as well as alto sax; he has done large compositions; he made a terrific recording with the guitarist Pat Metheny, *Song X*; and he formed a sometimes-free-sometimes-funk band, Prime Time, that includes his son Denardo on percussion. If his general popularity has never matched his critical acclaim, he is still a great musician with an enormously original voice in the twentieth-century Afro-American tradition.

Lonely Woman is a gorgeous and sad song, a dirge like Mingus's *Goodbye Pork Pie Hat* and the MJQ's *Django*. Again, the music is based on a melody—the elegiac, additive tune—and the melody's mood. The mood is set from the very beginning, with the soft drums and bass leading into the theme. The form of the song is basically aaba, but those phrases aren't smooth, continuous 8-bar units; rather, they sound additive, with solo breaks filling them out (remember the 2-plus-2 phrase structure so common in earlier jazz and blues). But the a phrases are all

Ornette Coleman. Courtesy of the Rutgers Institute of Jazz Studies.

like one another and contrast with the b̲ phrases. (The a̲ phrases are those arching, "lonely" sounding lines of the title; the b̲ phrases begin with that short rising figure in the trumpet.) Listen to the bass and the drums as well. The bass often plays dronelike figures, harmonically and melodically very static, but rhythmically keeping the music moving forward. What is the drummer doing? How does that fit with the bass and the soloists? Could you make any connections between *Lonely Woman* and Coltrane's *Naima* and *Alabama*?

The mood and feelings of *Congeniality* match the title just as exactly as those of *Lonely Woman*. The overall layout also resembles that of *Lonely Woman*. The solo improvisations here all come out of the various tunes and melodic motives, from the opening thematic chorus and from the new ones that evolve in the course of the solos. What you want to try to do here is breathe with the soloists: that will show you immediately where the phrases are, and (the same thing in different words) where the musical units or thoughts are. Once you've listened to the melodies and assimilated them, go back and tune into the rest of the ensemble. Not only are the texture and layout like those of *Lonely Woman*, they're exactly like those we've heard in bop; the rhythm work in the bass and drums also resembles what we heard in the 1950s. At the same time, from the very nature of the ensemble, the texture is like that of the "cool jazz" Lee Konitz/Gerry Mulligan *All the Things You Are*. You might want to remember Louis Armstrong, too, in the verve, the ebullience, and the swing of this music. *Congeniality* has a lot of connections to earlier jazz, and of different types of jazz. What's new here are the freedom and the irregularity in the melody and phrase lengths, the emphasis on tonal coloration (especially Coleman's wonderful and original combination of the sweet with the raspy). Even such "congenial" music as this is sometimes hard for newcomers to get a grasp on, because it doesn't give you the repetitive framework of regular choruses or even sometimes the bedrock of constant meter to hook into. At the same time, those same aspects are often absent in fusion, rock, and these days rap. It's a matter of learning a new dialect. Once you've done that, learned to hear it on its own terms, free jazz will speak to you as directly as any other kind of music.

Charlie Parker used to say about the days when he was moving from Kansas City-style Swing to bop (the "new thing" of its era) that sometimes he could hear it in his mind, but he couldn't play it. His achievement was learning to play, to produce, the music his mind had already intuited. Ornette Coleman made a similar often-quoted remark about his own evolution, to the effect that when he figured out that he could make *mistakes* in his new style, he knew he was onto something. In other words, freedom isn't chaos.

➤ *Free Jazz* (excerpt), Ornette Coleman. Ornette Coleman, alto sax; Don Cherry, Freddie Hubbard, trumpet; Eric Dolphy, bass clarinet; Scott LaFaro, Charlie Haden, bass; Billy Higgins, Ed Blackwell, drums. Recorded 1960.

This group, an octet (eight players), can be regarded as a double quartet, two similar groups of four:

alto sax	bass clarinet
trumpet	trumpet
bass	bass
drums	drums

They're identical except for the difference in reeds. Both alto sax and bass clarinet have wide ranges (especially with players like Coleman and Dolphy) and can overlap. But they have different timbres, and the bass clarinet's normal range is much lower than that of the alto sax.

The personnel on this recording is a combination of Coleman's quartet with Dolphy and Hubbard, whom we heard earlier on *Out to Lunch* and other tracks, Blackwell on drums, and Scott LaFaro, the bassist we heard with Bill Evans. LaFaro was one of the great modern bassists, and this is an example of his versatility.

Free Jazz is an excerpt from an album-long composition by the same title, some 10 minutes here from a total of about 37'. You might try to find a copy of the whole thing and listen to it. It's not unusual for free-jazz compositions to take up an entire recording as in this case, or a whole 60- or 90-minute live set in a club or concert. But the variety of styles and musics that one hears in the course of such an extended composition is tremendous, and the overall impact can be overwhelming.

I emphasized in the bop sections of Chapter Four that that is a multilayered music, and that one has to be able to take the layers apart and put them back together in order really to hear what's going on. It's the same thing for free jazz—but not only do you want to be able to separate all the strands that you hear at any one time, you also need to distinguish the short successive sections one from another. When are the basic rhythms straightforward and simple (there are even some very "funky" places in *Free Jazz*); when does the collective improvisation build up in polyrhythms? When are there ostinatos, when is everything freer? Also, contrast Coleman's playing with Dolphy's: Coleman often seems closer to bop-style playing, more lyrical and less further "out." How do the reeds work with the trumpets, all four of these horns used here as melodic instruments? All of this is to say: the general free-jazz characteristics that I noted in the introductory essay and under the selections above apply here as well. These questions are the sort that you can ask yourself to direct your listening and to hear this particular cut.

➤ *Enter Evening*, Cecil Taylor. Cecil Taylor, piano and reeds; Eddie Gale Stevens, Jr., trumpet; Jimmy Lyons, alto sax; Ken McIntyre, oboe; Henry Grimes, Alan Silva, bass; Andrew Cyrille, drums. Recorded 1966.

This is another extended selection, this time from Taylor's recording *Unit Structures*. You can apply here the same descriptions and questions that we've discussed earlier. But in addition, listen to the distinctive sounds of Taylor's unit. The beginning of *Enter Evening* is very gradual, very "pointillistic," to borrow a term from the visual arts, slowly building up from isolated notes and gestures to fuller textures, longer phrases and sections. The music itself is also "entering." The composition is very impressionistic in its way—the muted trumpet, the twilight-sounding figures from the other instruments, the quietness of the whole piece. Again, pay attention to the variety of timbres in this cut and to the *new* sounds whose like we haven't heard before. In some cases, you may not even be able to identify the particular instruments— but try. This expansion of instrumental possibilities was common to both jazz and "classical" music in the 1960s, and foreshadows the cooperation and mutual explorations by jazz musicians and younger "classical" composers and performers since the early 1970s. (This parallels the move of some fusion musicians into "classical" realms, too.) In many ways, *Enter Evening* sounds much "freer" than any of the other selections we've discussed here: is it still jazz? Why? What connections can you hear to other jazz, to the historical traditions of jazz?

➤ *Thème de Yoyo*, Beasley, Lester Bowie, Malachi Favors, Roscoe Mitchell. The Art Ensemble of Chicago: Roscoe Mitchell, saxes, clarinet, flute, percussion; Joseph Jarman, saxes, flutes, percussion; Lester Bowie, trumpet, fluegelhorn, percussion; Malachi Favors, acoustic bass, electric bass, percussion; Don Moye, drums; Fontella Bass, vocal and piano. Recorded 1970.

Thème de Yoyo (*Yoyo's Theme*) comes from the soundtrack to a French film entitled *Les Stances à Sophie* (*Sophie's Stanzas*). As I mentioned in the essay at the beginning of this chapter, the Art Ensemble turns to a range of sources for its music on this album—R & B, "funk," free jazz, a theme of the Italian Baroque composer Monteverdi, among others. One can also see the collective nature of ensemble from the number of composers listed for the music, and in the number of instruments each musicians plays. Take this cut as a small example of the Art Ensemble's virtuosity, and enjoy it. Separate the various elements—the basic riff, the free-jazz breaks, Fontella Bass's singing (she is known for both her gospel and her R & B work), the way she works over the instrumental sections, and so on—and then put them back together again. How do they all fit in?

If this section gives us only a taste of the variety and the possibilities of free jazz in general, this cut is only the barest introduction to the Art Ensemble of Chicago, whose motto is "Great Black Music: Ancient to Modern." Collectively and in the music they make individually, the Art Ensemble and their "parent" organization, the Association for the Advancement of Creative Musicians (AACM) are some of the most exciting contemporary music you can hear. Look out for their recordings and especially their live performances.

FUSION, BEFORE AND AFTER

➤   *Lalene*, Keith Jarrett. Keith Jarrett, solo piano. Recorded 1971.

Jarrett, like the pianists Herbie Hancock and Chick Corea (see the following selections), work in Miles Davis's groups and performed extensively as a soloist. More recently he has also turned to "classical" music, especially J. S. Bach, Mozart, and Shostakovich. Much of his earlier work, such as this tune, is closely related to the general 1970s fusion trend, but he can't be shut completely up in that box. (One of my purposes here anyway is to demonstrate the musical variety of the players too often labeled and even dismissed with the epithet "fusion.") He also turns to earlier musics and jazz traditions, like the Art Ensemble, and his playing at any given time seems to depend on the format—solo, duet, small group, *which* small group specifically—and on the particular stage of his career. *Lalene* is a wonderful and compact performance from the days when Jarrett was better known and received in Scandinavia and Germany than he was generally in the United States. In this cut, the swing of the rhythms and the blue notes that he coaxes from the piano—reminiscent of the sort of playing Joe Zawinul did with Cannonball Adderley in the late 1950s—are always gentle, no matter how insistently they move. Jarrett alternates this main beginning section with swirling melodic runs and passages of big, full chords; and the

Keith Jarrett. Music Division, The New York Public Library for the Performing Arts, Astor, Lenox and Tilden Foundations.

effect of this is, in its way, like that of sectional free jazz, an ebb and flow of musical intensity. Jarrett is associated with fusion, with "funk," with various substyles of jazz, but like many other contemporary artists, he's primarily an individual voice on the general current scene.

➤ *The Law of Falling and Catching Up*, Chick Corea. Chick Corea, piano; Miroslav Vitous, bass; Roy Haynes, drums. Recorded 1968.

➤ *Bossa*, Chick Corea. Same personnel, same date, as *The Law of Falling and Catching Up*.

Both these tunes come from Corea's landmark 1968 recording *Now He Sings, Now He Sobs*. Corea's playing career has been every bit as varied as those of Jarrett and Herbie Hancock: in the early 60s he played hard bop and Latin-infused jazz; he played with Miles Davis; he has played with various electronic and acoustic groups under his own name, including the band called Return to Forever; and in recent years he has returned at times to a sort of post-Bill Evans kind of jazz tradition.

But these two cuts are entirely different in techniques and effects. *The Law of Falling and Catching Up* is done completely *inside* the piano, plucking strings, sweeping across them, stopping them directly with his hands to change the timbre, and so on. (These are techniques that appeared in American "classical" music with the compositions of Henry Cowell, a California composer, in the 1920s and 1930s. They were very common in American music especially in the 1960s.) These untraditional sounds are echoed by Vitous and Haynes for a real timbral continuity among the instruments, not the distinctions we're used to. The music is ametrical, which does not mean that it doesn't have rhythm. It also uses timbre and texture instead of melody. How would you compare or contrast this to Cecil Taylor's *Enter Evening* in the previous section? Keep these sounds in mind when we get to Weather Report, below. As ever in this chapter (and, indeed, with some of our examples going back to Ellington), is this jazz? Does the question matter?

Bossa is a more traditional tune, a lilting ballad that swings along at an infectious moderate tempo. Corea plays sustained chords with his left hand and lyrical, singable melodies with his right. The Latin flavor comes first from the drums, but then moves into Corea's playing as well. (Corea has always been known for his Latin playing.) Toward the end the bass becomes increasingly active, also with a Latin kind of swing, but the rhythms never become aggressive or hard-edged. All in all, this is the same sort of gentle romanticism that we've heard already from Jarrett and will also hear in this section from Hancock and Pat Metheny. Does it remind you at all of the piano playing of Bill Evans?

➤   *Maiden Voyage*, Herbie Hancock. Herbie Hancock, piano; Freddie Hubbard, trumpet; George Coleman, tenor sax; Ron Carter, bass; Anthony Williams, drums. Recorded 1965.

This cut includes a number of Miles Davis alumni and is an example of preelectric Hancock. (We also heard Hubbard and Williams in the free jazz sections, above.) This music might remind you of the Miles Davis of the late 1950s or the relaxed, modal music of Coltrane from the same era. What will feed into the fusion to come is the static, gleaming texture of the music, the filled-out backdrop for the various solos. This texture is the product, as it will be in fusion, of the steady, repetitive keyboard chords and bass, and especially of the drummer's use of the cymbals to create a sort of sheen, or "wash," around the sound.

Herbie Hancock. Music Division, The New York Public Library for the Performing Arts, Astor, Lenox and Tilden Foundations.

The melodies here are simpler than any we've heard in quite some time. In part, this has to do with the immediate musical concerns: Hancock's composition is an impressionistic portrait of the sea, as he makes clear in the liner notes, and in this particular section of the album *Maiden Voyage*, a portrait of the silent sea at dawn. But in a more general way, this new simplicity or directness in the melody is a sign of change from earlier music, a reaction to the more active complexity of bop and its succeeding styles. Such simplicity (or simple-mindedness, according to its critics) will continue in the jazz to come.

➤ *Miles Runs the Voodoo Down*, Miles Davis. Miles Davis, trumpet; Wayne Shorter, soprano sax; Bennie Maupin, bass clarinet; Chick Corea, Larry Young, electric piano; Jim Riley, percussion; Lenny White, Jack DeJohnette, Charles Alias, drums; Harvey Brooks, Fender bass; Dave Holland, bass; John McLaughlin, electric guitar;. Recorded 1969.

You may want, at this point, to go back and listen again to the Miles Davis music from the previous chapter to renew your acquaintance with him. It's also interesting to listen to Davis's work from the 1960s, which we've had to skip over in this book, and to follow his progression from *Kind of Blue* to *In a Silent Way*, his first electronic music (and, according to a few purists—or pedants—the last Davis album which a real jazz fan would be interested in). We'll pick up Miles Davis when the move to electronic jazz/fusion really occurs, with the 1969 double album *Bitches Brew*.

First of all, consider the instrumentation: trumpet; soprano sax and bass clarinet, the only reeds; electric guitar and Fender bass; acoustic bass; two electric pianos; three separate drummers; and one performer on percussion (again, various kinds of percussive instruments besides the conventional trap set). This roster of only three horns against all those chordal and percussion instruments, fusion's version of the rhythm section, should give you an indication of what this music is going to sound like, of what its textures are going to be. The background is going to be full, from bottom to top. It will be more sustained than that of other kinds of jazz, since electric instruments don't die away immediately like acoustic piano, bass, and guitar. This sustained, constant background will be activated by the rhythms of drums and percussion and the funky ostinatos of the Fender bass, taken over from rock. The texture will be full also because the electric pianos and guitars share much of their ranges, so there are anywhere from two to five people playing in the same register. Electric pianos and guitars are also slightly more similar in timbre than are the acoustic varieties, so there's less distinction of layers in this music than there is in free jazz or earlier styles.

The solos of fusion should present no problems to you at all: they come directly from the earlier jazz styles we're familiar with. But how are they placed over the new background? What sense of phrasing do you get? Can you connect Miles's playing here with his work from the 1950s?

Be sure at this point that you know, intellectually as well as from listening, the distinctions between fusion and free jazz. The two styles are somewhat alike in that compositions tend to be of extended lengths; both use expanded percussion sections and new timbres; both use ostinatos, though fusion music tends to insist on the ostinatos and keep them going throughout an entire work, not just for smaller sections; and both tend to avoid the standard forms, the blues or 32-bar aaba, of earlier jazz. Beyond that, however, the styles are vastly different. The textures, the overall sound, of fusion tends to be much less mobile or varied than those of free jazz, and in general, fusion's textures are much thicker, for the reasons I detailed above. Free jazz tends to concentrate more on melody and the collective improvisation of melodies, without the constant harmonic filler-material of fusion. Free jazz is also much more varied in its meters, rhythms, and tempos. It tends to bring in music from a greater variety of sources than does fusion, although as I said in the introduction to this chapter, fusion jazz also incorporates elements of Latin and European musics, both pop and jazz. Finally, one of the most obvious differences is the presence or absence of electronic instruments—they are usually the mainstay of fusion groups, and are generally *absent* in free jazz ensembles.

The apparent barriers between fusion, free jazz, and the still-continuing older styles have given rise to acrimonious debates among musicians, critics, and jazz fans. Such disputes aren't new to jazz or, in fact, to any sort of art. And they are probably not of much importance in the long run, either. Personal preferences are one's own business. The point is not to take sides, but to be able to appreciate all these styles: it shouldn't matter to anyone but ourselves whether we as individuals *like* fusion more than free jazz, more than bop or whatever. Jazz is such a rich music in all its aspects that we should learn to appreciate as much of it as we can, to know what's going on, to be able to listen as well as possible to its different styles, to expand our ears. Unfortunately, that is impossible for many people.

➤ *Milky Way*, Wayne Shorter, Joe Zawinul. Weather Report: Wayne Shorter, soprano sax, reeds; Joe Zawinul, electric and acoustic piano; Miroslav Vitous, bass; Airto Moreira, percussion; Alphonse Mouzon, drums. Recorded 1972.

➤ *Orange Lady*, Joe Zawinul. Weather Report: as for *Milky Way*.

➤ *Surucucú*, Wayne Shorter. Weather Report: Wayne Shorter, reeds; Joe Zawinul, electric and acoustic keyboards; Miroslav Vitous, bass; Eric Gravatt, drums; Dom Um Romao, percussion. Recorded 1972.

➤ *Directions*, Joe Zawinul. Weather Report: as *Surucucú*.

It makes some sense to treat these four selections as a group, as different manifestations of a single style and its possibilities, rather than as distinct compositions. These four selections come from Weather Report's first two albums, *Weather Report* and *I Sing the Body Electric*, two recordings which made an enormous impact with the general public and with musicians as well. These cuts exemplify Weather Report's early style, their concerns and innovations, and their energy.

Milky Way is a striking beginning (it is the first cut on their first album)—the sounds are impressionistic, galactic, but they are produced with only acoustic piano, soprano sax, and studio manipulation of the tapes. The other three cuts (the last two of them from a live recording) are more standard electronic jazz, closer to Miles Davis's

Miroslav Vitous. Music Division, The New York Public Library for the Performing Arts, Astor, Lenox and Tilden Foundations.

Bitches Brew but yet different from Davis's music in the variety of devices and musics they encompass.

Listen to these selections with the same guidelines that we've used all along in this section: what are the textures like? how do the soloists work over the percussion and drums? what's the role of the bass? of the keyboards? Next, how is the music put together in time? What distinguishes one section from another? (This has to do with the questions you've just asked yourself about textures.) What kind of phrasing do you hear? What are the melodies like? How about harmony and rhythm—are they static, moving, both in turn? Finally, as with free jazz above, what makes this jazz at all? Can you hear any connections with earlier styles, or has the jazz/rock hybrid developed into a new music which is really in fact neither?

➤ *Yolanda, You Learn*, Lyle Mays, Pat Metheny. The Pat Metheny Group: Pat Metheny, sitar, slide guitar, synclavier guitar; Lyle Mays, piano, synthesizers; Steve Rodby, bass guitar; Pedro Aznar, voice, bells; Paul Wertico, drums. Recorded 1984.

Pat Metheny has been one of the most famous fusion musicians since he arrived on the scene in the 1970s. He is also very versatile, having toured and recorded (as leader) with Dewey Redman, better known as a free-jazz tenor sax player, and done the widely noted album with Ornette Coleman, *Song X*. He is best known, of course, as a guitar virtuoso and a musical romantic. He likes melodies, and his tunes are lyrical, forthright, and listener-friendly. All of this, except perhaps for his technical virtuosity, is exemplified on this cut from his 1984 recording *First Circle*.

The tune begins with real rock-and-roll drumming, followed by the rest of the rhythm section, and leading into the soaring, Latin-esque principal melody. The point here, as with many Metheny compositions, is the tune, whence comes much of the joy of the music. The melody is propulsive through its long phrases and the sustained notes over fast and energetic rhythm work. The texture of the whole cut is clear, emphasizing light, transparent sounds. The harmonies are equally open and uncomplicated. What you hold in your mind's ear after the tune is over, in fact, may be just the melody and the underlying rhythm playing. The youthful freshness of this music is infectious.

➤   *Little Rock*, Sonny Sharrock. Sonny Sharrock, electric guitar; Pharoah Sanders, tenor sax; Elvin Jones, drums; Charnett Moffett, acoustic bass. Recorded 1991.

We close out this chapter with a very different sort of "fusion" music, one that stems from a different kind of earlier rock and with direct connections to contemporary free jazz. The music on this recording, *Ask The Ages*, comes from the R & B, funk, and soul of the 1950s and 1960s, the rock-guitar playing of Jimi Hendrix, and the free jazz of the 1960s to the present. Given the personnel of the recording, this isn't surprising: Pharoah Sanders was a free-jazz sax player with Coltrane and others in the 1960s; Elvin Jones also played as part of Coltrane's "classic" quartet, having come from hard-core hard-bop Detroit with his brothers Thad and Hank; the young Charnett Moffett comes from a family at home in all jazz styles, but especially dedicated to progressive jazz. Some of the tunes on the recording emphasize one of these elements at the expense of others. The cut *Who Does She Hope To Be?*, for example, sounds very much like a 1950s kind of slow-dance R &B number. The present number, *Little Rock*, emphasizes the R & B and the post-Hendrix kinds of rock, over rhythm-section textures and sounds of free jazz.

The main lick of *Little Rock*, played four times in succession at the beginning of the tune and then again three times toward the end, sounds like a Memphis or Southwestern soul riff, from the funky swinging rhythm to the unison sound of electric guitar and tenor sax. This riff kicks us into Sharrock's extended solo, using fuzz-tones and jazzy (or jazz/rocky) rhythms that sometimes recall Hendrix at his most ecstatic and bluesy. Sharrock's range is enormous, and he exploits it to the utmost. His playing is intense in a way that we really haven't heard in this fusion section, and that, too, can be heard as coming from the free jazz side of the street, as well as from rock guitarists. The backdrop to Sharrock's playing is the driving textures, more like free jazz than like any rock or any other fusion, of the bass/drums rhythm section. This continues under Pharoah Sanders's solo, very much post-Ornette Coleman in its style. We then hear a duet from the bass and drums—and it is a real duet, neither taking precedence—the original riff (three times), a return to the bass and drum duet, and then, a little surprisingly, a quick fade.

It should be glaringly obvious at this point that, as labels, neither "free jazz" nor "fusion" tells us much about whatever music they're applied to. Given the similarities that one might point to—kinds of ensemble, texture, presence or absence of electric instruments, any two given musicians' biographies—as *groups*, neither the recordings in the first half of this chapter, under the rubric "Free Jazz" nor those in the second half really form a coherent and distinct style comparable to the Swing of the 1930s and 1940s. Indeed, as I've indicated, the question "What kind of jazz is this?" can often lead these days directly to the question "Is this jazz?" And that is a swamp it usually does not pay to enter.

To a certain degree, that situation continues to the present day. On any given night in a music capital like New York, or in an area that has a number of college jazz radio stations, you can still hear everything from "traditional" (i.e., New Orleans) jazz through swing and bop to free and fusion. But the past ten years or so—the last half of the 1980s and the beginnings of the 1990s—have produced a kind of retrenchment movement. Very different musicians are looking at jazz's history and heritage and using these to rather different ends. These returns to, and reuses of, jazz history will be the subject of Chapter Five.

➤ Chapter 5

Recent Events
(That's It)

To describe current situations in any format intended to last longer than the time it takes to read those descriptions is asking for trouble. This chapter does not pretend to be comprehensive. What I do want to do is indicate some of the trends of jazz in today's clubs and studios, and to describe some of the most recent examples. My perspective, like any contemporary writer's, is incomplete; what you can do as a corrective is go to any concerts in your area, turn on your local (especially college) radio stations—television, alas, doesn't know what to do with jazz except try to pretend it doesn't exist—and talk to people at your local record store. Wherever you live, I'm certain you will hear the kinds of contemporary jazz I describe here. You will also hear much more.

Everything that has happened in jazz's almost 100 years can be heard today—not just on historic recordings, but live as well. Many musicians are returning to earlier styles or material, and there is as well a "jazz repertory movement" that aims to keep historic compositions and arrangements alive. The best-known examples of this are probably the Lincoln Center Jazz Orchestra, led by trumpet player Wynton Marsalis; the Carnegie Hall Jazz Orchestra, led by trumpet player Jon Faddis; and the big band at the Smithsonian Institute in Washington, D.C., cofounded by Gunther Schuller and David Baker, and now led by Baker.

This jazz repertory movement has also been a matter of great contention. This is not just the usual reinterpretation of earlier standards by current players, like Ella Fitzgerald doing an up-to-date version of *St. Louis Blues*. Rather, musicians return to the very arrangements of an earlier band, rehearse and perform them anew, usually with solos (if there are any in the original) that are not note-for-note copies, but new improvisations still in the style of the original. Some musicians and writers have said that such a repertory movement is in fact the death of jazz, placing its relics in glass museum cases instead of continuing and developing its traditions and making new music, that enshrining jazz as "America's Classical Music" is in fact stifling it. Those in favor of the jazz repertory movement, of course, feel that they have no apologies whatsoever to make for resuscitating great compositions and arrangements, which have been long unheard, and performing them live for the first time in decades. What has been unpleasant, though, is accusations of jealousy from one side or the other and the fairly bitter recriminations that have occasionally overshadowed the musical concerns. Along with this has been the even more unpleasant racial antagonism that has sometimes bubbled to the surface in recent debates, with accusations of racism coming from both black and white musicians. However, such discussions, arguments, and recriminations are also part of everyday life in the United States; the situation in jazz is a focused and specific example of American society at large.

To return to the discussion of today's extraordinary musical variety: it is often impossible to place any jazz musician within a particular school, since (perhaps because of the growth of formal jazz education) even the young players are expected to be able to handle "the fundamentals"—usually standards performed in a 1950s or post-1950s style— as well as be able to express themselves in a more personal idiom. Some of the greatest and most noted musicians of the day—for example, Wynton Marsalis and Lester Bowie, to choose two very different trumpet players from the selections below—are at home in any number of styles. Many players associated with Miles Davis in the 1960s and fusion in the 1970s have "returned" to earlier styles, or even moved into playing "classical" music or working with "classical" musicians. As has happened in jazz history since its very beginnings, what particular musicians play often depends on the venue and the audience.

In any case, today's principal jazz language, its mainstream, is still the bop style that developed in the 1940s and 1950s. This has become jazz's "classical" language, and anyone who is familiar with the music called jazz in the 1950s will still be at home in clubs and concerts today. But many dialects and new voices exist, and there seem to be two major trends in contemporary jazz. The first of these is usually called "neo-

classic" (sometimes dismissed as "neoconservative") or "the jazz repertory movement" that I mentioned above; this movement is based on the
belief that such great music as is available in the history of jazz should
not be left to languish in somebody's attic, but should be heard. Not
everything that is available in scores is equally available on recordings.
In addition, live performances almost always, if they're any good, have
more presence, more passion and drive than studio recordings. So if it's
not possible for today's audiences to hear, say, Duke Ellington live, it is
still more than worthwhile to hear his music performed live by a band
that knows what it's doing. Furthermore, for those younger players still
coming up in the ranks, the experience of playing earlier music will
seep into their own work; this has been the case since Fletcher Henderson and Louis Armstrong played blues behind Bessie Smith in the
1920s. For some musicians and writers who dislike recent directions
like free jazz and fusion, this is heaven-sent: jazz will *finally* get back to
business. For others, as I've said, this represents musical ossification,
since for them the essence of jazz tradition is its constant change, and
"neoclassicism" means death.

A second principal current trend is also one that returns to jazz's
roots, or indeed may never have left them. This is the movement that
goes back to the sounds of work songs and gospel, or of other black
musics, but uses these sounds for new and original compositions and
improvisations. The Art Ensemble of Chicago was an example of this in
Chapter Four. Other bands use the music of James Brown, Janet Jackson, and other contemporary black artists. The end result is often
unpredictable: you may get a straight-ahead gospel or soul tune; you
may move into free-jazz kinds of improvisation; you may hear anything. The singer/pianist Nina Simone used to say frequently, "With
me you never hear the same show twice, and when I'm flying, you
never hear it once." This trend of returning to, or at least emphasizing,
black roots might also be expanded to the recent interest among all
kinds of U.S. musicians in music of other cultures, the so-called World
Music (or World Beat, sometimes World Pop) phenomenon. It is not
uncommon to hear especially the younger generation of jazz musicians
bring in licks from Latin, African, Asian, and European folk musics and
incorporate them into their compositions and improvisations.

So, herewith a handful of examples of the current jazz scene.
Because of the fluid nature of today's scene, and because of the dangers
inherent in trying to single out any particular artist, composition, or CD
as "representative," the format of this chapter will not be that of the
earlier ones. Instead, I want to discuss certain trends, cite examples at
greater or lesser length, and make a few comparisons. Again, I make no
pretense of these selections being completely representative. They are

meant only to exemplify some of the things that have happened in the jazz universe since the 1970s. To find out what has really happened, you'll have to take over. Turn on the radio, read music magazines, talk to your friends, go to concerts. As I've tried to stress since the very beginning of this book, jazz is a *living* phenomenon. Until you've heard it live, in fact, I don't believe you've heard it. So don't stop now: keep listening.

THE JAZZ REPERTORY MOVEMENT

The most famous example of this is no doubt the trumpet player Wynton Marsalis, one of jazz's current "stars" beyond the jazz world and a highly influential and active musician. He is also a "classical" trumpet virtuoso and a composer, and in fact was awarded a Pulitzer Prize for his large-scale jazz oratorio *Blood on the Fields*. In 1991 Marsalis and the Lincoln Center Jazz Orchestra did a concert, recorded live, of musical portraits by Duke Ellington, including a *Portrait of Louis Armstrong* with Marsalis playing the "Armstrong" part. Ellington, as we know, did musical "portraits" throughout his life. The *Portrait of Louis Armstrong* comes from Ellington's *New Orleans Suite*, first performed at the New Orleans Jazz Festival in 1970 and recorded later that year. (Other portrait subjects from the suite include Sidney Bechet and Mahalia Jackson, the "second line" of jazz bands and the "Bourbon Street Jingling Jollies," as well as a movement entitled "Thanks for the Beautiful Land on the Delta.") The piece was originally written with the trumpet of Cootie Williams in mind.

The piece is an aaba. Marsalis leads the first two choruses, the band sounding much hotter and brassier than does the Ellington original recording. It's a much more 1990s sound than a strict recreation of the Ellington band, and the Lincoln Center Jazz Orchestra also plays this tune at a slightly faster tempo than the Ellington orchestra did. Marsalis's solo in the first chorus is high and burning, occasionally using some of Cootie Williams's growls, driving the band on, and with a tone much closer to Louis Armstrong's than to, say, Diz's or Clifford Brown's. (Marsalis is also from New Orleans.) All this continues into the second chorus, where in the bridge Marsalis quotes the "Habañera" from Georges Bizet's opera *Carmen* (1875), a favorite of Armstrong's and of many bop trumpet players as well. (It gets an appreciative chuckle from the audience.)

This is followed by an ensemble chorus that yields to a trumpet cadenza over a bass pedal, with "stop-time" chords from the rest of the orchestra. During this cadenza Marsalis may or may not quote *When You're Alone* and other standards; again, as that music lover noted years ago, "We've only got 12 notes—everything is going to sound like something else." The end of the cadenza is a teaser, like the end of Ella Fitzgerald's *Air Mail Special*, before Marsalis hits the high, hard one to close out.

In what way is this music a "portrait" of Louis Armstrong? If you heard it without knowing the title, would you have thought of him?

A different sort of repertory band is the Mingus Big Band, which plays weekly in New York and has put out a number of terrific recordings. The band is bigger than almost any ensemble Mingus himself was able to put together during his lifetime, some 20 players. It was started in 1991 and as its name implies dedicates itself to the compositions of Mingus. Three of their most popular recordings are *Nostalgia in Times Square* (1993), *Gunslinging Bird* (1995), and *Que Viva Mingus!* (1997). Most of this music was rarely performed after Mingus's death in 1979 until his widow founded the band. The group is a real generational (and racial) mix, and their music is extraordinary. Mingus, of course, like Ellington encompassed the whole history of jazz and its black roots in his compositions and performances, as well as his "Latin" music as portrayed in *Que Viva Mingus!* The Mingus Big Band makes that all live again—sort of a double repertory movement, Mingus himself being an original one.

The music on the Mingus Big Band's recordings is much more varied than that which I discussed above in Chapter Three. This has to do primarily with the size of the group. The colors and mix of colors may remind you of Ellington, although the Mingus group often has a heavier feel. The charts include Mingus's love of stacking up melodies and his unusual, *sui generis* musical forms. Here too, as in the small group charts, he is not afraid to switch gears in the middle of a piece, to juxtapose different meters, tempos, and textures (cf. *Don't Be Afraid, The Clown's Afraid, Too* from *Nostalgia in Times Square,* or indeed almost any of the charts). Mingus's music really has a message—it has a lot of messages—and the Mingus Big Band conveys them with real panache and excitement. It is this excitement, as well as the enormous variety of the music itself and its connections to all kinds of other musics, that helps swell the band's audiences. They often pull a younger crowd than you might see in other jazz clubs. Even though this is a kind of revival of music from an earlier generation, there is not the slightest whiff of the museum in the band's performances. The Mingus Big Band makes his music contemporary.

Another kind of return to the past is the so-called Swing revival, accompanied by an increased interest in ballroom dancing, especially Swing-era dances like the lindy. (I've read a number of newspaper articles about this new interest in social dancing on the part of college students and people in their 20s. The articles usually go on at some length, quoting various professional sources, about young people's desire for more societal and sexual structures, and how this desire is achieved in ballroom dancing. For all I know, that's perfectly true; but the articles never seem to mention that doing the lindy is a lot of fun as well.) One example of such music is the group Squirrel Nut Zippers, who started as a garage band in Chapel Hill, North Carolina, and have recently hit the big time. They do a lot of different kinds of music, however; so a more representative example of this "Swing revival" might be the Brian Setzer Orchestra.

To my ears, Setzer's music isn't really Swing. (Remember my frequent cautions about applying labels. They're not interesting in themselves; only the music is.) Sometimes it's reminiscent of a kind of New Orleans sound, but for the most part it's a kind of 50s-retro, but without any post-modern irony or self-consciousness about it. Another way of characterizing it would be as a sort of fusion for the 90s—the rhythm section sounds like 1950s rock & roll or R & B; the use of the sections is straight out of Swing big bands, usually keeping them separate but with lots of call and response and a hot Swing-era timbre; Setzer's singing also sounds like the 1950s, maybe Vegas out of R & B; the instrumental solos are good jazz-funk. Some of the arrangements recall brass writing of the Maynard Ferguson band and the big show bands of the post-World War II era. The group does a lot of numbers written in the 1950s (*Sleepwalk*, a classic slow-dance number, Louis Prima's *Jump, Jive and Wail* from the 1998 CD *The Dirty Boogie*) and a number of Setzer originals in the same mode. Much of the music is also blues or blues based, although Setzer's harmonies are often a lot more varied and original than the music's 1950s roots. And it certainly swings—or jumps.

TRADITIONAL MEANS, NEW MUSIC

Ultimately, virtually every artist working today could be put into this box. But what I have in mind here is music that somehow emphasizes jazz's traditional elements and its black roots while at the same time pushing the music forward, recombining those elements and emphasizing jazz's eternal newness. Just as Ellington was one of the first composers to write "classical" jazz in his suites and portraits, he was one of the first to do this as well, in his "jungle style" and throughout his career. We heard it as well in Mingus's *Haitian Fight Song* and *Hora Decubitus*, in much free jazz, and in the Art Ensemble of Chicago's *Thème de Yoyo*.

A 1998 recording by the Art Ensemble (actually recorded in 1995–1996), *Coming Home Jamaica*, continues this tradition. The tune *Grape Escape* is built over a boogie-woogie bass. *Strawberry Mango* and *Lotta Colada* have the Caribbean sound promised by the recording's title. The Art Ensemble's patented variety in textures, instrumentations, colors, and so on, comes through on every tune, perhaps especially so on *Jamaica Farewell*. All the tunes on the recording are originals, by members of the group, but all of them use musical elements that have been part of jazz since its inception.

The members of the Art Ensemble of Chicago wear other hats as well. Lester Bowie's Brass Fantasy is a brass band, such as we haven't thought of since the early New Orleans days. The differences are its repertory—it plays everything from marches through Swing tunes through Billie Holiday's *Strange Fruit* and James Brown's *Papa's Got a Brand New Bag*, up to Art Ensemble-like new compositions—and the way it plays that repertory, sometimes straight and sometimes in con-temporary guise. Sometimes it does more than one of these things at the same time. An example is the tune Rahsaan Roland Kirk's *Inflated Tear*, taken from a 1989 album called *Serious Fun*; the latter title is a good indication of what's going on.

The music is structurally like a lot of recordings in this chapter. It begins with a gradual intro, sliding into the tune, from the bells, gongs, solo trumpet, and then the rest of the brass. We then hear the tune stated by the brass in close harmony. This is followed by a trumpet solo over brass harmonies and the rhythm section, and a trombone solo over a tuba pedal. This then builds up to the full band texture for the last part of the arrangement, and the end brings back the bells of the begin-ning. What kind of jazz—or maybe what kinds of jazz—does this sound like to you? Can you hear this as related to the fullness and rich variety of the Ellington band?

M'Boom is a percussion ensemble founded and directed by Max Roach, whom we've been listening to since the early 1940s. *That's It*, from the 1992 recording *Live at S.O.B.'s—New York*, is a piece that is not too com-plicated formally, but listen to the rhythms, the interplay of different instruments, the interplay of solo and ensemble, the different colors!

Various percussion instruments come in one by one as an intro—cow bells, traps, bass drum, bells, vibes, marimba and so on, up to the whole group. (For the present, anyway.) The band moves into a series of vamps, built up from the bottom. (Remember the riffs of the Swing-era bands and of Charlie Mingus's *Hora Decubitus*.) The last phrase in what is the thematic chorus is a rising figure in the bass line that also works like a vamp in its repetitive buildup of tension to the final release. Once all these are introduced and put together, listen to how

Max Roach. Music Division,
The New York Public Library
for the Performing Arts,
Astor, Lenox, and Tilden
Foundations.

everything continues to work together, but at the same time everything
remains clear because of the different timbres of the instruments and
their very different rhythms. This is yet another version of contemporary group improvisation. In fact, sometimes it's not clear what's solo
and what's improvisation. How would you tell, with this group, and
with the close association between vamps as main theme and a tune or
two as a theme?

The weird instrument you hear in the second half of the cut is the
musical saw. What's it doing here? Could you connect it with a vocal?
Or is it doing something else?

David Murray, whom we hear elsewhere in this chapter with the World
Saxophone Quartet, was one of the leading composers and performers
of his generation, as soloist, in his quartet and octet, and as leader of
this big band. Two original compositions from his 1984 *Live at Sweet
Basil, vol. 1* (Sweet Basil is a major jazz club in New York), *Lovers* and
Bechet's Bounce, both pay direct tribute to earlier jazz, in their textures,
harmonies, and colors. Having made your way to this point in jazz history, you will doubtless need little guidance from me to find your way
through these formally uncomplicated tunes. But I would like to say a
few words about their general worlds.

Lovers, it will be obvious from the first note, comes from a musician deeply imbued with the work of Ellington and Mingus. The love

of rich, dark colors, the elegant beat that is both relaxed and forward moving, the often thick and always inviting textures, the immediate emotionality of the music, all these are directly in the tradition of Ellington and Mingus, among jazz's pantheon. By the same token, *Bechet's Bounce* goes back to Bechet as one of the first great clarinetists (or reed men in general) and to the "bounce" pieces of his era. The "bounce" of the music is irresistible, and so is the contrast between the old-timey sound of the band and the free-jazz sound of the solos. This is not unlike Mingus's *Hora Decubitus*, but in a lighter vein. One could begin a class in jazz history with these two tunes, pointing out textures, instrumentation, rhythms and colors, all the things we've talked about since the beginning, using these recordings as a kind of summary combination of what the class will cover from start to finish. But at the same time, both tunes are completely of their era, especially in their solos and in their textures.

The World Saxophone Quartet is four men who play all the reeds in various combinations. Usually they play unaccompanied; sometimes they bring in a percussion section or a rhythm section. They have done recordings of Ellington's music and of soul, including a cover of Otis Redding's *Sittin' on the Dock of the Bay* that got a fair amount of air time. This live recording shows their linear descent from the front line of New Orleans jazz, their direct descent from free jazz, and some more evanescent references to other kinds of black music.

Their recording called *Steppin'* begins with a rhythmic pedal in the alto flute and bass clarinet, with a tune in the saxes; this is the thematic chorus of the composition. Then, as with some free jazz, we move from one section, one kind of music, to another; rather than being additive and successive, you have the feeling that there's a large pool of music that these players are moving around in. These sections contrast in texture, tunes, harmonies, and so on. The Quartet alternates sections that are lyrical and legato with music that is rhythmically hopping. As we move along, these things all tend to happen at shorter intervals, or even at the same time; this is modern-day collective improvisation. After moving in the direction of thicker texture and more activity, there comes a section of solos and duets. We hear the group improvisation again, and then we hear an out chorus, a repetition of the opening thematic chorus.

When you're used to the general sound and layout of *Steppin'*, you should listen to it closely for all the resemblances to other kinds of jazz and black music that you know. These are four guys who know their stuff inside and out; what they play, they do not do lightly. How much of the history of jazz can you connect this to? What else is there— what's new?

Amina Claudine Myers is a musician who was associated for many years with the AACM, the same group that gave rise to the Art Ensemble of Chicago in the late 1960s. She comes from strong gospel roots, having performed with Martha Bass, Fontella Bass, and others. She also shares the AACM's dedication to new music springing from traditional roots, and to the Art Ensemble's motto, "Great Black Music—Ancient to Modern." Like much current music, especially that which is closely related to what turned (at least in part) into free jazz, her own compositions defy easy labeling. Her composition *Do You Wanna Be Saved?* (recorded 1983) is an example.

It will be obvious on first listening—on the first ten seconds of the first listening—that this comes straight out of gospel. Myers's singing is like gospel in that it never strays too far from the original tune—since one of the main points of this music is communication, you want to make sure your audience is close to you at all times—but its intensity is unsurpassable. The piano playing also stems from gospel and soul (the latter out of gospel, too, of course), but with maybe a detour through Bud Powell along the way. It's what's always called two-fisted playing, with thick chords, harmonic pedals that (unlike Coltrane's) are energized by the rhythmic drive. Myers's playing in the middle section (more choruses of the strophic tune) is like her singing: the melodies are only longer and more sustained, since neither piano or organ has to breathe, and the whole sounds more like one unit rather than singer and accompanist (even if those two are the same person). She's also overdubbing on herself, so she sets up a kind of call-and-response between piano and organ, also reminiscent of a full gospel texture.

In her performances, Myers does numbers like this, Bessie Smith blues, original "free" tunes, and more, all cheek by jowl. Besides the immediacy of her performance, this makes you hear all the more quickly the close connections between traditional black music and the latest "new" compositions. The same thing happens with other people in this unit—the Art Ensemble, David Murray, the World Saxophone Quartet. It cannot be recommended too strongly that you hear this music in live performance, because you'll realize how everything they play infuses everything else they play, and what an extraordinarily *intra*connected musical universe they (and their listeners) live in.

A final recording I should simply mention in passing is Herbie Hancock's 1998 *Gershwin's World*. Dedicated to George Gershwin compositions, virtually every selection is a different type of arrangement for a different ensemble, and Hancock defines Gershwin's "world" (and his own, as well) as pop, jazz, and classical as well. Hancock has been concentrating on standards with a trio for some years now, rather than continue in the fusion vein of the 1970s and 1980s or the more world-music-oriented work of others, such as Joe Zawinul and Orange Then Blue (see below). But *Gershwin's World* is a step far beyond that kind of jazz mainstream, or any sort of mainstream. It's a fascinating recording.

OTHER GROUPS AND SOLOISTS: "YOUNG LIONS" AND OTHERS

The most recent generation of up-and-coming jazz players is often referred to as the "Young Lions." To a person, they have formidable technical abilities and usually a thorough knowledge of jazz history and traditions. They cover the entire range of jazz instruments. Many of the pianists went through the "University of Betty Carter," but their training and their approaches are extremely various. Most are composers as well.

It proved impossible to pick among the many first-rate young pianists working today. I can simply list the names of Geri Allen, Cyrus Chestnut, Brad Mehldau, Myra Melford, Renee Rosnes, Marcus Roberts. There are many more as well. What does follow below is some notice of young soloists or groups that have attracted a lion's share of ink in recent years.

Unfortunately, I've never heard an Orange Then Blue recording that comes close to the fire and energy of their live concerts. They're an exciting band out of Boston, young people in their 20s and 30s, playing a mix of post-40s big-band jazz (Ellington, Mingus, Gil Evans, the Miles Davis Nonet, George Russell) with new influences and interjections from World Beat or World Music sources—folk songs from Bulgaria or Venezuela, instruments from all over, or as in their tune *Panama*, from the 1989 CD *Funkallero*, simply importing the flavor of Latin America into their original tunes.

Panama begins with a pedal in the trombone, bass, and piano—all a little out of sync, not to make fun of folk musicians but to get the flavor of communal music making—that is always associated with a Latin American dance, the *habañera*. This builds into the first appearance of the tune, aa'bba, in the sax, doubled softly by the trumpet. We also hear a lot of folk or folk-ish instruments—whistles, all the percussion, the bass sounding like a guitar, and so on. What's new, or non-folky, in this chart is its harmonies, especially in the b phrase, and the solos, which are in contemporary jazz idioms. The first solo, on sax, builds up in texture to a climax; this is followed by a trombone solo, with another parallel buildup. Under all this is the continuous pedal figure in the bass.

A section of group improvisation leads into a chordal section, the

Orange Then Blue. Courtesy of Linda Rutenberg.

middle part of the arrangement. The tempo gets faster, and what's interesting here is the rhythm and meter: you'll hear that the "stop-time" chords in the band are offbeat, but can you hear the beat stated anywhere? Finally we get a thematic chorus in close harmony and a fuller texture that builds up to the climax of the arrangement as a whole, and the final fade.

The notes to this recording connect the music to Panamanian folk music and its instruments, and direct the listener to follow a sort of musical journey from the lowlands through the jungles and into the mountains. Is that an appropriate program for this tune?

Orange Then Blue is an exciting, out-of-the-ordinary band. They're also an example of what's going on around the country, away from the New York mainstream, and another case in point of the diversity that is coming into jazz with a new generation of players. The last time something on this scale happened was in the 1970s, with fusion. What are the differences between that generation and this one? Have we had any other non-jazz injections into the jazz mainstream since the 1920s?

Two young tenor men around whom many writers seem to want to build a rivalry (like that between Lester Young and Coleman Hawkins in the 1930s and 1940s) are James Carter and Joshua Redman. Both Carter and Redman are virtuosos on almost all the reeds, not just tenor. Both demonstrate the range of styles that one can expect from almost any first-rank player of their generation. Both are also—obviously, in the best jazz tradition—committed personal voices as well. Carter is usually thought of as the quasi-Hawkins in that particular dichotomy: his playing can be both rougher and more "out" than Redman's usually is, and he is less noted for concentrating on the standards of the jazz tradition. Redman's tone and delivery are often less aggressive than Carter's. He seems to have been easier for older jazz listeners, as well as his own generation, to warm to.

But these generalizations are just that. Carter's playing is always arresting and highly original. Two of his more acclaimed recordings are *In Carterian Fashion* (1998) and *Conversin' with the Elders* (1996). The former is largely originals, with a few traditional or other compositions, using organ and drums (and sometimes bass) as a rhythm section, and other horns on some tunes. *Conversin' with the Elders* is all over the map: Carter does compositions by Buddy Tate, Benny Moten, Lester Young, Harry "Sweets" Edison, Charlie Parker, John Coltrane, Lester Bowie, Anthony Braxton, and himself. His guest soloists are appropriate to the composition: in the same order of pieces, they are Buddy Tate (clarinet and tenor sax) on his own tune and the Benny Moten, "Sweets" Edison (trumpet) on *Lester Leaps In* and his own tune, Larry Smith (alto sax) on the Parker, Hamiet Bluiett (baritone sax) on Coltrane's *Naima* and the Braxton, and Lester Bowie (trumpet) on Bowie's tune and the Carter original. Carter plays both with and against his guests. The music swings; and it's honest and deeply felt.

Like Carter, Joshua Redman has put out a number of recordings; his best known seems to be the 1998 *Timeless Tales (for Changing Times)*. As the title implies, the selections are mostly standards. But they're not necessarily *jazz* standards: Redman also includes tunes by Stevie Wonder, Joni Mitchell, Bob Dylan, Lennon/McCartney, and (the artist formerly known as) Prince. Each of the tunes, jazz standard or no, is given a wonderful treatment that makes it unmistakably contemporary jazz. In addition, Redman also composed interludes that connect many of the tunes to create a longer and more complicated emotional picture. Redman's playing, as I've said, is not usually aggressive, but it is extremely attractive and full of joys. His melodic ideas are very rich and he puts together meaningful solos. His playing has a great deal of variety and his rhythms are particularly exciting. He and Carter are both players to listen to.

Another new voice on the scene is the jazz/funk/power organ trio Medeski, Martin & Wood. They, too, use a lot of elements of earlier jazz, but the sound is new. On the 1998 CD *Combustication* you hear funky organ sounds that may remind you of Amina Claudine Myers (see above), but combined with the contemporary sound of a DJ with a turntable. In some tunes the textures and the variety of rhythms are reminiscent of Weather Report in the early 70s, but also bring in Latin sounds as well. Occasionally their textures are very thick, as in 1960s Coltrane. Some of the tunes, such as *Hey-Hee-Hi-Ho*, are built on riffs and bristle with soul-jazz energy. Their music isn't retro, like that of Brian Setzer; but it is another 1990s kind of fusion of all sorts of elements from various sources, brought into a synthesis that rocks as much as it swings.

The variety of big bands working today mirrors the variety of the jazz scene as a whole. So far in this chapter I've mentioned the various repertory orchestra, Brian Setzer, the Mingus Big Band, the David Murray big band, and others. Two more that are difficult to characterize are those led by Toshiko Akiyoshi and Maria Schneider. Akiyoshi's band is based in New York and well known in this country and her native Japan, as well as in Europe. Schneider stays mainly in Europe and is better known there than in the United States; but she is beginning to get more attention in this country.

Both bands, like the Ellington orchestra, the Mingus Big Band, and others, are primarily the voice of their leaders as composers. Beyond that, they are difficult to categorize. Akiyoshi's band will probably sound more mainstream or traditional to you in its textures and kinds of compositions. Schneider also uses a wide variety of instruments, and her musical voice has echoes of many sources. For some American critics she has been an acquired taste, but her music is fascinating and a wonderful addition to contemporary jazz.

JAZZ AT THE MOVIES

Jazz in the movies goes back to "soundies" in the 1920s, and encompasses concert films, documentaries, biopics about real or fictional jazz musicians, and non-jazz-related movies that have jazz soundtracks. It's impossible even to begin the topic here—those who are interested should start with Krin Gabbard's *Jammin' at the Margins* (see the Bibliography)—but three recent films have been notable for their use of jazz, and the recorded soundtracks make exemplary recordings as well.

The makers of Clint Eastwood's 1988 *Bird*, about Charlie Parker, made a musical decision which has occasioned a great deal of headscratching and commentary by various critics and writers. They returned to Parker's original recordings, but they kept only his playing, to be mimed by the actor playing Parker, Forest Whitaker. The rest of the music was played live by musicians in the film. The resulting sound is a little strange, and it's also a little difficult to know why the film-makers made their decision. In passing, the film is also very unfortunate in its treatment of Parker as a sort of Romantic "noble savage," emphasizing his difficulties and drug problems at the expense of crediting him with the intelligence and the general mind that in fact he had.

Much more satisfying are the 1986 *Round Midnight*, about a fictional sax player based on Bud Powell and Lester Young, and Robert Altman's 1995 *Kansas City*, largely set in a black nightclub, the Hey Hey Club, in the Kansas City of 1934. *Round Midnight*'s soundtrack uses standards of the story's era, played by Dexter Gordon but, as he said, in his own style, not in any imitation of Lester Young or any other 1950s musician. The title cut from the movie, played by Herbie Hancock (piano), Ron Carter (bass), and Tony Williams (drums), with a vocal by Bobby McFerrin, is an example of the mastery by younger musicians of an older style of jazz with which they had not been much associated before. All three of the instrumentalists are known to us, for their work with Miles Davis, fusion, and, in the case of Tony Williams, free jazz as well. But all have become equally adept with this kind of post-bop mainstream sort of music, as well—and not just able students but fluent in the language.

This particular recording is also marked by a kind of smoky French romanticism, due no doubt to its use in the movie. You might want to go back to Chapter Two to listen again to Ella Fitzgerald's version. McFerrin and the trio produce the midnight indigo color of the music through timbre and texture. McFerrin is especially arresting, his voice sounding sometimes more like a muted trumpet (Miles?) than like a singer. In the first of two choruses he stays very close to the original melody, curling around it, as Hancock plays countermelodies against him. All the players exhibit a tremendous rhythmic elasticity that keeps this infinitely slow tune still in motion and gives it pulse. In the second chorus, McFerrin lays out for the first two phrases, and the trio picks up the tempo. This will not sound to you like the Hancock we listened to in Chapter Four: it's much more bop in style, with post-Bill Evans chords and a floating rhythmic freedom above the bass and drums. With the bridge of the second chorus, McFerrin reenters, and the last two phrases gradually return to the emotional world of the first chorus.

What kind of movie would you expect from this title cut? Find it, and see what you think!

An even better example of Young Lions playing old music is *Kansas City*. The music underscores much of the action of the movie and plays a major part in creating its fictional world and its emotional impact. The musicians include 21 first-rate talents over a wide age span, but largely of the new generation: the sax players James Carter and Joshua Redman (here acting out the sort of Coleman Hawkins/Lester Young duel that I mentioned above), David "Fathead" Newman, Craig Handy, and David Murray; bassists Ron Carter, Tyrone Clark, and Christian McBride, still in his early 20s; pianists Geri Allen and Cyrus Chestnut; vocalist Kevin Mahogany as bartender/blues shouter; and many others. Yet all the music of the film is firmly set in the style and time of the story, the wide-open Kansas City of the Depression, just after the repeal of Prohibition. The tunes are from the Kansas City/Southwest Swing era—*Moten Swing*, Ellington's *Solitude*, a number of blues, the standard *I Surrender, Dear*; and the arrangements—almost all new, and some by players Geri Allen and Craig Handy—are equally consistent with time and place. James Carter combines his penchant for "out" playing with solid references to the honking and wailing sax players of the Southwest. All the music sounds contemporary, in both senses: it's fresh today but sounds as equally hip and fresh as it must have in 1934.

It's hard to imagine that such a thorough recreation of a bygone style and setting could have been accomplished by any younger generation of musicians at any point before the present. But this is a testament to today's jazz scene and the knowledge and musicianship of our best contemporary players. As I said in the second paragraph of this chapter, the whole history of jazz can be heard live today. Whatever the merits and demerits of the jazz repertory movement and everything else on the current scene, this situation has existed perhaps only in the 1940s and 1950s, when it was possible to hear on the same night, in the same city, music ranging from the latest bebop to the Swing of the previous era, to the "traditional" jazz that had been revived in part as a reaction against bop. What didn't work with "traditional" (New Orleans) jazz in the 1940s was that some of those whom other musicians called "moldy figs" fell into stagnation precisely because they refused to live through their music; they played only what had already been played. The musicians of *Kansas City*, indeed all those in this chapter, may play old tunes or old-style tunes, even in arrangements of the past. But they all still manage to make it new.

The listener who likes David Murray or Amina Claudine Myers or the Art Ensemble of Chicago or Joshua Redman or Medeski, Martin & Wood can go back and hear, on the one hand, the eternal newness and fresh appeal of the most "traditional" kinds of music, at the same time perhaps learning to hear the traditional elements in the newest. The listener who wants to hear only Ellington, or only Armstrong, or only Billie Holiday, or only Mingus performed as the music was by its originators will end up in the same position as too many of today's "classical" music listeners: able to hear only what they already know, unable to understand, even to begin to decipher anything with an element of the new. These are dinosaurs.

The point, which I have tried to stress throughout these pages, is not that you have to like everything. Promiscuity is not open-mindedness. But I do think it vital, almost literally, that one try to be aware of, and even *understand* every kind of music in the world today, for that is how we learn about the world we live in. To turn your back on people's music is to turn your back on people. Given the world we inhabit, that way lies disaster. It is much more fruitful, I believe, to listen to those musicians who make history as they tell it; for doing so may help us carry our own histories with us throughout our lives. As I have said repeatedly in these pages, keep listening.

Glossary of Musical Terms

additive form: building up a piece by successively adding on phrases and new melodies as the musician wishes, not according to any present patterns such as <u>aab</u> (the form of the blues) or <u>aaba</u> (the form of many jazz and popular compositions). Additive form is most common in prejazz, "folk" music and in post-bop jazz.

attack: the way a note is "hit," or begun.

bar: see **measure**.

blue note: a note played or sung a little bit below its "correct" pitch to give it a more expressive color. Used not only in blues and jazz, but also in much rock and popular music.

break: usually the last 2 measures of a 4- or 8-measure phrase, when the ensemble stops playing and a soloist improvises. The phrases of vocal blues are often 2 measures sung and 2 measures instrumental break.

bridge: the contrasting <u>b</u> phrase in a 32-bar <u>aaba</u> chorus.

cadenza: a virtuoso solo section, usually free in form.

call and response: a way of building up a piece in which a leader calls out a phrase and a group (or another soloist) responds with an answering phrase. This can be heard in prejazz folk music and also in Kansas City swing. An example: one section of the band will "call" out a 2-bar phrase or riff, and another section will answer with a second 2-bar phrase or riff.

chord: three or more notes that are played simultaneously. The main chording instruments in jazz are piano, guitar or banjo, and organ; but sometimes, as in Duke Ellington's *Mood Indigo*, three or more instruments are combined to play chords together.

chorus: see **strophic form.**

circular form: a form in which there is no strong feeling of division into choruses, since the last measure of the basic formal unit feeds seamlessly into the first again. This is in contrast to the *strophic form* (for example blues or aaba), in which there is a strong sense of closure or return at the end of each chorus.

circumlocution: sliding around or embellishing a pitch, instead of attacking it cleanly and holding it.

cross-phrasing: instead of staying within the usual 4- or 8-bar phrase-units, a soloist's melodies fall across those dividing lines, and often result in asymmetrical groupings.

cross-voicing: mixing instruments from different families, for example combining trumpet and trombone (brass section) with clarinet (reed section), as in Duke Ellington's *Mood Indigo.* This is in contrast to the more usual opposition of instrumental sections.

downbeat: the first beat of a measure.

dynamics: relative loudness or softness.

glissando: sliding directly from one pitch to another.

head: an introductory melodic figure, especially in bop.

homophony: see **texture.**

improvisation: creating music spontaneously during performance, as opposed to playing previously composed and written-down music. In jazz there are two principal types of improvisation: 1) *thematic improvisation* is the decorating or embellishing of a given tune, of a melody previously written; 2) *harmonic improvisation* involves discarding the original melody of a piece and creating a new one, using the original piece's chords.

legato: the smooth connecting of notes, with no silences or breaks between them; as opposed to **staccato.**

measure: the unit into which the pattern of strong and weak beats or pulses is grouped. (See the section on ragtime in Chapter One.) Also called **bar.**

meter: the organization of beats or pulses into a regular recurring pattern. (See the section on ragtime in Chapter One.)

modal jazz: a compositional style associated first with Miles Davis, in which a piece is built not on a series of chords, as in earlier styles, but rather on a scale or *mode* from which the musicians can choose the notes for their melodies and chords. Modal jazz is characterized by a very restricted use of chords—only a few chords in a whole chorus, in contrast to the change of chord every measure or half-measure in bop.

monophony: see **texture.**

ostinato: a melodic or rhythmic pattern repeated over and over without interruption. See also **pedal** and **sequence.**

pedal: also known as *drone;* a note or chord that is sustained, usually in a low register, while melodies and rhythms change above it. See also **ostinato** and **sequence.**

phrase: a section of a musical unit or melody, somewhat akin to phrases in language. Most phrases in jazz are 2, 4, or 8 measures long. They are combined into choruses (strophes) or sections.

polymeter: the use of more than one meter at the same time.

polyphony: see **texture.**

register: relative highness or lowness of a note (for example, a trumpet plays in a higher register than a string bass).

rhythm section: the section of a jazz group (small combo or big band) that provides the basic chords and meter. It consists of any or all of the following: piano (sometimes organ); string bass (tuba in early jazz bands); guitar or banjo; and drums.

riff: a short, usually 2-bar rhythmic, melodic, and/or harmonic pattern which serves as the basic musical material of a given phrase or chorus.

scat singing: singing with nonsense syllables instead of words, so that the voice becomes an improvising jazz instrument.

sectional form: building up a piece with a succession of contrasting large sections, as in marches and ragtime. As opposed to **strophic form,** in which the same basic section (called the chorus or the strophe) is repeated over and over.

sequence: the repetition of a melodic figure at a higher or lower pitch level. In contrast to **pedal,** a single sustained note or chord, and to **ostinato,** the repetition of a melodic figure at the same pitch level (not higher or lower than the first time).

staccato: the playing or singing of notes in a short, clipped-off style, so that they are not smoothly connected; as opposed to **legato.**

stop time: a kind of ensemble playing in which one melody instrument plays alone, while the rest of the ensemble comes in with chords only on the downbeat or on every other downbeat.

stride piano: a playing style with an "oom-pah" left hand and a syncopated right hand; often used by ragtime pianists.

strophic form: building up a piece by repeating the same music over and over, the repeated unit being the *strophe* or, more commonly, the *chorus.* In vocal music, each chorus usually has new words. In purely instrumental jazz or blues, each chorus will have a differently improvised melody. The two most common strophic forms in jazz are the 12-bar blues (where the chorus is 12 measures long) and the 32-bar aaba (four 8-bar phrases, each chorus thus 32 measures long).

substitute chords: chords which are substituted for, or added to, the original chords of a composition; usually more complex than those original chords.

syncopation: accentuation of a beat that is normally weak.

tempo: the speed of the basic pulse or beat of a piece.

texture: the number and relationship of instruments or melodic lines. The four principal kinds of texture are: 1) *monophony*, only one melody with no accompaniment at all; 2) *homophony*, one principal voice or melody, with accompaniment; 3) *polyphony*, more than one melody of equal importance at the same time; and 4) *heterophony*, a melody and simultaneous variations of that melody (just variations; not a different melody). Heterophony is relatively rare in Western musics, including jazz.

Notice that it doesn't matter how many voices or instruments are playing any of these melodies. If everybody in a ball park is singing *The Star-Spangled Banner* together, and there's no accompanying organ or band, that's monophony—even if there are 50,000 people singing. If they're all singing *and* they're accompanied by the organ or band, that's homophony. If, say, the game is in Toronto and fans from the United States sing *The Star-Spangled Banner* at the same time that the Toronto fans sing *O Canada*, that would be polyphony.

Texture also has a general, nontechnical sense, referring to the relative fullness or sparseness of sound. In this loose sense, a loud big band is said to have a "fuller" or "thicker" texture than a small combo.

third stream jazz: a style that developed in the early 1950s, associated mainly with the pianist/composer John Lewis, the composer Gunther Schuller, the Modern Jazz Quartet (whose pianist was Lewis), and a few others. It is called "third stream" because it combines "classical" European forms, on the one hand, with jazz harmonies and improvisations on the other. Third Stream has not lasted as a major jazz genre, but it helped broaden jazz's horizons in the 1950s, and many of its contributions have remained in the jazz mainstream.

timbre: the distinctive, characteristic sound of any instrument or voice—the difference in sound between, for example, a trumpet and a saxophone. Also called **tone color.**

tone color: see **timbre.**

trading 4s: two instruments, or a solo instrument and an ensemble, take turns playing 4-bar phrases in alternation. (If they're "trading 8s," their alternating phrases are 8 bars long.) A specific format for **call and response.**

vamp: a short instrumental chord progression played over and over as an introduction (for example, to set the mood until the soloist is ready to start); sometimes appears as a transition section or as an ending.

Discography
Sources of Musical Selections

Of the almost 200 recordings discussed in this book, virtually half are included in *The Revised Smithsonian Collection of Classic Jazz*, a 1987 multi-CD anthology compiled by the critic and writer Martin Williams. (The anthology is not available in record stores, but it may be ordered by writing to: Division of Performing Arts, Smithsonian Institute, Washington, D.C. 20560.) There are also a few recordings from the first version of the *Smithsonian Collection* (1973) which were not retained in the second collection. These appear below marked 1973 *Smithsonian Collection*. Finally, I have also used some recordings from the Smithsonian's 1983 anthology *Big Band Jazz: From the Beginnings to the Fifties* and the 1998 anthology *The Jazz Singers*.

I have listed only the *Smithsonian Collection* for all recordings in the book from that anthology, regardless of whether they are also available on other current recordings. For selections not in the *Smithsonian Collection*, I have used insofar as possible recordings commercially available at the time this book was being written. Unfortunately, of course, this situation changes with the winds, as does what is available on CD at any particular time. For these unanthologized selections, I give the title and manufacturer's serial number for the CD or LP from which they are taken. This should enable the interested listener to track down any recording currently in print.

CHAPTER 1: THE BEGINNINGS

Afro-American Roots

Ol' Hannah, Juliana Johnson, and *John Henry*
  Jazz, vol. 1: *The South.* Folkways FJ 2801.
Freedom Song
  Soul to Soul. Atlantic SD 7207.
Come On Children, Let's Sing
  Mahalia Jackson, *How I Got Over.* Columbia 34073.
Beautiful Dreamer
  Jan DeGaetani, Leslie Guinn, and Gilbert Kalish.
  Songs by Stephen Foster. Nonesuch 71268.

Ragtime

Joplin, *Maple Leaf Rag* (3 versions)
  1. Scott Joplin, piano. *Smithsonian Collection.*
  2. The New England Conservatory Ragtime Ensemble, Gunther
     Schuller, conductor, *The Red Back Book.* Angel 36060.
  3. Jelly Roll Morton, piano. *Smithsonian Collection.*
Morton, *Grandpa's Spells* (2 versions)
  1. The New England Conservatory Ragtime Ensemble, Gunther
     Schuller, conductor, *More Scott Joplin Rags.* Golden Crest
     31031Q.
  2. Jelly Roll Morton's Red Hot Peppers. *Smithsonian Collection.*

The Blues: Early and Classic

Blackwell, *Down South*
  Jazz, vol. 1: *The South.* Folkways FJ 2801.
Johnson, *Hellhound on My Trail*
  1973 *Smithsonian Collection.* Also in Robert Johnson, *The Complete
  Recordings,* Columbia C2K 46222.
Rainey, *Countin' The Blues*
  The Blues, vol. 1: *A Smithsonian Collection of Classic Blues Singers.*
  Sony RD 101-1 A 23982/A 23987.
Wallace, *(I'm a) Mighty Tight Woman*
  Women of the Blues. RCA LPV-534.
Smith, *Lost Your Head Blues*
  Smithsonian Collection.
Smith, *Young Woman's Blues*
  Bessie Smith, *Nobody's Blues But Mine.* Columbia G 31093.

Smith, *St. Louis Blues*
    Smithsonian Collection.

Early Jazz (I)

Morton, *Black Bottom Stomp*
    Smithsonian Collection.
Morton, *Dead Man Blues*
    Smithsonian Collection.
Morton, *King Porter Stomp*
    Smithsonian Collection.
Oliver, *Dippermouth Blues*
    Smithsonian Collection.
Bechet, *Blue Horizon*
    Smithsonian Collection.
Red Onion Jazz Babies, *Cake Walking Babies from Home*
    Smithsonian Collection.

Early Jazz (II)—Louis Armstrong

West End Blues
    Smithsonian Collection.
Weather Bird
    Smithsonian Collection.
Hotter Than That
    Smithsonian Collection.
Big Butter and Egg Man from the West (abridged)
    Smithsonian Collection.
Potato Head Blues
    Smithsonian Collection.
Struttin' with Some Barbecue
    Smithsonian Collection.
Sweethearts on Parade
    Smithsonian Collection.
I Gotta Right to Sing the Blues
    Smithsonian Collection.

Early Jazz (III)

Frankie Trumbauer and His Orchestra, *Singin' the Blues*
    Smithsonian Collection.
Frankie Trumbauer and His Orchestra, *Riverboat Shuffle*
    Smithsonian Collection.

Eddie Lang/Joe Venuti and Their All Star Orchestra, *After You've Gone*
  The Golden Horn of Jack Teagarden. MCA 227.
Johnson, *Carolina Shout*
  Smithsonian Collection.
Lewis, *Honky Tonk Train Blues*
  Smithsonian Collection.
Noone, *Four or Five Times*
  Smithsonian Collection.

CHAPTER 2: BIG BANDS, SMALL COMBOS, AND SWING

Introduction to Big Bands and Swing

Henderson, *Copenhagen*
  Big Band Jazz: From the Beginnings to the Fifties
  (Smithsonian/RCA).
Henderson, *The Stampede*
  Smithsonian Collection.
Henderson, *Wrapping It Up*
  Smithsonian Collection.
Ellington, *East St. Louis Toodle-Oo*
  Smithsonian Collection.
Moten, *Moten Swing*
  Smithsonian Collection.
Basie, *Shout and Feel It*
  Count Basie, *Super Chief*. Columbia CG 31224.
Goodman, *Stompin' at the Savoy*
  This Is Benny Goodman. RCA Victor VPM-6040.
Nichols, *Dinah*
  Smithsonian Collection.
Lunceford, *Lunceford Special*
  1973 *Smithsonian Collection*.

Duke Ellington

Black and Tan Fantasy
  This Is Duke Ellington. RCA Victor VPM-6042.
Mood Indigo
  This Is Duke Ellington. RCA Victor VPM-6042.
Daybreak Express
  RCA Victor LPV-506.
The New East St. Louis Toodle-Oo

Smithsonian Collection.
Diminuendo in Blue, Crescendo in Blue
   Smithsonian Collection.
Ko-Ko
   Smithsonian Collection.
Concerto for Cootie
   Smithsonian Collection.
Take the "A" Train
   This Is Duke Ellington. RCA Victor VPM-6042.
Cotton Tail
   Smithsonian Collection.
In a Mellotone
   Smithsonian Collection.
Blue Serge
   Smithsonian Collection.
The Clothed Woman
   The Carnegie Hall Concert, December 1947.
   Prestige 2-PRCD-24075-2.
Prelude to a Kiss
   Ellington Indigos. Columbia CK 44444.
Stompy Jones
   Duke Ellington and Johnny Hodges, *Side by Side.*
   Verve 82158-2.

Count Basie

One O'Clock Jump
   Big Band Jazz: From the Beginnings to the Fifties
   (Smithsonian/RCA).
Doggin' Around
   Smithsonian Collection.
Taxi War Dance
   Smithsonian Collection.
Sent for You Yesterday
   Big Band Jazz: From the Beginnings to the Fifties
   (Smithsonian/RCA).
Jumpin' at the Woodside
   Big Band Jazz: From the Beginnings to the Fifties
   (Smithsonian/RCA).
Lester Leaps In
   Smithsonian Collection.
Shiny Stockings
   Big Band Jazz: From the Beginnings to the Fifties

(Smithsonian/RCA).

Benny Goodman and Others

Goodman, *Don't Be That Way*
  The Carnegie Hall Concert of 1938. Columbia G2K-40244.
Goodman, *Sing, Sing, Sing*
  The Carnegie Hall Concert of 1938. Columbia G2K-40244.
Goodman, *Body and Soul*
  Smithsonian Collection.
Goodman, *I Found a New Baby*
  Smithsonian Collection.
Goodman, *Breakfast Feud*
  Smithsonian Collection.
Krupa, *Rockin' Chair*
  Smithsonian Collection.
Chocolate Dandies, *I Can't Believe that You're in Love with Me*
  Smithsonian Collection.
Hampton, *When Lights Are Low*
  Smithsonian Collection.
Miller, *In The Mood*
  Big Band Jazz: From the Beginnings to the Fifties
  (Smithsonian/RCA).
Dorsey, *Opus No. One*
  Big Band Jazz: From the Beginnings to the Fifties
  (Smithsonian/RCA).

Some Soloists from the 1930s

Fitzgerald, *'Round Midnight*
  Clap Hands, Here Comes Charlie. Verve 835 646-2.
Fitzgerald, *You'd Be So Nice to Come Home to*
  Smithsonian Collection.
Fitzgerald, *St. Louis Blues*
  Ella in Rome: The Birthday Concert. Verve 835454-2.
Waller, *I Ain't Got Nobody*
  Smithsonian Collection.
Tatum, *Willow Weep for Me*
  Smithsonian Collection.
Tatum, *Too Marvelous for Words*
  Smithsonian Collection.
Tatum, *Tiger Rag*
  Art Tatum: Piano Starts Here. Columbia CS 9655.

Quintette of the Hot Club of France, *Dinah*
    Smithsonian Collection.
Hawkins, *Body and Soul*
    Smithsonian Collection.
Hawkins, *The Man I Love*
    Smithsonian Collection.

Billie Holiday

Miss Brown to You
    Billie Holiday's Greatest Hits. Columbia CL 2666.
These Foolish Things (1936 recording)
    Billie Holiday: The Golden Years, Vol. 1. Columbia C3L 21.
Billie's Blues
    Billie Holiday's Greatest Hits. Columbia CL 2666.
Swing, Brother, Swing!
    Billie Holiday: The Golden Years, Vol. 1. Columbia C3L 21.
He's Funny That Way
    Smithsonian Collection.
All of Me
    Billie Holiday: The Golden Years, Vol. 1. Columbia C3L 21.
God Bless the Child
    Billie Holiday's Greatest Hits. Columbia CL 2666. Also in
    Billie Holiday: The Golden Years, Vol. 1. Columbia C3L 21.
Strange Fruit
    The Billie Holiday Songbook. Verve 823 246-2.
These Foolish Things (1952 recording)
    Smithsonian Collection.

CHAPTER 3: FROM BIRD TO TRANE

Bird Lives! Charlie Parker

Now's the Time
    The Genius of Charlie Parker, Vol. 3. Verve 6-8005.
KoKo
    Smithsonian Collection.
Lady, Be Good
    Smithsonian Collection.
Klacktoveedsedsteen
    Smithsonian Collection.

Embraceable You (2 versions)
    Smithsonian Collection.
Crazeology (2 versions)
    Smithsonian Collection.
Parker's Mood
    Smithsonian Collection.
Ornithology
    The Very Best of Bird. Warner Brothers 2WB 3198.
Night in Tunisia
    The Very Best of Bird. Warner Brothers 2WB 3198.

Diz and Monk

Gillespie, *I Can't Get Started*
    Smithsonian Collection.
Gillespie, *Shaw 'Nuff*
    Smithsonian Collection.
Gillespie, *Salt Peanuts*
    The Greatest Jazz Concert Ever: The Massey Hall Concert.
    Prestige 24024.
Gillespie, *Things to Come*
    Big Band Jazz: From the Beginnings to the Fifties
    (Smithsonian/RCA).
Monk, *Misterioso*
    Smithsonian Collection.
Monk, *Evidence*
    Smithsonian Collection.
Monk, *Criss-Cross*
    Smithsonian Collection.
Monk, *Bag's Groove* (excerpt)
    Smithsonian Collection.
Monk, *I Should Care*
    Smithsonian Collection.
Monk, *Straight No Chaser*
    Thelonious Monk: The Complete Genius. Blue Note BN-LA579-H2.

Some Soloists of the 1940s

Dameron, *Lady Bird*
    Smithsonian Collection.
Powell, *Night in Tunisia*
    Smithsonian Collection.

Powell, *Un Poco Loco*
  The Amazing Bud Powell, Vol. 1. Blue Note BST-81503.
Powell, *Glass Enclosure*
  The Amazing Bud Powell, Vol. 2. Blue Note
  BST-81504.
Garner, *Fantasy on "Frankie and Johnny"*
  Smithsonian Collection.
Byas/Stewart, *I Got Rhythm*
  Smithsonian Collection.
Norvo/Getz, *Body and Soul*
  Smithsonian Collection.
Gordon, *Bikini*
  Smithsonian Collection.

Some Soloists of the 1950s; Charles Mingus

Vaughan, *All of Me*
  Sarah Vaughan, *Swingin' Easy.* Trip TLP-5551.
Vaughan, *All Alone*
  Smithsonian Collection.
Vaughan, *I Ain't Got Nothin' But the Blues*
  The Duke Ellington Songbook, vol. 2. Pablo
  PACD-2312-116-2.
Carter, *By the Bend of the River*
  Betty Carter. Bet-Car MK 1001.
Carter, *Frenesi.*
  The Jazz Singers. (Smithsonian/Sony).
Carter, *This Is Always*
  The Jazz Singers. (Smithsonian/Sony).
Rollins, *Blue 7*
  Smithsonian Collection.
Rollins, *Pent-Up House* (abridged)
  Smithsonian Collection.
Brown/Roach, *I'll Remember April*
  Clifford Brown, *The Quintet, Vol. 2.* Mercury
  EMS 2-407.
Silver, *Moon Rays*
  Smithsonian Collection.
Mingus, *A Foggy Day*
  Mingus. Prestige PR 24010.
Mingus, *Haitian Fight Song*
  Smithsonian Collection.

Mingus, *Goodbye Pork Pie Hat*
    Better Git It In Your Soul. Columbia
    CG 30628.
Mingus, *Hora Decubitus*
    1973 *Smithsonian Collection.*

Into The Cool

Herman, *Four Brothers*
    Big Band Jazz: From the Beginnings to the Fifties
    (Smithsonian/RCA).
Tristano/Konitz, *Subconscious Lee*
    Smithsonian Collection.
Davis, *Jeru*
    The Complete Birth of the Cool. Capitol C21Y-92862.
Davis, *Boplicity*
    Smithsonian Collection.
Davis, *Israel*
    The Complete Birth of the Cool. Capitol
    C21Y-92862.
Konitz/Mulligan, *All the Things You Are*
    Gerry Mulligan and Lee Konitz, *Revelation.* Blue Note
    BN-LA-532-H2.
Modern Jazz Quartet, *Django*
    Smithsonian Collection.
Montgomery, *West Coast Blues*
    Smithsonian Collection.

Miles Davis, Gil Evans, and Bill Evans

Davis, *Oleo*
    Miles Davis. Prestige 24001.
Davis/Evans, *My Ship*
    Miles Ahead. Columbia CK-40784.
Davis/Evans, *Summertime*
    Smithsonian Collection.
Davis/Evans, *Concierto de Aranjuez*
    Miles Davis, Gil Evans Orchestra, *Sketches of Spain.*
    Columbia CK 40578.
Davis, *So What*
    Smithsonian Collection.
Davis, *Blue in Green*
    Miles Davis, *Kind of Blue.* Columbia
    CK 40579.

Bill Evans, *Blue in Green*
　　Smithsonian Collection.
Bill Evans, *My Foolish Heart*
　　Bill Evans, *The Village Vanguard Sessions.*
　　Milestone 47002.

John Coltrane

Good Bait
　　Soultrane. Fantasy/OJC-021-2.
Giant Steps
　　Giant Steps. Atlantic 1311.
Naima
　　Giant Steps. Atlantic 1311.
My Favorite Things
　　My Favorite Things. Atlantic 1361.
Bessie's Blues
　　The Best of John Coltrane. His Greatest Years. Impulse
　　AS-9200-2.
Alabama
　　Smithsonian Collection.

CHAPTER 4: FREE JAZZ AND FUSION

Free Jazz—"The New Thing"

Abbey Lincoln, *When Malindy Sings*
　　Straight Ahead. Candid CCD 79015.
Dolphy, *Out to Lunch*
　　Out to Lunch. Blue Note 84163.
Coleman, *Lonely Woman*
　　Smithsonian Collection.
Coleman, *Congeniality*
　　Smithsonian Collection.
Coleman, *Free Jazz* (excerpt)
　　Smithsonian Collection.
Taylor, *Enter Evening*
　　Smithsonian Collection.
Art Ensemble of Chicago, *Thème de Yoyo*
　　Les stances à Sophie. Nessa 4.

Fusion, Before and After

Jarrett, *Lalene*
    Facing You. ECM 827132-2.
Corea, *The Law of Falling and Catching Up*
    Now He Sings, Now He Sobs. Blue Note CDP 7 90055 2.
Corea, *Bossa*
    Now He Sings, Now He Sobs. Blue Note CDP 7 90055 2.
Hancock, *Maiden Voyage*
    Herbie Hancock, *Maiden Voyage*. Blue Note B21Y-46339.
Davis, *Miles Runs the Voodoo Down*
    Miles Davis, *Bitches Brew*. Columbia G2K-40577.
Weather Report, *Milky Way*
    Weather Report. Columbia CK-48824.
Weather Report, *Orange Lady*
    Weather Report. Columbia CK-48824.
Weather Report, *Surucucú*
    I Sing the Body Electric. Columbia CK-46107.
Weather Report, *Directions*
    I Sing the Body Electric. Columbia CK-46107.
Metheny, *Yolanda, You Learn*
    First Circle. ECM 823 342-2.
Sharrock, *Little Rock*
    Ask the Ages. Axiom 422-848 957-2.

CHAPTER 5: RECENT EVENTS

Wynton Marsalis/Lincoln Center Jazz Orchestra
    Portrait of Louis Armstrong, Portraits by Ellington. Columbia CK
    53145.
Mingus Big Band
    Mingus Big Band 93: Nostalgia in Times Square.
    Dreyfus FDM 36559-2.
    Gunslinging Bird. Dreyfus FDM 36575-2.
    Que Viva Mingus! Dreyfus FDM 36593-2.
The Brian Setzer Orchestra
    Guitar Slinger. Interscope INTD-90051.
    The Dirty Boogie. Interscope INTD-90183.
The Art Ensemble of Chicago
    Coming Home Jamaica. Atlantic 83149-2.
Lester Bowie's Brass Fantasy, *Inflated Tear*
    Serious Fun. DIW-834.

M'Boom, *That's It*
   Live at S.O.B.'s—New York. Blue Moon/MR R2 79182.
Murray, *Lovers*
   Live at Sweet Basil, Vol. 1. Black Saint 120085-2.
Murray, *Bechet's Bounce*
   Live at Sweet Basil, Vol. 1. Black Saint 120085-2.
World Saxophone Quartet, *Steppin'*
   Smithsonian Collection.
Myers, *Do You Wanna Be Saved?*
   The Circle of Time. Black Saint BSR 0078.
Orange Then Blue, *Panama*
   Funkallero. GM 3023CD.
James Carter
   Conversin' with the Elders. Atlantic 82908-2.
   In Carterian Fashion. Atlantic 83082-2.
Joshua Redman
   Timeless Tales (for Changing Times). Warner Bros. 9 47502-2.
Medeski Martin & Wood
   Combustication. Blue Note CDP 7243 4 93011 2 2.
McFerrin, *Round Midnight*
   Columbia CK 40464.
   Kansas City
   Verve 314 529 554-2.

Suggestions for Further Reading

The books listed below are general studies—history and/or criticism—of jazz. I have not included biographies of musicians, since many of these tend to focus on everything in their subject's life except the music. (There are also, of course, some excellent biographies. But the reader interested in learning more about a given individual musician can easily find books available in local libraries, bookstores, *Books in Print*, and on the World Wide Web.) I have also not listed periodicals, such as *Downbeat*, *The Journal of Jazz Studies*, or *The Black Perspective in Music*. Such periodicals are also worth exploring, and they can be found in many college and local libraries. Finally, there are a huge number of websites dedicated to record labels, individual musicians, types of music, and so on. I have not attempted to list any of these, either, because they can change so quickly and simply because there are so many of them. A good search engine will get you started.

Barlow, William. *Looking up at Down: The Emergence of Blues Culture*. Philadelphia: Temple University Press, 1989.

Berendt, Joachim. *The Jazz Book: From Ragtime to Fusion and Beyond*. Translated by H. and B. Bredigkeit with Dan Morgenstern. Revised edition, Westport, CT: Lawrence Hill & Co., 1992.

Brask, Ole, and Morgenstern, Dan. *Jazz People*. New York: Harry N. Abrams, 1976; reprinted Da Capo, 1993.

Buckner, Reginald T., and Weiland, Steven, eds. *Jazz in Mind: Essays on the History and Meanings of Jazz*. Detroit: Wayne State University Press, 1991.

Charters, Samuel. *The Roots of the Blues: An African Search*. Boston and London: Marion Boyars, 1981.

Chilton, John. *Who's Who of Jazz: Storyville to Swing Street*. New York: Da Capo, 4th revised edition, 1985.

Collier, James Lincoln. *The Making of Jazz: A Comprehensive History*. Boston: Houghton Mifflin, 1978.

Coryell, Julie, and Friedman, Laura. *Jazz-Rock Fusion: The People, the Music*. New York: Dell, 1978.

Davis, Angela Y. *Blues Legacies and Black Feminism: Gertrude "Ma" Rainey, Bessie Smith, and Billie Holiday*. New York: Pantheon, 1998.

Davis, Francis. *Bebop and Nothingness: Jazz and Pop at the End of the Century*. New York: Schirmer, 1996.

————. *In the Moment: Jazz in the 1980s*. New York: Oxford University Press, 1986.

Deffaa, Chip. *Swing Legacy*. Metuchen, NJ: Scarecrow Press, 1989.

DeVeaux, Scott. *The Birth of Bebop: A Social and Musical History*. Berkeley: University of California Press, 1997.

Feather, Leonard. *The Encyclopedia of Jazz*. New York: Da Capo, 1988.

————. *The Encyclopedia of Jazz in the Sixties*. New York: Da Capo, 1988.

————. *The Jazz Years: Eyewitness to an Era*. New York: Da Capo Press, 1987.

————, and Gitler, Ira. *The Encyclopedia of Jazz in the Seventies*. New York: Da Capo, 1988.

Gabbard, Krin. *Jammin' at the Margins: Jazz and the American Cinema*. Chicago: University of Chicago Press, 1996.

Giddins, Gary. *Rhythm-a-ning: Jazz Tradition and Innovation in the '80s*. New York: Oxford University Press, 1985.

————. *Riding on a Blue Note: Jazz and American Pop*. New York: Oxford University Press, 1981.

————. *Visions of Jazz: The First Century*. New York: Oxford University Press, 1998.

Gioia, Ted. *The History of Jazz*. New York: Oxford University Press, 1998.

————. *West Coast Jazz: Modern Jazz in California, 1945–1960*. New York: Oxford University Press, 1992.

Gitler, Ira. *Swing to Bop: An Oral History of the Transition in Jazz in the 1940's*. New York: Oxford University Press, 1985.

Gourse, Leslie. *Madame Jazz: Contemporary Women Instrumentalists*. New York: Oxford University Press, 1995.

Hentoff, Nat. *Jazz Is*. New York: Random House, 1976.

————. *The Jazz Life*. New York: Da Capo, 1975. (Reprint of London: P. Davies, 1962.)

————, and McCarthy, Albert J. *Jazz*. New York: Da Capo, 1975. (Reprint of New York: Holt, Rinehart & Winston, 1959.)

Hobsbawm, E. J. *The Jazz Scene*. New York: Pantheon Books, 1993.

Hodeir, André. *Jazz: Its Evolution and Essence*. Translated by David Noakes. New York: Grove Press, 1956.

Jones, LeRoi (now Amiri Baraka). *Black Music*. New York: Da Capo, 1998.

————. *Blues People*. New York: William Morrow, 1963.

Keepnews, Orrin, and Grauer, Bill, Jr. *A Pictorial History of Jazz*. New York: Crown, 1966.

Lees, Gene. *Meet Me at Jim & Andy's: Jazz Musicians and Their World*. New York: Oxford University Press, 1988.

————. *Waiting for Dizzy*. New York: Oxford University Press, 1991.

Litweiler, John. *The Freedom Principle: Jazz after 1958*. New York: William Morrow, 1984.

McRae, Barry. *The Jazz Handbook*. Harlow, England: Longman, 1987.

Murray, Albert. *Stomping the Blues*. New York: McGraw-Hill, 1976.

Nicholson, Stuart. *Jazz-Rock: A History*. New York: Schirmer, 1998.

Palmer, Robert. *Deep Blues*. New York: Viking, 1981.

Peretti, Burton W. *The Creation of Jazz: Music, Race, and Culture in Urban America*. Urbana: University of Illinois Press, 1992.

Placksin, Sally. *American Women in Jazz, 1900 to the Present: Their Words, Lives, and Music*. New York: Seaview Books, 1982.

Rose, Al, and Souchon, Edmond. *New Orleans Jazz: A Family Album*. Baton Rouge: Louisiana State University, 1967.

Rosenthal, David. *Hard Bop: Jazz and Black Music, 1955–1965*. New York: Oxford University Press,

Russell, Ross. *Jazz Style in Kansas City and the Southwest*. Berkeley: University of California Press, 1971.

Schuller, Gunther. *Early Jazz: Its Roots and Musical Development*. New York: Oxford University Press, 1968.

————. *The Swing Era: The Development of Jazz, 1930–1945*. New York: Oxford University Press, 1989.

Shapiro, Nat, and Hentoff, Nat. *Hear Me Talkin' To Ya*. New York: Dover, 1955.

Sidran, Ben. *Black Talk*. New York: Da Capo, 1971 (reprinted 1981).

Simon, George T. *The Big Bands*. New York: Macmillan, 1971.

Southern, Eileen. *The Music of Black Americans*. New York: W. W. Norton and Company, 3rd edition 1997.

Stearns, Marshall W. *The Story of Jazz*. London: Oxford University Press, 1956.

Stokes, W. Royal. *The Jazz Scene: An Informal History from New Orleans to 1990*. New York: Oxford University Press, 1991.

Tirro, Frank. *Jazz: A History*. New York: W. W. Norton and Company, 1977.

Walser, Robert, ed. *Keeping Time: Readings in Jazz History*. New York: Oxford University Press, 1999.

Weinstein, Norman C. *A Night in Tunisia: Imaginings of Africa in Jazz*. Metuchen, NJ: Scarecrow Press, 1992.

Williams, Martin T., ed. *The Art of Jazz: Essays on the Nature and Development of Jazz*. New York: Oxford University Press, 1959.

Williams, Martin T. *Jazz Changes*. New York: Oxford University Press, 1992.

————. *Where's the Melody? A Listener's Introduction to Jazz*. New York: Da Capo Press, 1983. (Reprint of 1966 publication.)

Wilmer, Valerie. *As Serious as Your Life: The Story of the New Jazz*. Westport, CT: Lawrence Hill & Company, 1980.

Index

This index gives page references to all proper names and titles in the book, but not to stylistic terms or other words to be found in the *Glossary*. **Boldface numbers** refer to pages with photographs.